John Ella

Musical Sketches

Abroad and at Home. Third Edition

John Ella

Musical Sketches
Abroad and at Home. Third Edition

ISBN/EAN: 9783744679503

Printed in Europe, USA, Canada, Australia, Japan

Cover: Foto ©Thomas Meinert / pixelio.de

More available books at **www.hansebooks.com**

MUSICAL SKETCHES,

ABROAD AND AT HOME.

Ballantyne Press.
BALLANTYNE, HANSON AND CO.
EDINBURGH AND LONDON

MUSICAL SKETCHES,

ABROAD AND AT HOME.

BY

PROFESSOR ELLA,

HON. MEM. PHIL. ACAD., ROME (1842); FOUNDER OF THE MUSICAL UNION, LONDON (1844)
HON. MEM. OF THE PHIL. SOCIETY, PARIS (1872);
Author of
"*Personal Memoir of Meyerbeer, with Analysis of 'Les Huguenots,'*" &c. &c.

WITH

ORIGINAL MUSIC BY MOZART, CZERNY, GRAUN, ETC., VOCAL CADENZAS, AND OTHER MUSICAL ILLUSTRATIONS.

"Toute histoire qui n'est pas contemporaine est suspecte."
PASCAL.

Third Edition,

REVISED AND EDITED BY

JOHN BELCHER, Esq.
Author of "Lectures on the History of Ecclesiastical Music."

LONDON:
WILLIAM REEVES, 185 FLEET STREET
(PUBLISHER OF MUSICAL WORKS).
1878.

DEAR MRS. TOM TAYLOR,

In Yorkshire, the native country of your family and mine, I first became acquainted with you—then Miss Laura Barker—and your rare musical accomplishments. Our acquaintance has, since your marriage, ripened into a cherished friendship for you and your husband. As a tribute to that friendship, and to my admiration of your musical acquirements and compositions, I feel gratified in dedicating to you this volume of "Musical Sketches."

I remain, dear Mrs. Tom Taylor,

Very sincerely yours,

J. ELLA.

January 1*st*, 1869.
9 *Victoria Square.*

PREFACE TO THIRD EDITION.

THE contents of the present Volume, with the exception of certain additions and alterations, remain the same as in the former Editions. But in order to give increased facility of reference, the various Articles and Anecdotes have been, as far as possible, arranged and classified, and where it seemed necessary, the date inserted.

It is hoped the reader may share in the pleasure and interest which this revision has afforded to

THE EDITOR.

PREFACE.

THE frequent demands for complete sets of the Musical Union "Records" have induced me to collect a variety of historical, anecdotal, biographical, and critical extracts, contained in some numbers out of print, and to add others which are published in this volume for the first time. My Musical Diary, extending over a period of fifty-six years of my life, is full of details of Italian Opera incidents. Mr. Chorley, however, by his "Thirty Years' Musical Recollections" of the Italian Opera, has rendered it superfluous to do anything for this part of my subject, beyond giving a few personal anecdotes. I have endeavoured, to the best of my ability, to select from my collection of musical anecdotes such as have more than a common interest. In this third edition the whole has been revised and classified with numerous additional extracts from my Diaries.

My motto says, All history that is not contemporary is open to suspicion.

The ancient historians of Egypt and China were not contemporaries of the events they related, and although no one doubts that the tale of Troy is, in its details at least, a fiction, yet the beauty of Homer's epic, says Pascal, will ever make it the companion of scholars and the delight of mankind. Voltaire regarded as a fable that Xerxes had *one million seven hundred thousand* men engaged in the Persian war, although this statement was made by Herodotus, who was in a manner a contemporary. As to the actual number of persons who inhabited ancient Rome, neither at school nor in Rome itself have I ever read or found any two authorities that expressed the same opinion. Music, too, which boasts of great antiquity, has not been very fortunate in the accuracy of its historical records. Mainzer, a learned man and instructed musician, with whom, some years ago, I had the good fortune to be acquainted, was sceptical as to the thousands of trumpeters and harpists assisting in the services of the Jewish Temple of Solomon, as related by Josephus. When I described to a circle of Hungarians, in Pesth, 1866, the monster gathering the same year of 30,075 children and adults, including a band of 500, in one county only of England, at Halifax, on Whit-Tuesday, my hearers betrayed doubts of the fact that in a country without a National School of Music such a choir could be educated by the voluntary efforts of the people. Fortunately, I had a copy of my "Record" containing full particulars, with the programme including four-part strict counterpoint of the immortal Handel, which an informant present assured me was sung with wonderful effect. Public men and artists are constantly the subject of misrepresentation. The sketches of personal incidents in this collection will be confined to what I have actually seen or heard. In the case of other anecdotes I have given the best guarantee I can of their authenticity by quoting the source from which they have been obtained.

J. ELLA.

CONTENTS.

*Those marked * are new or additional articles.*

PART I.

PART II.

PART III.

PART IV.

MUSICAL ILLUSTRATIONS.

MUSICAL SKETCHES.

—o—

JUDGMENT AND CRITICISM.

ÆSTHETICAL writers mostly agree in the analysis of mental and sensitive taste, and an English essayist observes that there are as many degrees of refinement in the intellectual faculty as in the sense. "Il musico sente più che non può esprimere," say the Italians; and a passage in Juvenal, in speaking of a sensation, is thus translated: "I cannot define, though I feel it." This explains the true state of an executant of superior mind and poetical sense engaged in realising his beau-ideal of a great work, and likewise expresses the sensation of an auditor moved by some passage of a vague, though suggestive character.

As Mrs. B. Stowe, in her "Sunny Memories," observes, "Every true painter, poet, and artist, is in some sense so far a prophet that his utterances convey more to other minds than he himself knows; so that, doubtless, should all the old masters rise from the dead, they might be edified by what posterity has found in their works."

In our intimate relations with musicians, we are made sensibly aware of the separate existence of those attributes, the aggregate of which *alone* attests the power of a truly great genius; and for one that excels in the ideal, a thousand attain excellence only in the mechanical of art. Unhappily, a fondness for any pursuit does not imply aptitude; hence we find a large proportion of skilful musicians to whom nature has been less bountiful than to their more fortunate rivals. Quintilian, Cicero, and Schiller, in much the same words, have stated that "the public in general are not bad judges, though not good critics;" but in the development of a faculty, we sometimes recognise an approximation in merit to a more successful competitor, which does not always elicit a due share of public appreciation; in such instances the impartial critic has to perform a pleasing duty and a great service. The vague expression of sound affords persons afflicted with that incurable distemper, *cacoëthes carpendi*, a great latitude for plausible sophism: but the generous nature of an educated public, able to appreciate the subtle meaning of a profound composition, is more disposed to discern a beauty, than to mark a fault.

The English public is said to be slow in its perceptions of excellence in executive genius, but the immediate acknowledgment of the powers of a great artist only proves the folly of continental critics drawing conclusions from false premises, and generalising on exceptional cases at speculative concerts, with a mixed and often ignorant public. Never since the last appearance of Mendelssohn at the Philharmonic Concert, in 1847, was so much enthusiasm expressed by a musical audience, as at the *début* of Rubinstein in 1857, at the Musical Union. This, however, satisfactorily proves that an organised institution for a special purpose is a safe tribunal for rendering justice to talent, which must eventually claim recognition from the general public.

A ploughman can distinguish the sun from the moon, but interrogated on the planets that complete our solar system, silence betrays his ignorance. Thus it is in common life, the great luminaries of the intellectual world receive homage from the illiterate, who are incapable of estimating the merits of minor constellations.

How rarely do we find a new artist, or a composition by an unknown hand, fairly appreciated at a *first* hearing, even by experienced musicians!

LATENT APPRECIATION OF TALENT.

"No compound of this earthly ball
Is like another, all in all."

—TENNYSON.

IT is the natural disposition of mankind to view through a flattering medium the virtues and excellencies of those they esteem, and it is hard to divest one's self of personal feeling in listening to the performance of rival artists. In playing, as in composition, one musician excels in the serene and placid, another in the more stirring and passionate style; both artists great in different ways. The *Atlas* reviewer, an experienced musician, commenting upon the above passage, remarked, 185 —"Nothing could be more happily expressed, whether as a genial *bonhommie*, or as a profound artistical truth. What one artist wants, the other possesses; and both together give us more than we could have obtained from either singly. Is it not better, then, to encourage them to mutual helpfulness than to raise up a barren rivalry which cannot but be disastrous to the best interests of the art? We have the more insisted on this amiable and truly artistical quality of Mr. Ella's mind, because we regard it as one of the principal causes of his signal success; but he has another qualification that also does him good service in his arduous and responsible office—a ready and cordial recognition of individual genius, under whatever guise it may present itself. He does not await the public judgment. Keeping an open sense for merit in every walk of the art, he forms his own opinion, and, what is more, dares act upon it. How rare and inestimable a quality this is will be best known to those who are most fully aware how indolent, unstable, and vacillating is public opinion not fully formed—what slothfulness of intellect, what craven fears of self-committal, and what illogical references to former misjudgments exert their paralysing influence on the great majority, even of educated minds."—Perhaps no more startling illustration of the above compliment can be mentioned than the fact of Hallé's *début* at the Philharmonic Concerts in 1852, after I had introduced him to the Musical Union in 1848. "The audience," said the *Times*, "could not but remember that, although he had played on twelve different occasions at the *Musical Union*, to the great satisfaction of Mr. Ella's subscribers, this was his first appearance at the Philharmonic Concerts." This is not a solitary instance of latent appreciation of talent introduced to the English public. The executive powers of Rubinstein, Jaell, and Lubeck, so thoroughly appreciated in Paris and other continential cities, are only now beginning to be fairly recognised in London, beyond the circles of the Musical Union. In spite, however, of personal prejudices and party influences for sinister purposes, notwithstanding the alleged dull appreciation of new works and new artists in England, genius will ultimately assert its pre-eminence, and conquer the obstacles that beset it on every side.

EXECUTIVE GENIUS IN MUSIC.

"Heureux celui que la nature a doué d'une profonde sensibilité."

—BAILLOT.

THE mind, by constant study of the antique, itself becomes antique; and ears trained to the exclusive appreciation of one style of music and playing, are apt to prejudice persons in the admiration of a false standard of the *beau-idéal.* Each executant musician, master of his instrument, has some speciality, either in *tone* or *style*, which distinguishes his talent from that of others; and when engaged in the performance of music congenial to his feeling and taste, every unbiassed critic must acknowledge his merit. Genius in execution adapts itself to music in a style best suited to express its varied character; in this lies the secret of triumphs achieved by great artists in playing compositions that have wearied the public in the hands of mechanical executants. "It is the high privilege of art," says M. Guizot, "that it has fallen to its lot to contribute to the happiness and prosperity of men in the most different epochs and states of society." It is equally a source of satisfaction that "neither clime nor race" denies to any country the production of genius to excel in art; and in opposition to the speculative theory of a great philosopher, eminent musicians spring up from regions remote from the sunny south, endowed with the most perfect organisation, and the most ardent temperament. It is true, that amateurs often mistake sensibility for genius; but no unprejudiced person, educated to the appreciation of the beautiful in art, falls into this error. The more contemplative arts of poetry and painting may be studied, and their merits ultimately felt by the unlearned; in music it is otherwise, and those flashes of genius in execution which fire the soul and rouse the enthusiasm of its auditors, completely set logic at defiance, and disarm all criticism. No wonder that the public in general has more sympathy for the genius-executant than for the genius-creative, and that the experienced professor, in his desire to bring forward new works of merit for the advancement of art, should meet with little encouragement.

An artist of sensibility without judgment takes you by surprise; but the intellect of a man of genius surprises by an excess of beauty, and imparts to the general effect of concerted music some unexpected degree of novelty by its presiding influence in the leading part. Hence, one always receives from the repetition of known works new emotions at fresh combinations of executants; and this compensates, in some degree, for the great self-denial in foregoing the pleasure of hearing music less familiar than that which is selected to gratify the taste of members. The septets this day of Beethoven and Hummel are assigned to executants chastened and ripened by age and experience, the best that can be obtained for their respective parts. Here ends my task; a patient rehearsal ensures that perfect *ensemble* which Baillot justly observes does not rely solely upon the efficiency of every performer to a part, "mais de son intelligence et *liaison avec le tout*."—July 3, 1866.

INTELLECT AND SENSIBILITY.

STOIC natures, unmoved by the glowing impulses of an executive genius in music, are much to be pitied. Considering the different constitutions of mankind, and that a passion for art does not always co-exist with intellect and sensibility to comprehend and feel its truth, it is a matter of congratulation to artists, that so much unanimity exists on questions of taste among the educated and thinking portion of the community at large.

Intellect, however exalted, without strong feelings, can never achieve the high purposes of art, and the musician who betrays no emotion in playing the inspired and inspiring *chefs d'œuvre* of the classics is not to be envied. The player, absorbed in the earnest "labour of love," alike indifferent to appearance or manner, at once enchains the heart and captivates the willing auditor. It is the same in an actor, "whose rare talent, after all," says Erskine, "has its seat in the superior sensibilities of the mind, which identify him for the moment with the characters he represents." Without this nature, even with *irritable* sensibility, an orator, in public discourse, arising out of sudden occasions, could never be eloquent. The musician, alike animated by the excitement of his theme, by some sudden stroke of impulse makes captive his hearers, and triumphs over their feelings. This is the power of genius in musical expression. "Que l'élève devenu habile dans le mécanisme ne se croie donc pas à la fin de ses travaux. *L'expression* vient ouvrir à son talent une carrière qui n'a de bornes que dans les sensations du cœur humain ; il ne suffit pas qu'il soit né sensible, il faut qu'il porte dans son âme cette force expansive, eette chaleur de sentiment qui s'étend au dehors, qui se communique, qui pénètre, qui brûle. C'est le feu sacré qu'une fiction ingénieuse fait dérober par Prométhée pour animer l'homme." "L'expression, enfin, consiste à rendre avec énergie toutes les idées que le musicien doit rendre et tous les sentimens qu'il doit exprimer."—ROUSSEAU.

THE PEDANT AND THE ARTIST.

"The poetical eye is early busied with imagery, and its reveries with passions; as early will the painter's hand be copying forms and colours; the young musician's ear will wander in the creation of sounds; and the philosopher's head will mature its meditations. It is, then, the aptitude of the appropriate organ, however it varies in its character, in which genius seems most concerned, and which is con-natural and connate with the individual, and, as it was expressed in old days, is *born* with him."—I. DISRAELI.

MUSIC, distinctly a science and an art, includes among its votaries theorists of stolid nature and persons of artistic temperament. The one mistaking means for the end, the other frequently disregarding the laws which should regulate their practice. "*La sensibilité fait tout notre génie*," says M. Piron; but sensibility without aptitude does not constitute the artist, or there would be a world of artists among amateurs who have never cultivated their natural feeling. The union of knowledge with sensibility is the absolute *sine quâ non* of every true artist—executive and creative. In every profession are found pedants jealous of their more gifted and successful fraternity; for, although a man may be skilled in the principles and theory of music, he may not be endowed with the faculty which commands public favour in works of genius. Hence, it is well said, that for one that excels in the ideal, a thousand are masters of the mechanics of art. An apt illustration of this distinction of acquirement, and *le feu sacré*, is shown in the life of Petrarch, who, at the age of eight years, was a pupil of Convenola, at Pisa, 1314. "Though he had taught rhetoric and grammar for sixty years, Convenola possessed only the theory of his profession. He sometimes, however, thought of composing; but, scarcely had he conceived the plan and written the preface, when he changed his design and began another book. Petrarch compared him to the stone which sharpens knives, but is dull itself. It was from this master, however, he received the first lessons in poetry."

Musical theorists, without too lively an imagination, are the best instructors; but, as critics, they are frequently cynical and unjust. The most gifted composer is rarely a logical instructor of the principles of his art; nay, more, it is said that no eminently successful composer ever wrote a well-digested treatise on the theory of music. Cherubini, perhaps, may be considered the only exception.

During my studies with Attwood, I wrote all the exercises of harmony which he had learnt from his instructor in Vienna—Wolfgang Mozart. I confess that I have seen more useful progressive exercises. "Men advanced far in knowledge," we are told, "do not care to repeat the elements of their art." Of the true artist, as distinct from the mere artisan, I will conclude this sketch with a definition expressed by Ary Scheffer in Mrs. Grote's Memoirs and Life of this remarkable man and painter:—"Pour être artiste, il faut avoir en soi un sentiment élevé, ou une conviction puissante, dignes d'être exprimé par une langue qui peut être, indifféremment, la prose, la poésie, la musique, ou la peinture. C'est que réellement, l'artiste le plus éminent n'a rein créé ni rien inventé ; il a seulement rendu fidèlement les impressions du beau, du sublime, et du bon, qu'il a reçues de la nature entière. Je dit *expressément* la nature entière, parceque à côté des parties palpables qui s'adressent à nos yeux et à nos sens, il y a cette partie qui parle directement à notre âme, sans interprète, ou matériel visible," &c.

MUSICAL TRIADS.

THE cabalistic number of *three* is fertile in musical associations. Within three centuries the complete development of the science has been established. Perfect concord consists of three intervals. The art itself is composed of three separate parts:—melody, harmony, and accent. Three unisons are the maximum of resonance in keyed instruments. The human voice is chiefly characterised by three most distinct qualities:—soprano, tenor, and bass. The attributes of musical genius in execution are three—instinct, perception, and individuality. Practically developed, these qualities are recognised by the expression, judgment, and phrasing (*distinction*) of the performer. Three qualifications are required for an efficient conductor:—active sensibility, self-control, and practical experience. The complete orchestra is composed of three classes of instruments, of animal, vegetable, and mineral production, viz., stringed, wood, and metal. The faculties to excel in music are three—intelligence, sensibility, and taste; and what is most essential to an earnest enjoyment of good music of every class, are the three qualifications of a healthy mind—liberality, impartiality, and intellectuality. To sum up these hasty reflections in a few words, I must here remark that although opinions are suddenly formed on the merits of a new vocalist or executant, too frequently in excess of praise or detraction, reason soon gets the better of prejudice, and time ultimately awards justice to the artist.

The musical genius of Germany is divided into three eras, each identified with a Triad whose works have successively enlarged the domain of Art, viz., Bach, Handel, and Gluck; Haydn, Mozart, and Beethoven; Weber, Mendelssohn, and Spohr.

One problem connected with the fate of music has long ago been solved, and every true artist must feel the force of the poet's language:

> "What shines and glitters has its birth
>   But for the present hour alone.
> The *real*—the thing of truth and worth—
>   To all posterity goes down."
>
> —GOETHE.

IMAGINATION, TASTE, AND FEELING.

" Si l'on a une imagination dure, on n'y entend rien ; si on l'a faible et trop sensible, on comprend trop."—GRETRY.

" Si la musique, dans certains cas ne signifie rien, ce n'est donc point la faute de l'art, mais bien celle du compositeur."—LE SUEUR.

THE growth of taste is slow ; but the ear acquires, by habitual training, a method of correspondence with what is agreeable, beautiful, and elegant ; and, like the eye "versed in the works of the best painters, it soon learns to distinguish true expression from false, and grace from affectation : quickened by exercise, and confirmed by comparison, it outstrips reasoning, and feels in an instant that truth which the other develops by degrees."

" The imagination in its first setting out ever prefers extravagance to justness, or false beauties to true ; it kindles at the flashes of —— ; and flutters at the sentimentalism of —— ; this is its childhood. As it grows in vigour, it refines in feeling ; till, superior to its first attractions, it rests on the tender pathetic of Mozart, or the manly spirit of Beethoven."

Every enthusiastic musician who reflects on the wild extravagant opinions of his early career, his indifference to works that in aftertimes engage his fondest contemplation, will acknowledge the above truthful description of his first impressions and matured taste. In their relative degrees of combination, the different species of composition, as addressed to the powers or the understanding, may be thus classified :—the diatonic progression of consonant harmonies in old simple chants; the rigorous counterpoint of the complete services of Palestrina and his successors; the mixed style at the dawn of modern harmony; the more perfect development of discords with nervous melodic counterpoint by Bach, Handel, and the learned masters of the eighteenth century; and lastly, the more impassioned and varied employment of the resources of the advanced progress of science in Oratorios, Operas, Concert Music, and Chamber Compositions by the composers of the present age. It is this latter species of music that Rousseau specified as distinct from all others, where *remplissage* is totally inadmissible, as the substitute for tangible and thoughtful matter.

The art of condensing musical ideas to four real parts, original and effective, implies an amount of genius and scholarship that few possess, or the schools of Europe would more frequently enrich the library of Chamber Music with the triumphs of their aspiring students. In concluding this imperfect notice of the specific character of music, I cannot but regret that the science of harmony, so easy of acquirement, so profitable in economising practical attainment in vocal or instrumental art, should so rarely engage the study of English *dilettanti*. It is a great error to imagine that the sensibilities of the heart are blunted by a knowledge of musical science, or that our pleasures are diminished by a refinement in musical taste: the imagination, on the contrary, in its exalted flight on the pinions of wisdom, views art in a world of ethereal beauty.

The captious votary who revels in roulades and mediocrity in art, tauntingly jeers the enthusiastic devotee to the higher regions of the divine muse, and is totally wanting in sympathy with the admirers of those intellectual productions which engage the executants at the Musical Union; to him I commend the following known anecdote for his reflection:—

"A silly young fellow, seeing an aged hermit go by him barefoot, '*Father*,' says he, '*you are in a very miserable condition if there is not another world.*' '*True, son*,' said the hermit, '*but what is thy condition if there is?*'"

FANCY AND IMAGINATION.

"So full of shapes is fancy."—*Twelfth Night.*

"Il y a chez les Allemands plus d'imagination que de vraie passion."
—MME. DE STAEL.

MY readers, I hope, will be gratified by the perusal of the following extracts from Coleridge's Introduction to the Study of the Greek Classic Poets, containing a clear and satisfactory definition of terms, which, although distinct in their application, are commonly used as synonymous. The definition of Coleridge will no doubt find a musical parallel in minds of a poetical nature. The French composers may be said to excel most in a species of music that fascinates without inducing reflection; whilst the Germans surpass all other nations in musical creations of a deeper character; the difference between these two characteristics of French and German composers, is identified, to my thinking, with fancy and imagination—the existence of which, affecting in some degree all sorts of intellectual operations, has a direct and perpetual bearing on poetry. There is, perhaps, no difference in metaphysics so necessary to be known by an accomplished critic, and yet none so generally neglected as this. A knowledge of this difference may be used, more than any other, as the touchstone of power, and the sure key by which to open the various chambers of genius.

"With very few exceptions, indeed, in books and in conversation, the fancy and the imagination are taken to be either absolutely synonymous, or at the utmost as differing degrees of the same faculty. Fancy, therefore, will be a term for a light and airy kind of imagination; whilst imagination will be another word for an ardent and concentred fancy. But certainly if there do exist two such different faculties in the mind, we ought, for the sake of perspicuity, to be careful in using the two words distinctly and appropriately.

"It is seldom that any man can be supposed to possess either of these faculties to the absolute exclusion of the other; yet it is, perhaps, not improper to characterise many of the eminent poets by that *one* which predominates in their works. Hence we may say that there is more of fancy in Sophocles, more of imagination in Æschylus; so more of the first in Horace, more of the last in Lucretius; the same again of Ariosto, as compared with Dante; and we may with great accuracy call Cowley a fanciful, and Milton an imaginative, poet; whilst both epithets must be given, where they are both most due, to our single Shakespeare alone. Be this distinction, however, sound or not in point of metaphysical truth, I am persuaded the principle involved in it will be found, if borne in mind, a very useful rule for, or aid to, a discriminating criticism."

Glück, Handel, and other writers of the last century, afford copious illustrations of the above thesis. I prefer, however, to quote examples from modern composers.

No one who hears for the first time the *tremolo* of dissonant chords in the introduction of the overture to "Der Freyschütz," with the mysterious *pizzicato* of the basses on the unaccented part of the bar, can fail to recognise the strong imaginative faculty of the poet, whilst many other parts of the opera, such as the Laughing Chorus, the Bridesmaids' Chorus, and Waltz, exhibit the most obvious and striking instances of musical fancy.

These two powers, indeed, constitute the very elements of the poetry of music, and there is not a standard composition extant in which their presence may not be distinctly traced by the intelligent connoisseur.

INTRODUCTION—OVERTURE—"DER FREYSCHÜTZ."

There is, also, in the opera of "Der Freyschütz," a beautiful illustration of these distinctions in music, occurring simultaneously in the duet of Agnes and Anne, where the maiden's cheerfulness and her mistress's sadness of heart are most happily conceived, and distinctly expressed with charming effect.

Want of space precludes me quoting several other examples; but enough, I trust, has here been shown to make the parallel of poetry and music perfectly clear, according to Coleridge's definition of fancy and imagination.

Cherubini, of all the profound musical thinkers, perhaps, had the least fancy. The one faculty of deep imagination predominates in most of his sacred and secular music. To my mind, there is no more striking effect of powerful imagination suggestive of the darkest imagery of tragic incidents than the whole of the introduction to "Les Deux Journées." After the two lovely cadences of serene placid harmony, come the basses with powerful unisons in a grand figure of a vague character reposing on a deep pedal note. How touching are the bewailing short melodic phrases so tenderly expressed, with the penetrating chord of the augmented fifth in its simple structure!

The mysterious tremolo of the violins, the wailing effect of the flutes, the tragic responses of the basses, and the terrific utterance of the corni *ff* in the fifth of the dominant, until the grand climax of the allegro, are in the highest degree suggestive, and have served Weber and Mendelssohn to good purpose. This introduction I have always considered one of the most poetical creations of Cherubini.*

* Cherubini's introduction to "Les Deux Journées."

INTRODUCTION TO OVERTURE—"LES DEUX JOURNEES."

Flute 8o........
Oboe.
♯5
♯5
fr.
p
Flutes.
p
p
fr. p
Vcello.
Bassoon. 8o. lower.
f
p
p
Cello.

Wind Instruments.
fr.
p
Cello.
tutti.
f
pp
Corni.
ff
cres

tutti.
ff
f

Allegro.
cre.
ff

MUSICAL EXPRESSION AND TASTE.

THE indefinite power of music in expressing ideas, has often afforded mere matter-of-fact reasoners a plausible excuse for preferring what are termed more profitable and useful studies; seeking for knowledge instead of pleasurable emotion, they attempt to decry the art for that vagueness which constitutes one of its greatest charms. To such disbelievers in the divine Muse as pollute her sacred temple with utilitarian prejudices, the learned theorist, Fétis, in his treatise on counterpoint, thus replies: "Et qu'on ne croit point que le défaut positif soit une imperfection de la musique; car c'est de là que vient la puissance de ses effets. N'ayant de règle que l'imagination du compositeur, et de bornes que les sensations de l'auditoire, son domaine est immense, ses formes inépuisables, et, bien que les impressions qu'elle laisse soient fugitives, la faculté qu'elle a de les reproduire, en les variant sans cesse, assure son triomphe sur tout homme bien organisé."

Associated with poetry and painting, music may be elevated or debased; but, alone in the glory of her intrinsic merits, she is all pure and incorruptible; and, notwithstanding the *apparent* advantages of other arts, in an intellectual point of view, the study of music has never ceased to engage the attention and command the admiration of the wisest and most virtuous of mankind in all ages. The conventionalities which characterise the melodic forms and harmonies of national and descriptive music are understood by every well-educated musician. The peculiarities of the Scotch gamut, with the omission of the 4th and 7th, the Swiss appoggiatura of the 6th, the pedal-pastoral bass, and the quaint progressions of old masters, form a language which never fails to speak to his mind as intelligibly as positive scenes do to his ocular sense. By the practised ear of an amateur these differences are easily felt; and having his attention once directed to the composer's purpose, a composition like that of the "Pastoral Symphony" would not in vain appeal to his imagination, in presenting the most captivating scenes in nature. The full indulgence of a composer's invention being fettered by the limits of vocal capabilities, once elicited the confession from Beethoven, whose "conscience était sa muse," that if he could enjoy a certain income, he would only write symphonies, masses, and quartets. The repeated quarrels of the conscientious Beethoven with vocalists for not adhering to the text of his cantabile, offer a singular contrast to those blissful hours he devoted to the Schuppanzigh Quartet Party, for whom he expressly composed most of his later compositions of that class. In large assemblies, or at ordinary musical entertainments, the lowest grades of art and the meretricious displays of vocal talent obtain the greatest favour. "Tone for the million, and style for the æsthetic few," is exemplified in the sensational effects of a few misplaced screaming notes in a final cadence, totally at variance with the expression of the poetry. This calls to mind the plea of a singer once executing a most elaborate cadenza in the final phrase of a pathetic song, on the word "*morire*," because it suited her voice, and produced a sensation. A really true artist of education and refined taste would not descend to such an artifice.

To submit to the choice of certain ballads that encumber the programmes of most concerts given in London, would be fatal to the success of the Musical Union; nor would I ever encourage the singing of grand dramatic scenes, without orchestral accompaniment. The repertoire of good English, French, and German chamber vocal music offers an abundant variety, and from this class of composition are usually selected the few pieces introduced in the miscellaneous programme of the Musical Union once every season. The omission of vocal performances at the ordinary meetings of the Musical Union is obviously necessary, since nothing short of perfection in vocalisation, so rarely to be obtained, could satisfy the exigencies of a fastidious audience, assembled to appreciate classical instrumental music delivered in the *highest style* of excellence.*

* In Paris, at the classical orchestral concerts of Pasdeloup and Colonne, rarely is *vocal music* introduced; and at the matchless concerts of the *Conservatoire*, the few vocal works introduced are choral.

DEVOTIONAL AND INSTRUMENTAL MUSIC.

"During the infancy of poetry, all the different kinds of it lay confused, and were mingled in the composition, according as inclination, enthusiasm, or casual incidents directed the poet's strain. In the progress of society and arts, they began to assume those different names under which we now know them."—BLAIR.

PRECISELY so, as described in the above quotation, was it in respect to instrumental music ere it became a separate branch of the muse. In its earlier stages, the combinations, restricted to diatonic progressions, assumed no specific character that could distinguish it from the severe vocal music of the Roman Catholic Church services. From the earliest period of their known existence, stringed instruments have but little changed in shape, and have always possessed qualities of accent, and modification of sustained tone, superior to those of the organ or any other instrument.

Admitting that the executive art has kept pace with the progress of musical composition—both orchestral and chamber—yet, until science extended her domain to the chromatic and novel harmonies of the present century, instrumental music could rarely excite intensity of emotion, nor was it capable of being invested with those infinite charms of modulation which beautify the scores of Haydn, Mozart,

Beethoven, Weber, Spohr, Onslow, Mendelssohn, and their followers.

The musical historian, Fétis, very naturally expresses his astonishment that the science of harmony should have so long retained its stately simplicity, while a simple aggregation of notes, towards the sixteenth century, gave to combinations a new and expressive character. After quoting examples of the first introduction of the dominant seventh by the inventor, Monteverde, and his contemporary, Marenzio, in their madrigals at Venice, Fétis adds, that "Toute la tonalité moderne repose donc sur cette succession inconnue à tous les musiciens jusqu'à la fin du sixième siècle." The seventh added to this major triad, as is well understood and felt by

all musicians, imparts to the third that expressive character, designated very appropriately "*note sensible.*" This at once, by its tendency to ascend, determines the keynote and settles the foundation of a system upon a sure and permanent principle; the ninths, their inversions, and other dissonants, which Rameau and subsequent theorists added, being all generated by this dominant fundamental chord.

Our historian proceeds thus, after a clear exposition of the influence of this dissonant in establishing a fixed key to music, and banishing the confused tones, eight in number, until then used in church compositions: "La musique prit un caractère dramatique à la naissance de cette harmonie;

l'opera véritable, la cantata, l'air accompagné des instruments, le recitatif, toutes ces nouveautés qui transformèrent l'art arrivèrent presque en même temps."

The free indulgence of this new harmony soon led to the introduction of compositions into the Catholic service, better adapted to the theatre than to a temple of worship, and which induced Artusi to assail Monteverde and other innovators for having, according to his opinion, ruined the character of devotional harmony. Fétis insists on the speciality of all kinds of music being strictly preserved; and in support of his own admiration for the old diatonic services, of which "Rome seul résista et conserva d'excellentes traditions, que plus de deux siècles n'ont pu détruire entièrement," quotes an expression uttered by Rossini, "Que la seule impression profonde et durable, qu'il ait éprouvée du caractère religieux dans la musique d'église lui fut faite à Rome."

Kandler, a German musical writer of eminence, during a long residence in Italy, twice visited Rome, and his observations, published forty years ago, on the then actual state of ecclesiastical harmonies introduced in modern masses, perfectly coincide with the impressions made upon me during a visit to the Italian churches in 1842. His veneration for the old services sung in the Papal chapel is expressed in the fervent language of religious enthusiasm.

"As music was formerly translated from the church to the theatre, so has she eventually returned to the church, with all the 'pomp and circumstance' with which she was invested, and even surcharged, on the stage; and the softness and sweet insipidity, which had their beginning at the end of the eighteenth century, exercise their pernicious influence even at the present day in all the churches of Italy. Formerly the ardour of faith and love influenced the mind of the composer, and the enthusiasm which elevated him to the most sublime ideas inspired those immortal productions, which have no relation to any earthly object, but which proclaim the praises and glory of religion and of the Supreme Being. Nothing can surpass the true, pious, and holy style of those old composers, whose noble simplicity and admirable art of seizing on the mind without the aid of unmeaning and meretricious ornament, is entirely lost in our days. This simplicity in music, by means of which the principal points are brought out in all their strength, produces incontestably a much finer and more imposing effect: for the faster sounds succeed each other, the more are they lost in elevated spaces, and the feebler is their impression. If the *plastic* art of the moderns, says an eminent author, yields to that of the ancients in vigour and force of design, we may observe the same difference between their sacred music and ours."

In the ordinary services of the English churches, I am opposed to individual display of vocalists in anthems, and I entirely agree with the above great authorities, French, Italian, and German, and am glad to find that the music of our English Protestant worship is becoming daily more restricted to simple combinations of pure and devotional harmony, whilst instrumental music still advances in developing the resources of harmony, with strikingly novel effects of instrumentation.

IMAGINATION, SUBLIMITY, AND BEAUTY.

THE effects of the different arts of taste are similar. The landscapes of Claude Lorraine, the music of Handel, the poetry of Milton, excite feeble emotions in our hearts, when our attention is confined to the qualities they present to the senses, or when it is to such qualities of their composition that we turn our regard. It is then only we feel the sublimity or beauty of their productions, when our imaginations are kindled by their power, when we lose ourselves amid the number of images that pass before our minds, and when at last we waken from this play of fancy as from the charm of a romantic dream. The beautiful apostrophe of the Abbé Delille upon the subject of gardening—

> " N'avez vous pas souvent, aux lieux infréquentés,
> Rencontré tout-à-coup, ces aspects enchantés
> Qui suspendent vos pas, dont l'image chérie
> Vous jette en une douce et longue rêverie ? "

is equally applicable to every other composition of

taste; and in the production of such trains of thought seems to consist the effect which objects of sublimity and beauty have upon the imagination.

ALLISON.

PISARONI IN "DONNA DEL LAGO."

THE accidental sight of a fine composition that has once excited in me powerful emotion, however remote the period of its execution, forcibly presents to my memory the precise time, the locality, the very features of the performers, and every minute circumstance of the scene where its performance took place. The portrait of any poetical artist that has ever performed in my hearing a suggestive work raises pleasurable images in my mind; whereas the recollection of a mere mechanical executant is but a chronological fact, void of interest. So is it with the impressions received from the effect of certain vocalists and instrumentalists. There is something peculiarly affecting in the quality of a contralto voice; and I have a vivid recollection of every contralto singer that appeared during the quarter of a century I played at the Italian Opera; their method of singing, style, cadenzas, defects, and excellences. Never shall I forget the intense emotion of Pisaroni's singing the opening of Malcolm's grand aria, in the second act of Rossini's "Donna del Lago." If Alboni possessed the most equal range of notes, natural and falsetto, the rich, elastic *timbre* of the deep *registre* of Pisaroni's voice far surpassed that of any contralto voice heard in London within my recollection. Each phrase was given *sostenuto* in one breath; and a better exercise for young vocalists, to sustain a few notes with taste and expression, cannot be chosen than the whole of the movement.

Aria—"Maestoso." Sung by Pisaroni, London, 1829,
in "Donna del Lago."—ROSSINI.

Sotto voce.
cres.
p
Ah! si pe-ra, ormai la mor-te
fia sol-liev-o a' ma-la miei fia sol-
pp

LINES FROM "THE LOTUS EATERS."

"There is sweet music here, that softer falls
Than petals from blown roses on the grass,
Or night-dews on still waters between walls
Of shadowy granite, in a gleaming pass;
Music that gentlier on the spirit lies
Than tir'd eyelids upon tir'd eyes;
Music that brings sweet sleep down from the blissful skies."

—TENNYSON.

THE soothing influence of a slow pathetic piece of music on certain natures induces total abstraction and somnolency. After severe mental exertion, I have watched its effect upon men of powerful intellect and keen sensibility listening with a placid smile of divine humanity beneath "tir'd eyelids upon tir'd eyes." The above lines were recalled to my memory on seeing the late accomplished *dilettante*, Mr. Bernal, with his gentle spirit wearied by the political turbulence of the House of Commons, dozing during the performance of the divine adagio of Mozart's Quintet in G minor at the Musical Union. Rogers, the poet, invariably dozed — intermittent sleep—at the Musical Union; and awakened on the cessation of sound.

DE GUSTIBUS NON EST DISPUTANDUM.

In 1865, after the programmes had announced the performance of Spohr's Concertante Trio, Op. 119, I received, by the same post, two notes containing the following remarks:—

No. 1. "I really cannot stand these chromatics of friend Spohr; so pray allow me to transfer my ticket for the next Union."

No. 2. "I anticipate a very great treat next Tuesday, as I see that Hallé is to play my favourite trio of Spohr."

During the season I usually receive a number of letters of friendly advice, what to select and whom to engage, with critical observations. In the midst of this conflict of opinions, although never loath to adopt any prudent suggestion of members, I am always reminded of the words of Dante:—

> "Segui il tuo corso, e lasciar dir le genti,
> Sta comme torre ferma che non crolla
> Giammai la cima per soffiar de venti."

When it is considered how greatly a fine work of music relies on the sensibility, perception, and knowledge of the auditor for the due appreciation of its manifold excellence, it is a wonder to find so much agreement of opinion among a large assembly of persons, differing in age, temperament, and degrees of intellect.

LE GOUT.

"LE goût n'est autre chose que l'avantage de découvrir avec finesse, et avec promptitude, la mesure du plaisir que chaque chose doit donner aux hommes."—MONTESQUIEU.

FASHION AND ARISTOCRACY.

FOR several seasons I had the direction of concerts at the residence of the late Sir George Warrender, Bart., on the plan of those interesting entertainments of the deceased Lord Saltoun, with a chamber band, chorus, and principals. The programmes were selected purposely to suit the tastes of the expected visitors. If the latter comprised the fashionable leaders of *ton*, the most popular and hackneyed music was chosen; if, on the contrary, the really musical families of the aristocracy accepted the invitations, the pieces selected were of a much higher order of composition, and new works were sure to be listened to with respectful attention. Count Flemming, one of the most accomplished amateurs that ever visited this country, and whose sudden recall and appointment to the Prussian embassy in Vienna was much regretted by a large circle of amateurs in London, more than once described an English fashionable concert as a *conversazione* with a musical accompaniment. "Had I not," said the Count, "attended the *matinées* of the Musical Union, I should have had a mean opinion of the musical taste of the higher classes of English society."

Experience, then, has long proved that a wide difference exists between the frivolous tastes of volatile fashionables, and the sterling qualities of the aristocracy devoted to pursuits of mental enjoyment.

ART AND ARISTOCRACY.

THE late Earl of Westmoreland and his accomplished lady, the one a *dilettante* composer, the other equally skilled in painting, were the most popular members of the English aristocracy, both at home and abroad. In Florence, Berlin, and Vienna, the remembrance of his lordship's diplomatic residence, and social reunions, is still fresh among the veteran artists of those cities. The last social gathering I attended at his residence in Cavendish Square, included members and friends of the family, Madame Clara Schumann,

Benedict, and Baron Marochetti. The ex-Lord Mayor Moon was in earnest conversation with Madame Schumann during dinner, and it was wittily remarked that although Madame Schumann all her life had been lauded to the skies, she probably never was before so near the moon.

After dinner most of the party dispersed, leaving Madame Schumann and myself with the Countess. On seeing a Viennese pianoforte, Madame Schumann sat down and delighted us with some choice solos of her husband's composition. Since the death of this lamented and beloved nobleman, the Earl of Westmoreland, I do not know, in all this leviathan metropolis, a single family of the aristocracy where such a social union of artistic talent is brought together, as in the above triad.

ENGLISH DILETTANTISM.

"Each pleasing art lends softness to the mind,
And, with our studies, are our lives refined."

WERE the imaginative faculty of our young men of rank and wealth directed to the moral and social advantages of æsthetical studies, the example of the late Prince Consort in fostering art would find more imitators in the splendid mansions of our nobility, and both music and musicians would be listened to with genial sympathy. If it were inconsistent with manly and other pursuits to acquire a right appreciation of an art which, in our forms of public worship, and most of our public places of innocent relaxation, engages so much of our attention, and appeals so frequently to our judgment, there might be some plausibility in the oft-expressed objection of young men of shallow understanding to the study of music, which is chiefly cultivated and supported by the female sex and the clergy in England. Happily the brutal sports and feudal pastimes of barbarous ages are now changed for more rational recreation, and the people in general begin to acquire a *liking* for good music. Were it necessary, however, to prove to the youth of the higher classes that a taste for music and art acquirements is not incompatible with severe mental occupation and masculine pursuits, I need only point to the names of the eminent divines, distinguished men of science and literature, statesmen and soldiers, which adorn the list of the members of the Musical Union. Did music, as a *science*, form a part of a gentleman's polite education, as illustrated among the various accomplishments of students in German universities, there would be fewer dupes among English patrons of art in general, and the instructed professor would enjoy that position in the society of the educated English amateurs which makes his continental life so much preferable to a residence in London.

Perhaps no *dilettanti* were ever more esteemed in England, or on the Continent, for their genial love and keen appreciation of music, painting, and literature, than the late Earl and present Dowager Countess of Westmoreland. At Florence, to this day, one hears of Il Conte Burghersh and his pleasant art gatherings. In Berlin, too, at a later period, 1846, his lordship's diplomatic residence was the rendezvous of the most notable intellects and artistic celebrities. Here I have met Humboldt, Meyerbeer, Mlle. Lind, Countess of Rossi (*née* Sontag), painters, sculptors, &c. In London, too, his lordship had the tact of bringing together the most gifted and accomplished members of the fine arts: amongst those I last met at his table were Meyerbeer and Marochetti: posterity now records their fame connected with the social virtues of the noble Amphytrion. Had we in London, as exists in Paris and Vienna, a national school of music liberally supported by Government, with a staff of well-educated professors, amply remunerated for their services, it would lead to more frequent social gatherings, much to the advantage of both the professor and the amateur of music. By the present system certain artists are obliged to rely, for their subsistence, on the precarious results of an annual benefit concert—of little use to the furtherance of the art, and often attended by disappointment to the so-called *beneficiaire*.

Indeed, the English have yet to learn that "en toute relation sociale entre l'artiste et l'amateur, l'avantage en résulte à l'amateur." This extract reminds me of the custom of the late Sir George

Cornwall's family, greatly distinguished as musicians and linguists, who never left town for their country mansion without a musician for their guest. Nor can I ever forget the happy days passed with this baronet, a capital amateur violoncellist, at Moecas Court, on the lovely banks of the river Wye. "There is more got out of a musician in one day in the country than during a whole season of bustle and excitement in London," was the worthy baronet's observation, and the accuracy of the remark cannot be questioned.

ENGLISH AMATEUR VOCALISTS.

IN a friendly discussion with Rossini at Bologna, in 1842, the maestro humorously apostrophised Albion and her women thus—"Bel paese! belle donne! bellissimi soprani!" Here the courteous maestro paused; but his alleged criticism on English amateur singers during his visit to this country in 1824, ended with "*cattivissimi cantatrici!*" as the antithesis of the compliment paid to our beautiful women and soprano voices. Music, however, has made rapid strides in England since Rossini, Fétis, Spohr, Weber, Prince Pückler, or Von Raumer published observations on English manners and tastes; although private concerts, where the most eminent artists are engaged, are still often concocted for no other object than that of assembling crowds of persons, totally irrespective of any taste for what they are invited to enjoy. But there is now evidently a desire on the part of amateurs to aim at something beyond the mere exhibition of hackneyed *roulades* and threadbare *ditties*, and to engage the sympathies of those who love to listen to, and can appreciate really beautiful concerted music. Female dilettantism is greatly in the ascendency in England, and recently I have heard gratifying displays of amateur vocal talent in music far above the average quality of works sung at the most costly professional concerts. I now hear of collegians at Oxford and Cambridge Universities acquiring some knowledge of musical theory, and forming choral societies; should they ever be sufficiently skilled to compete with the University Liedertafel of Vienna, it will be a good omen for music in England. The Italian saying, "*Buon dilettante non fa buon professore*," is perfectly true; but it may also be said, that whatever amount of art-acquirement is modestly displayed by the amateur, it never partakes of the vulgarity which is common to uneducated and presumptuous professors.

In Paris a much better education is obtained than in London, and in private houses may be heard vocalists and pianists of remarkable talent. During the siege of Paris, 1871, several families of good position sought refuge in London, and were supported by the exercise of their musical abilities in singing and giving instruction.

VOCALISTS AND VIOLINISTS.

MALIBRAN, being once asked to recommend a *finishing* master of singing, for taste and expression, replied, "Listen to my husband's (De Beriot) fiddling." The management of the *bow* and of the *breath* are quite analogous in their economy, and no more perfect examples of cantabile could the vocalist desire than the expression, taste, and phrasing of a first-rate violinist, with all the modifications of which sustained tone is susceptible. The celebrated vocalist, Mara, declared that, in learning to play the violin, she acquired all her experience in taste and musical expression. I am reminded by this anecdote of a flattering compliment paid me, some years ago, by the most accomplished lady amateur in London, after singing, under my direction, scenes from several operas, at the residence of the late Rt. Hon. Sir George Clerk, Bart. The lady in question presented me with a silver cup, containing a letter of thanks for the great benefit derived from my instruction. In most cases I find vocalists ignorant of the elements of harmony, and rarely safe in reading music of a mixed character. To avoid errors in taste, and to sing dramatic music with a thorough knowledge of the scenes expressed, the guidance of experienced and educated musicians is required. Were violinists to commit the errors in taste which I daily hear applauded in singing, they would cease to be considered "artists."

FEMALE INFLUENCE ON ART.

THE parallel so frequently attempted by politicians between nations, irrespective of the condition of the female sex in their educational and social position, often leads to false conclusions, and the fears of the unreflecting that all nations are doomed to share the fate of ancient Rome are altogether groundless.

The stability of our institutions and the permanent welfare of this rich and prosperous country are secured by the morals and manners of the people, as exemplified in the intelligent and virtuous class of the well-educated. It is needless to enumerate the sources from which one might derive the opinion of the efficacy of female influence on art, and on all that gladdens and gilds social existence, amongst which music ranks high, if not highest, in the catalogue. Even in the history of ancient Greece we are told, that "the degree of civilisation among any people may be judged from the condition of its women. Endued with less of physical strength, that sex can only assume its due place when the powers of the mind are more honoured than those of the body; and if we are to assume this as a criterion, we must place Athens low in the scale." But in England, where the state is making every effort to raise the character of the lower orders above their present ignorance and intemperance, there also women, in their quiet and unobtrusive sphere, lend a powerful aid, by example and taste, to excite a feeling for art in every way, and more especially in music, as most calculated to refine the manners of a people.

Our foreign and literary visitors who publish opinions on the performances of the Musical Union, in expressing astonishment to see ladies sharing with professors an equal amount of gratification, in listening to music of the severest order with score in hand, seem to overlook the known fact, that although excluded from the studies of our universities, music, both as a science and art, forms an essential branch of female education, especially among the wealthy and travelled classes in this country, and English female composers of works of merit are far more numerous than is generally believed.

Of our English female *literati*, it is no exaggeration to say that the refined sensibility of their taste sometimes marks a superiority of eloquent diction over the style of more masculine minds. Their delineation of the qualities of the female heart is tinged with a delicate perception of the beautiful and sublime in nature, which at once asserts the instinct of that poetical temperament which is an indispensable element of excellence in *all* arts.

It is the absence of this divine gift among some musicians that so often proves a barrier to the success of their laudable attainments, whilst others, of far less mechanical knowledge, more favourably organised, at once engage the sympathies and carry off the prize. The true artist and amateur, having mutual sensation, become, as it were, united by a supernatural agency simultaneously affecting kindred souls, and the cold indifference of a new audience melts at the first flash of genius. I am greatly averse to generalising on individual examples, but, so far, I agree with Doctor Burney, that no whole nation exclusively enjoys the best gifts of the Creator; and this admitted, I presume that music has been made a profession in England, too frequently as a means of easy existence, without sufficient regard being paid to a favourable organisation in the student—a *sine qua non* abroad, in admitting pupils to the national academies of music for gratuitous instruction.

Experience in continental society soon awakens travellers to the brilliant powers of conversation, in the saloons of Paris, Berlin, Vienna, and other cities, among the female sex, on matters of small interest and harmless compliment: *et verba valent ut nummi*, —*words are like money;* and when the current value of them is generally understood, no person is cheated by them. Let not, however, the foreign artist expect in this country the fleeting praise of an over-excited public, nor confound the less turbulent signs of emotion of the reserved and reflecting English with ignorance or indifference to art. It is natural, then, for highly educated minds to discard frivolous and useless pursuits; and whilst the masses clamorously vent their feelings of delight with the music given at popular concerts, congenial to an incipient taste, the *dilettanti* at the Musical Union and similar institutions, principally supported by ladies, well instructed in the true principles of art, more dispassionately enjoy in the better order of compositions that gratification which springs from the depths of a cultivated intellect.

MUSIC AND MORALS—MIXED CHOIRS.

DIOGENES speaks of "Musicians who keep the strings of their harps in tune, but neglect to tune their souls to good morals." Of all the arts, music, in its acquirement and practice in domestic life, exercises the greatest influence over the social habits of our lives, and frequently promotes the lasting friendship of virtuous and congenial natures. It is, therefore, of the highest importance that we should know the true character of those to whom is confided the education of our families. It is always sad to find artists recklessly selfish and indifferent to respect, in the exercise of their rarely bestowed gifts. In setting at defiance the observance of all moral principles, content with popular applause and mercenary reward, the musician places himself on the level of the "street acrobat," between whom and his gaping admirers there is no kindly sympathy nor care for his existence.

From my experience in the society of young men, both in Italy and Paris, I am not surprised that mothers are unwilling to allow their daughters to form part of "mixed choirs," as in Germany and England. The improved system in education promoted by the Government of Italy, will naturally tend to elevate the character and morals of the people.

France is eager in the fray, and the middle-class colleges for young females in Paris are crowded to excess, and the number of schools for children of both sexes is greatly increased. National Musical Academies are promoted in Italy and France, and in the latter country especially the Municipal Authorities are authorised to subsidise Choral Societies. In the twenty arrondissements of Paris there are twenty thousand choral students.

In my last visit to Florence, a friend interested in the formation of a "mixed choir" of amateurs, complained of the difficulty of enlisting the co-operation of Italian ladies,—mothers not being willing to trust their daughters.

In reference to "mixed choirs" of male and female voices, very seldom heard in Italy and France, I agree with Mr. Jos. Proudman's remarks: "It augurs well for *our social* system, that there is no hindrance to the union of the sexes in the pursuit of pleasant and healthful recreation, as found in our choral societies and classes. A very wonder we must have been to the startled Parisiens, at the Exposition, 1867, that so many young and fair *Anglaises* should be trusted, not only out of sight or out of town, but out of *our country* for days together. And we may hope that the moral lesson may not be lost upon them, but may influence them for good. Let us expect that France's sons and daughters may soon breathe together the same healthy atmosphere of the innocent enjoyment."—*The Musical Standard*, Feb. 8, 1868.

DILETTANTISM IN YORKSHIRE, 1823.

"The science of musical sounds is now, with justice, considered as the art that unites corporal with intellectual pleasure by a species of enjoyment which gratifies sense without weakening reason; and which, therefore, the great may cultivate without debasement, and the good enjoy without depravation."—Burney.

At the first great musical festival in York Cathedral, 1823, under the direction of Greatorex, conductor of the Concerts of Ancient Music in London, much confusion arose from the neglect of details in the organisation and accommodation of the 285 vocalists and 180 instrumentalists engaged.

Shortly before the commencement of an evening concert, it was discovered that a parcel expected from London with duplicate parts of Beethoven's C Minor

Symphony, for the stringed instruments, had not arrived. In this dilemma, it was agreed that the symphony should be omitted. No sooner, however, did Miss D. Travis begin with the Scotch ballad, "O! Charlie is my darling, my darling, my darling," than a general murmur arose among the audience, and one of the stewards, a grave-looking, bald-headed gentleman, with a stentorian voice, lustily called, "Symphony; none of your darlings; we can hear them any day in Yorkshire. I insist upon the symphony being played." Greatorex, at this unexpected interruption, turned deadly pale, and became painfully nervous. Appeal, explanation, or excuse was in vain; and at last the Symphony was scrambled through, with six and eight to a part. Crosse, in his account of the festival (p. 353), gives more particulars, and states, "The reader might naturally suppose that the performance must have failed in giving satisfaction; the contrary, however, was remarkably the case; every movement was listened to with attention, and hailed at its termination with prolonged applause." Mori led, and every musician, stimulated by the good taste of the steward, played his part with zeal and unflagging spirit. The greatest curiosity was expressed among the musicians to know the name of the *dilettante*, so conspicuous in this matter. Returning from the Norwich Festival in 1824, I recognised this Yorkshire amateur among my fellow passengers at dinner in Stamford. Upon this occasion I made his acquaintance, and he then exacted from me a promise to pay him a visit. At a villa, near Wakefield, well supplied with books and music, I found a member of his family, a daughter, an accomplished musician, who played Beethoven's pianoforte music with taste, feeling, and intelligence. To the end of his life I enjoyed the friendship of this steward of the Festivals in York, F. Maude, Esq., the late Recorder of Doncaster, a passionate lover of music, a kind-hearted man, a liberal patron of the art, and a most sincere and affectionate friend. In the list of patrons to my "*soirées musicales*" in 1829-1830, my first attempt and *failure* to establish, by subscription Chamber Concerts in London, stood the name of F. Maude, Esq.; and I became first acquainted with several families now belonging to the Musical Union during my frequent and enjoyable visits to Hatfield Hall, near Wakefield. Prince Pückler Muskau and other writers have remarked that, "to appreciate the virtues of the English character, and know the extent of accomplishments among the females of the noble and educated families in England, social life in country houses must be witnessed." Musicians engaged in giving lessons during the short London season,—too jaded, and often unwilling, to promote the social enjoyment of friendly unions of amateurs and artists, as in Paris, Vienna, St. Petersburgh, and Florence,—have no right to complain of absence of sympathy for art and artists in England. The truth is, as Czerny observed, that during the flying visits of foreign artists to London, their motto is "*Point d'argent, point de Suisse.*" The late Earl of Liverpool more than once declared that his official, senatorial, and domestic duties in a London season deprived him of those quiet hours of musical enjoyment which made life so pleasant in the country.

Some Russian nobles manage to have a *suite* of servants in their country residences, able to take part in an orchestra. Although instrumental music has not made much progress in the provinces of England, I have known a small number of artisans, *suddenly* brought together during my visit at Hatfield Hall, sing the choruses of *L'Allegro ed il Pensieroso*, of Handel. With all this passion and aptitude for the art in the great manufacturing districts of this music-loving country, it is sad to think that England has no National School for Music! no Library! no Institute!

SUNDAY SCHOOL JUBILEE.

(The Seventh Commemoration, held in the Piece Hall, Halifax, May 22d, 1866.)

WHILST one branch of the art was being illustrated by the perfect rendering of a choice selection of chamber music, on Whit-Tuesday, at the Musical Union, with one performer to a part, another branch of the art was illustrated by the zealous co-operation of teachers and scholars, at Halifax, singing the praises of "*God omnipotent*," aided by a band of 500 performers, with a total of 30,075 of both sexes. Verily, such a musical congress, so well organised and disciplined (judging from the accounts received orally from a learned member of the Musical Union present at the commemoration), justly entitles Yorkshire to the distinction of being considered the Germany of England in musical cultivation. This congress consisted entirely of Dissenters—Baptists, Independents, Methodist Free Church, Methodist New Connection, Primitive Methodists, Wesleyans, and various philanthropic institutions (seven in all). The total number of schools was 94. There is no instance, within my recollection, of so vast an assemblage brought together for musical purposes. What was the effect of the myriads of musicians, as recorded in holy writ, at the Jewish rites in Solomon's Temple, with instruments of percussion and of tubular form, and harps, it is difficult to say, in ignorance of the music of that remote period, but it is easily imagined what was the effect of 30,000 voices and instruments at Halifax, on Whit-Tuesday, 1866. The programme contained the following compositions: No. 1, Hymn, "Iona." No. 2, Hymn, "Devotion." No. 3, Hymn, "Old Hundredth." No. 4, Hymn, "Spring." Chorus from "Samson." "Around the Bright and Starry Throne," Handel. No. 5, Hymn. "Widdop." Chorus, "Hallelujah" (Messiah), Handel. National Hymn. The whole of these pieces, in score of four parts, were neatly printed in a small brochure of eight pages, with an appropriate pictorial illustration on the cover, representing "The Good Shepherd," with groups of children carrying banners on which were inscribed texts from Scripture. In point of musical effect, the 5000 charity children, annually brought together under the dome of St. Paul's, must naturally be more satisfactory than 30,000 spread over a vast area. The above Sunday school commemoration occurs once in five years. It is a pity the fine Cathedral of York, with its splendid organ and able organist, is not devoted to similar gatherings in the cause of humanity. The Dissenters of the manufacturing districts have long directed their exertions to promote singing in their infant schools. When the author of Sacred Melodies, an Unitarian, forty years ago, presented his first volume to the Archbishop of York (Vernon Harcourt), his Grace acknowledged the benefits rendered to the Church by opening new sources of melody for religious musical services. Upon all occasions where monster choirs are engaged to sing sacred music, plain harmony, diatonic and *consonant*, only should be used. The 100th Psalm and the National Hymn, I have heard greatly damaged in effect by the intrusion of dissonances and untonal harmony. The old system of unisons is preferable to such invasions of secular art, disturbing the devotional feelings of a congregation. The vocal arrangement and accompaniments of Handel's choruses for this jubilee were by the Conductor, Mr. A. Dean, and Mr. T. Wadsworth.

PRECOCIOUS TALENT.

EVERY season it devolves upon me to answer a number of letters on the subject of musical education. As the future destiny of precocious talent is mainly influenced by the course adopted in forming the youthful mind, under the tuition of able masters, I cannot too strongly impress upon parents the importance of one observation in particular (in italics) in the following extract, which most forcibly strikes at the root of an evil that, in nine cases out of ten, nips the bud in its growth, and blights its prospects for ever.

"Les talens précoces sont une exception à la marche lente et graduée de la nature; les uns sont le produit d'une organisation plus parfaite et plutôt développée, les autres sont le résultat d'un travail forcé: dans le premier cas, cette marche contraire à la loi commune, a toutefois quelque chose de naturel, puisqu'elle tient à un développement de facultés, indépendant de l'éducation; elle n'est dangereuse que si l'on veut ajouter les efforts de l'art aux avances que la nature a faites; dans ce dernier cas, ce n'est mise à contre temps à la place d'un ordre que l'on ne peut changer impunément. *Ainsi, loin de hâter les progrès des enfans doués d'une intelligence extraordinaire, on doit plutôt s'appliquer à les rallentir, autrement, c'est fatiguer leurs organes aux dépens de leur constitution, et se presser d'en faire des hommes, c'est s'exposer à en faire de vieux enfans.* Cette précocité n'est point d'ailleurs un gage pour l'avenir. Il est sans doute néccssaire de profiter de la souplesse des organes et des muscles, souplesse beaucoup plus grande chez les enfants que chez les hommes faits, et que favorise leurs progrès en tout ce qui tient au mécanisme, mais il faut proportionner le travail à leur âge, à leurs forces, à leur taille."—BAILLOT.

NATURE AND ART.

CHILDREN brought up in musical families soon acquire a musical sense, which thus shows that the formation of the musical ear depends on early impressions. Sailors are quicker than landsmen in descrying objects at sea; and the astronomer detects phenomena in the heavens which elude the sight of ordinary observers. The early cultivation, therefore, of a particular sense absorbed in any genial pursuit is associated with impressions that cling to memory throughout life, often to the abnegation of pleasure to be derived from other pursuits. By force of habit and association, the feelings are affected by natural sounds, which to a musician would suggest no poetical imagery.

Without multiplying examples to illustrate this thesis, one anecdote must now suffice. In the neighbourhood of the Melton Hunt once lived a goodly squire, the lord of the Manor of Wimeswould, a genuine sportsman from his youth. His ear, trained to the music of nature, found no pleasure in listening to the refined music of art, and the full cry of the hounds was to the squire the climax of earthly delight. Upon one occasion, during his visit to London, he was presented with an admission to the Italian Opera to hear *La Gazza ladra*, when Ninetta was first personated by Grisi—at that time the most lovely and bewitching of youthful *prime donne*. The squire, apparently, enjoyed the incidents of the drama, and was moved to admiration for the fascinating Grisi. When questioned about the music, and the effects of the orchestra, he honestly confessed that, to his ears, there was better harmony in the cry of the Melton hounds. Some years elapsed before I again saw the old squire; he was then prostrate with rheumatic gout, and having no taste for literature and art, I could not but commiserate his condition. True to the instincts of his second nature, he insisted upon my accompanying his daughters to Ella's Copse—the scene of the well-known engraving of the Melton Hunt. Here a fox was speedily found, and the hounds, in full cry, soon left me in the lurch upon the squire's old hack. On our return to the manor house, the gouty sportsman inquired my opinion of the music of the hunt. I replied that it was perfect in its way, and the skill of the huntsman in recognising each hound by the tone of its voice surprised me greatly—reminding me of the alleged faculty of the shepherds in the Holy Land of detecting a particular animal by the note of its bleat. "Well," said the squire, "after fiddling all the season to that pretty Miss Grisi, it will do you good to come and stay with us, and I will give you a mount." I replied, "So long as I can have the opportunity of killing a salmon, I much prefer the music of the reel to that of your hounds, and I have heard the Melton sportsmen, in the Highlands, declare that there was more intense excitement in killing a fine salmon than galloping after a sly old fox." "Well, well, it is all a matter of taste; I prefer the music of the hounds to fiddling and fishing." There are, I fear, very many country squires of this opinion, or the musical wants of England would not lack champions to support the Chancellor of the Exchequer in his modest grant of £500 to the Royal Academy of Music. —1865.

MUSICAL ASSOCIATIONS.

CASTIL-BLAZE, in his essay on ballet music, observes that no lady in advanced years ever allows modern dance music to possess the charms of the stately minuets and gavottes, which captivated her innocent mind at her *début*. I am acquainted with an amateur who imbibed in his youth an affection for the music of

Corelli, and to this day it awakens in his mind scenes which his memory loves to dwell upon. Since the music of *Corelli* has no longer any place in the programmes of our orchestral concerts, this Septuagenarian Corellite believes that the taste of the public is degenerated.

THE SALZKAMMERGUT.

"Que nos plus doux plaisirs sont dans nos souvenirs."
—JOUBERT.

SALZBURG and Vienna have much the same attractions for musical pilgrims as Florence and Rome for painters. The birth-place of Mozart and the cradle of musical genius—Vienna—are associated with the noblest emotions of a musician's life. Mrs. Shelley somewhere calls the Salzkammergut country the Paradise of Europe; and Murray remarks that, few travellers who annually visit Salzburg and Linz, or who merely pass rapidly along the high road connecting these places with Vienna, are aware that they have skirted and turned their backs upon one of the most picturesque districts in Europe. The Salt mines alone produce a net revenue of £2,200,000 to the Austrian Government. Sir Humphrey Davy wrote his *Salmonia* on the banks of the Save and Traun, and thus speaks of the Salzkammergut: "If I were disposed to indulge in minute picturesque descriptions, I might occupy hours with details of the various characters of the enchanting scenery." The mountain of Dachstein and the valley of the river Save, once seen, are never obliterated from memory. The lakes, too, in the neighbourhood of Salzburg and Ischl, are also very beautiful, and the retired village of Golling, with its grand waterfall, is most picturesque. After a grand parade, in a camp near Vienna, 1845, of 60,000 troops, a regiment passed me singing lustily a melody, at the end of which, from a thousand throats, I recognised the words, "Dieses schönes Land ist der Steirer Land. Ist mein liebes, theüres, Heimathsland." I followed this tuneful regiment to their distant quarters, and had to wend my way back several miles in the dark.

The melody haunted me for some time. In the year 1850, a party of ten Hungarians arrived in London, and sang capitally together various national and characteristic compositions; and, among others, a Styrian melody, which I recognised as the one that I had heard near Vienna, at the camp. Re-visiting Styria in 1852, after a day's fatigue, I arrived at Salzburg with two companions, and had no sooner begun supper, than the nine-o'clock chimes of the Cathedral, opposite the inn, played this Styrian melody. One of my fellow-travellers, the late Sir Carpenter Roe, struck with the effect of the chimes, commenced writing down the tune; but news suddenly arrived by a telegram of the death of the Duke of Wellington, and created a panic among all English travellers at Salzburg. Thus, the melody I

LOVELY STYRIAN LAND.

English Words by G. LINLEY. Music by GRATZ.

now present to the members is pregnant of many and various associations. When it is considered that the two first lines express the most striking features in scenery of their native country, it is no matter of wonder that the native mountaineers, shouldering muskets in a camp on the plain of the Danube, should sing with pride and zest this national song. Whether Mozart, who lived close by, ever listened to the chimes playing this tune, I cannot say, but Rossini probably was well acquainted with Styrian and Swiss melodies, when he produced "Guillaume Tell."

FACULTIES OF THE EAR.

"The knowledge we obtain of surrounding bodies depends upon the practice and use we make of our senses, and it may be justly said that we learn both to see and hear."—GARDENER.

"Notre oreille est inhabile à saisir les combinaisons de l'harmonie, si l'exercice ne les y a disposés. Sans doute l'habitude d'entendre suffit en beaucoup d'occasions pour sentir les beautés de la musique ; mais l'habitude est elle même une éducation."—FÉTIS.

IN the preface to his treatise on the Theory and Practice of Harmony, containing the doctrine of the science and the art of music, the learned Fétis exposes the fallacy of systems based on erroneous principles, and cites the opinions of physiologists on the faculty of the organ of hearing. In respect to the ear, Fétis quotes definitions by French, American, and German writers, giving to this sense a natural power of analysis which it does not possess. According to M. de Baer (of Kœnigsberg, 1824), "*L'oreille a la faculté de distinguer les sons*, en raison de leur gravité et de leur acuité ; la relation de deux sons est d'autant plus agréable *à l'oreille* que leur rapport numérique est plus simple ; et, enfin, l'oreille a des désirs (Begierden), des exigences (Erforderungen)." Fétis justly observes, "Si l'oreille a tout cela dans son domaine, quelle est donc la part de l'intelligence ? Evidemment, dans cette hypothèse, la musique n'est qu'un jeu de sensations; elle ne saurait devenir un art." Certain intervals immediately please the ear ; these intervals are the 5th and 8th. They are called perfect consonances—that is, consonances of conclusion.

The author of the *Music of Nature*, Gardiner, had a keen perception of sounds and a remarkably well-trained ear. In his list of songs of birds he tells us that the cuckoo sings always in D ; and White, of Selborne, says, "I have tried all the owls in this neighbourhood with a pitch pipe, and found them hoot in B flat, and the cuckoos to sing in the key of D." It matters little in what key the song be sung, provided the intervals are recognised by the ear. Beethoven, in his Pastoral Symphony, makes the cuckoo sing in B flat—in each case the song consists of the third of the key and the tonic note. Judging these sounds by the normal pitch established in France, which is about half a note lower than that of London, the English cuckoo sings G and E flat, and Beethoven's symphonic bird, D sharp and B. Gardiner was wont to relate that on his way home West-endwards, from the City, after a Lord Mayor's feast, he noted down the cries of watchmen, "past twelve o'clock," in every key of the gamut, and, with one exception, consisting of the same intervals, the tonic and dominant.

Ex. 
Past twelve o' - clock.

The exceptional case excited his curiosity and compassion—an aged guardian, worn out in the service, who had not strength to reach the upper tonic note, and commenced on the octave below with this chant—

Lento.
Past twelve o' - clock and clou - dy night.

These intervals and their rhythm form the introduction to the Symphony in D, of the Salomon set of twelve, composed in London by Haydn. Passing along the Strand, Haydn is said to have been struck with the melodic intervals sung by men delivering bundles of firewood, which he made the subject of his Finale to the above Symphony.

Ex. 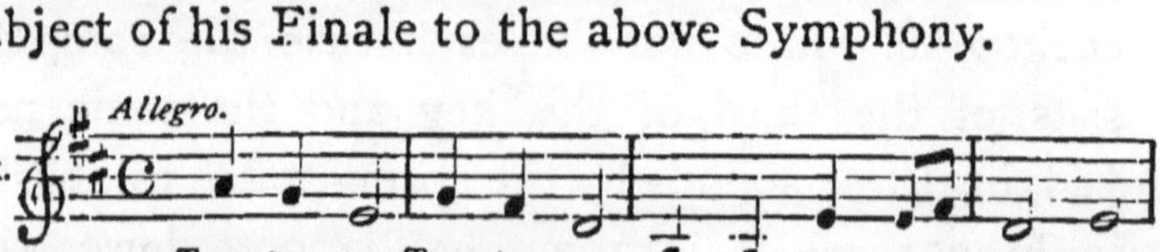
Allegro.
Twen-ty - one, Twen-ty - two.

So eagerly does the musically trained ear of a composer seize upon any succession of sounds susceptible of melodic interest and rhythmical order, that it would be no troublesome task to multiply instances wherein the greatest masters have adopted them for the themes of their compositions.

ON THE ART OF LIVING.

"THE consideration of the want of something to do besides talking, leads naturally to that branch of the art of living which is connected with accomplishments. In this we have hitherto been singularly neglectful; and our poor and arid education has often made time hang heavy on our hands, given opportunity for scandal, occasioned domestic dissension, and prevented the just enjoyment we should have had of the gifts of Nature. More large and general cultivation of *music*, of the fine arts, of manly and graceful exercises, of various minor branches of natural philosophy, will, I am persuaded, enhance greatly the pleasure of society, and mainly in this, that it will fill up that want of something to do besides talking, which is so grievously felt at present. A group of children, with their nursery chairs as playthings, are often able to make a better and pleasanter evening of it than an assembly of fine people in London, where nobody has anything to do, where nothing is going on but vapid conversation, where the ladies dare not move freely about, and where a *good chorus*, a childish game, or even the liberty to work or read, would be a perfect God-send to the whole assembly. This, however, is but a very small part of the advantage and aid to the art of living which would flow from a greatly-widened basis of education in accomplishments, and what are now deemed minor studies. I am persuaded that the whole life would be beautified and vivified by them; and one great advantage which I do not fear to repeat, though I have urged it two or three times before in different places, is, that from this variety of cultivation excellencies would be developed in persons whose natures, not being suitable for the few things cultivated and rewarded at present, are thick with thorns and briers, and present the appearance of waste land, whereas if sown with fit seed, and tended in a proper manner, they would come into some sort of cultivation, and bring forth something good, perhaps something which is excellent of its kind. Such people who now lie sunk in self-disrespect, would become useful or ornamental, and therefore genial; they would be an assistance to society instead of a weight upon it."—*Friends in Council.*

The author of the above extract, A. Helps, Esq., was well acquainted with the best society in this country, and no one who has had access to the brilliant circles of Germany, Austria, Italy, and France, will deny that we are far behind our neighbours in social accomplishments, and in estimating the moral obligations which society owes to literary and artistic genius. In no country but England do persons talk loudly whilst good music is being skilfully rendered in a private assembly; and, judging from the definition of "well-bred society," in which Edmund Burke asserts that "talent is always safe," I am disposed to infer that such examples of want of proper feeling towards talent consist of supercilious individuals, who, in the language of the continental satirist, "ape the follies and not the virtues of their superiors in rank." One anomaly must, however, cease before we can expect much improvement—namely, the congregating together of persons to hear music who have no ears, and consequently no perception of its charms. On comparing notes in my diaries on musical society in England and on the Continent, the more genial sympathy of the latter is quite conclusive. Some years ago, after the performance of selections from "Zelmira," very effectively sung and accompanied, a person, aping the supercilious slang of fashionable life, remarked to me, "That's fine stuff, Ella; *there's* '*go*' in that music."

At a Philharmonic Concert in Vienna, 1866, a gentleman sat next to me whose critical remarks induced me to set him down as a professor. To my astonishment, on exchanging cards, with a mutual desire to become better acquainted with each other, I discovered my neighbour to be the wealthy and gallant Bohemian, Count de Wilczek, chamberlain to the Empress of Austria. This Count, who had followed the hounds at Melton, was well acquainted with English field-sports. I am still honoured by his friendly remembrance of our accidental acquaintance, and a more accomplished and amiable *dilettante* I have rarely met with in my rambles abroad.

MUSIC OF THE PAST AND PRESENT.

REFERRING to my diary of some thirty years back, I find during the season in London that my orchestral engagements included twelve Concerts of Ancient Music on Wednesday evenings, and twelve public rehearsals on the Monday mornings previous; six concerts of the "Società Armonica," and eight concerts of the Philharmonic Society, for symphonies, overtures, solos, and vocal music. At Her Majesty's Theatre the season included sixty subscription nights —Tuesdays and Saturdays—with a few extra benefit nights on Thursdays. Most of the benefit concerts, too, at the Hanover Square Rooms, were given with an orchestra; but at present they are simply a tedious compound of chamber music and opera songs with pianoforte accompaniment. Compared with the terms then paid to an orchestral performer at Her Majesty's Theatre and concerts, they are now more than one-third less, whilst to soloists and singers the terms are increased to more than double.

The Concerts of Ancient Music, after an existence of more than half a century, under the especial patronage of royalty and the noblest families of England, ceased to exist, *partly* on the refusal of managers to allow the Italian singers to appear at public concerts out of Her Majesty's Theatre. These entertainments were highly interesting, and afforded our young English singers an arena for acquiring a good and traditional style of singing the works of Handel and selections from masses and secular works of the German and fine old Italian composers. The style in which the above music is now *occasionally* sung at monster choral meetings, would not be tolerated by the polite ears of the Ancient Concert audience. The noble director of each concert usually entertained at dinner, on the evening of the performance, the conductor and a large circle of distinguished guests, who accompanied their Amphytrion to the concert. In this exclusive circle I remember having seen Sir W. Scott, Moore and Rogers the poets, Sir Humphry Davy, Sir Thomas Lawrence, and the notable political, military, and naval lions of the day. Had the directors nominated Costa, instead of the late Sir Henry Bishop, to the conductorship of these concerts, he would have re-organised the choral and orchestral forces, and infused vitality into the venerable institution, in conjunction with the Prince Consort and the late Earl of Westmoreland.

As in literature, so it is in music—new institutions and new publications create new patrons. What is quite certain is, that the Concerts of Ancient Music, with their compact band, professional chorus, and choice variety of English and Foreign standard works sung by the best native and foreign vocalists, have left behind no orchestral performances of equal interest, and, moreover, that the noblest and richest *dilettanti* have now partially ceased to actively exercise their sympathy for musicians, and to continue their liberal contributions to the musical charities of England. Here I should mention that a public rehearsal and performance of the "Messiah," for the benefit of the Royal Society of Musicians, was included in the engagement for the twelve ordinary concerts, under the patronage of the directors and subscribers. The library of old masters, once belonging to the Ancient Concerts, is now at Buckingham Palace; the old organ has disappeared; the Philharmonic Concerts are now given at St. James's Hall, and the late Hanover Square Room, the best in London for music, has been converted into a West End club.

In imitation of the defunct Concerts of Ancient, Secular, and Sacred Music in London, a society has been recently formed in Paris, which is zealously promoted.

LONDON BENEFIT CONCERTS.

THESE entertainments without orchestras annually increase in number, and deteriorate in quality of talent and works to be heard. To use a familiar description of their mongrel character, many of them are neither fish, flesh, nor fowl.

The programmes usually consist of heterogeneous compositions—grand orchestral music without an orchestra, and drawing-room songs not suited for public rooms. Vocalists and soloists, importuned to lend their kind assistance, are sometimes troubled with sudden colds or short memories, and treacherously disappoint the *bénéficiaire.* The order of the programme is deranged, and the indulgence of the good-natured public fervently appealed to. Occasionally at the eleventh hour, just as the singer is about to ascend the orchestra, the volunteer accompanyist is called upon to transpose a song, or, what is equally inconvenient, to read a badly-written copy, full of errors. The accompanyist does his best, the singer also does his best; both fail to satisfy the public, and the blame, of course, is thrown upon the volunteer "gran maestro al pianoforte." In some concerts, strongly impregnated with commercial interests, the name of the actual speculator is represented by that of a professional receiving a douceur, the singers are paid to sing particular songs, "gran maestri" are invited to accompany them, a valiant body of *claqueurs* are instructed to *encore*, and a flattering notice of the event, somehow or other, gets into print. *Bénéficiaires*, relying solely upon the gratuitous assistance of their fraternity and sisterhood, are never so exigent as to require rehearsals; this, truly, would be an abuse of good-nature. It happens, therefore, that concerted music, for want of preconcerted arrangement, not unfrequently disconcerts the unhappy *bénéficiaire*, and renders him nervous and totally unfit to sustain his share in the concert, either as vocalist or soloist, with self-possession and credit.

If the *bénéficiaire* introduce a severely classical piece of music, the mixed audience of lovers of the art, pupils, relatives, friends, and tradesmen, listen with profound reverence, gape, and at the end, applaud. If they recognise a favourite piece heard at the gatherings of the said *bénéficiaire*, an *encore* is inevitable. The majority of benefit concerts are attended chiefly by the *clientelle* of the *bénéficiaire*, under some obligation for contributions of musical entertainment for their "at homes." Families, out of respect to the professor, instructor of their children, often purchase a dozen tickets for an evening concert which they are unable to attend; and a peeress has been brought into social contact in the reserved stalls with her neighbour's waiting-maid, both enjoying the banquet set before them. An audience, composed as described above, is easily pleased, and slow to anger. The judgment, therefore, of such an assembly is worthless to a really conscientious artist; hence the impatient desire to appear before a tribunal of competent judges, uninfluenced by personal obligations and partial feelings.

Monster concerts in hot, crowded rooms are simply monstrous nuisances, involving very great expenditure—if the artists be paid for their services—and, for a time, making the life of the anxious *bénéficiaire* miserable, which no pecuniary result can sufficiently indemnify. There are other entertainments which, under the title of *Matinées d'Invitation*, cheat both the artists and the public. The former are never paid, and the latter, entrapped by an invitation to what they imagine to be a private, gratuitous entertainment, are subsequently reminded of their delusion by a packet of benefit concert tickets. M. Comettant supposes that 20,000 persons get their living in Paris by teaching the piano. According to his humorous method of classifying these 20,000 teachers, it might be said that 40,000 would be a safe calculation of those who teach the young idea how to finger the pianoforte in this vast population of four millions.

Concert givers may be classed in much the same category as piano teachers, so varied are their accomplishments, so mysterious are their claims—

1. Artists who both compose and play.
2. Composers who do not play.
3. Players who do not compose.

4. Beneficiaires who neither compose, nor sing, nor play.

The entertainments may generally be classified thus:—1st, Orchestral and vocal. 2nd, Vocal and pianoforte. 3rd, Pianoforte (recitals) and no vocal.

The choice programmes of exceptional concerts given by the first-class artists are alone enjoyable to a connoisseur. But what I wish to prove is, that the benefit concerts now given in public rooms and halls, of no specialty of character, are very inferior to those which were given in days gone by, when no musician of any talent would venture to invite his friends, pupils, and patrons, to sit out three hours of mixed music and singing without the relief and support of a complete orchestra. As a sample bill of fare presented to his friends by a pianist of celebrity in his day, Edward Schulz,* I present my readers with the following choice selection of music, singers, and players, heard at his benefit, at ordinary prices, 10s. 6d. the admission, and when every artist, with the exception of Costa and Herz, received payment for services rendered on the occasion.

GREAT CONCERT ROOM, KING'S THEATRE,

June 7th, 1836.

PART I.

Overture (*Midsummer Night's Dream*)..........*F. M. Bartholdy.*
Duetto, Signor TAMBURINI and Signor LABLACHE
"Un segreto" (*Cenerentola*)..............................*Rossini.*
Aria, Madame GIULIETTA GRISI, "Dal asilo"..............*Costa.*

* Died 1876, leaving legacy of £1000 to the Royal Society of Musicians.

Fantasia, Pianoforte, Mr. E. SCHULZ, "Montechi e Capuletti" (first time of performance) ....*Thalberg.*
Air, Signor IVANOFF, "O care imagine" (*Zauberflöte*)...*Mozart.*
Trio, Signor RUBINI, Signor TAMBURINI, and Signor LABLACHE (*Guillaume Tell*)..................*Rossini.*
Solo, French Horn, Signor PUZZI (first time of performance)..*Puzzi.*
Aria, Signor RUBINI (*Adelaida*)..........................*Beethoven.*
Polacca, Madame GIULIETTA GRISI, Signor RUBINI, Signor TAMBURINI, and Signor LABLACHE (*I Puritani*)..................................*Bellini.*

PART II.

Tartini's Dream for Voice and Violin, Madame MALIBRAN and M. DE BERIOT........................*Tartini.*
Grand Duet for Two Pianofortes, Monsieur HENRY HERZ and MR. E. SCHULZ...............................*Herz.*
Aria, Madame MALIBRAN DE BERIOT, "La tremenda ultrice spada" (*Capuletti*)....................*Bellini.*
Duetto, Signor IVANOFF and MR. BALFE, "Li Marinari"...*Rossini.*
Solo, Violin, Monsieur DE BERIOT.......................*De Beriot.*
Aria, Signor TAMBURINI......"Vi ravviso"......(*La Sonnambula.*)..*Bellini.*
Tarantella, Signor LABLACHE..............................*Rossini.*
Overture (*Fidelio*)..*Beethoven.*
Leader, Mr. MORI. Conductor, Signor COSTA.

Contrast this phalanx of talent and a complete orchestra with the guinea concerts of the present day, and I shall not be accused of overestimating the class of concerts given formerly in London.

With the exceptions of Malibran, Lablache, Rubini, and Mori, the celebrities who took part in this admirable concert are still living (1868.) Most of them are rich, and some have retired.

MUSICAL COMMONWEALTHS.

GREAT enterprises for the amusement of the people generally come to grief under the management of joint authority. Jullien's account of the board meetings of the disastrous Surrey Gardens speculation is amusingly true of boards in general—"One has all the talk, and the others sit still as *mouses*."

A committee of musicians, in the management of the first successful series of London promenade concerts, quarrelled among themselves and ruined the undertaking. The failure, too, of the late London Musical Society, which could once boast of its one thousand four hundred subscribers, was attributed to the deeds of a council of many heads; and I cannot but think if the Philharmonic Concerts were managed by one active, intelligent, and experienced musician, instead of seven heads, that they would be more successful. Experience has proved the wisdom of appointing only óne directing mind in managing the Crystal Palace; and the results of individual responsibility, in the direction of the South Kensington Museum, are strikingly evident to every visitor. Sydney Smith's suggestion to a vestry-board squabbling about wood pavement, "to lay their heads together and the thing was done at once," is a wholesome satire. But far more humorously true is the solution of the following Italian anagram, expressive of contempt for the government of corporate bodies—

M	U	N	I	C	I	P	A	L	I	T	A
5	8	9	10	1	4	3	2	7	12	11	6

The numerals indicate the satire—*Capi mal uniti.* In many towns and parishes, where the governing power is intrusted to many disunited heads, this anagram is quite applicable.

Persiani and Delafield, having both sunk their fortunes in establishing the Royal Italian Opera, were succeeded by a small commonwealth of artists, staking their talent, time, and money to direct the affairs of the theatre. This joint direction very soon terminated, and left Gye, the present lessee, sole minister of the lyrical State, and I trust he has "feathered his nest."

MONSTER CONCERTS.

BEYOND certain limits sound does not travel without a difference being perceptible between the time of its reaching the ear, and the motion of the baton and the bow of the performers as *seen* by the audience. To some persons of a peculiarly sensitive organisation, this non-agreement of sound and motion is unpleasant. In the least complex music, the effect of the vocal and instrumental forces is at times sublime; and in simultaneous expression of syllabic canto with the full power of the band and organ, and in the utterance, too, of short detached sentences, the effect is majestically grand. The pathetic melodies of the solo vocalists are totally lost to the ears of the majority of the audience. As an exhibition of art, these gatherings on so large a scale in vast edifices can never be wholly satisfactory. The vocalists strain their voices, and, to please the "mixed public," they are apt to improvise cadences of equivocal taste. In a moral and social point of view, musical gatherings of town and provincial amateurs and artists have a beneficial result; and, for my own part, I would never fail to be present, if the selections were limited to choral music.

DEMONSTRATIVE AUDIENCES.

> " Ut qui conducti plorant funere, dicunt
> Et faciunt prope plura dolentibus ex animo, sic
> Deriso vero plus laudatore movetur." *—HORACE.

THESE lines are ever recalled to memory when claqueurs, cliques, partisans of artists, paid hirelings at theatres and concerts, persist in violent and prolonged demonstration of feeling. Encores, recalls, ovations, garlands, and bouquets, in many instances, more particularly in England, are the manifestations of interested parties. Emotion waits not on the

* " As those who mourn at funerals for pay, do and say more than those who are afflicted from their hearts; so the sham admirer is more moved than he that praises with sincerity."—C. SMART.

morrow; and the first burst of spontaneous applause, said Lablache, is the most welcome to a true artist. The audience at the Musical Union is even less demonstrative than is desirable, partly owing to the great preponderance of the female sex. Nevertheless, involuntary criticisms are expressed by members in letters which often surprise me by the depth of feeling they exhibit in admiration of the performances, and by the judicious remarks made on the merits of the compositions. No work of genius satisfactorily executed has ever escaped recognition, nor has any executant of talent failed to command approbation at our *matinées*.

ENGLISH AND FRENCH AUDIENCES.

THE distrustfulness of an English public, and its reluctance to countenance any new enterprise requiring its patronage, is a remarkable trait in the character of this country, whilst by the French, every novelty of excellence, particularly in the arts, is enthusiastically supported, and the artist crowned with glory and honour.

That most popular, if not the most original and effective lyrical production of modern times, Gounod's "Faust," whilst played to crowded and enthusiastic audiences in Paris and all over the Continent, actually remained shelved in London seven years before it delighted the ears of an English public. As to executive talent, more than one foreign resident musician is now in the receipt of a large income who failed to earn his expenses the *first* season in London. Partly in apology for our apparent reluctance to seize upon every new comer with the same avidity as our neighbours, it might be admitted that the English public is often the victim of impudent *charlatanerie*, and its patronage shamefully abused by the importunities of the most mediocre foreign talent with letters of introduction. Ill-bestowed patronage, we all know, is most productive of the jealousies and bickerings of rival artists, and whilst the really conscientious and independent musician confidently relies on his known reputation for a passport to public support, the letter-bearer digs the ground from beneath his feet—himself a *parvenu*, whom the trump of fame never thought worthy of a blast!

The unprecedented phalanx of musical genius and talent which visited London in 1851,* is singularly contrasted with the little of either, in point of *novelty*, that has since braved the struggle of London seasons.

* *Vide* Baugniet's Group of Eminent Artists, Portraits published by Hanhart, London:—

Ernst	(Austria).	Bottesini	(Lombardy).
Vieuxtemps	(Belgium).	Seligmann	(France).
Sivori	(Sardinia).	Menter	(Bavaria).
Sainton	(France).	Bennett	(England).
Deloffre	(France).	Hallé	(Prussia).
Laub	(Bohemia).	Eckert	(Prussia).
Hill	(England).	Pauer	(Austria).
Piatti	(Lombardy).		

ENCORES AND CADENCES.

"Civil or vulgar happiness is to covet and enjoy much. Philosophical happiness is to be content with little."—EDMUND BURKE.

HAD I authority to regulate the duration and laws of musical entertainments, I would suppress all encores. They fatigue the artists, protract the performances, and are sure to displease some portion of the audience. In classical works of grand dimensions, the repetition of any one movement damages the effect of that which follows. The greedy appetite of mixed audiences at theatres and concerts is never satisfied; and at a recent benefit of a popular singer, nearly every item in the programme was encored. Jullien was wont to say that an encore was a matter of hands at five or a hundred shilling the pair persisting in plaudits, a royalty which no publisher would grudge to popularise a new song. John Bull, with all his boasted liberty, is the veriest slave in respect of the manners and customs of ordinary life. In sacred and secular works, familiar to the public, certain favourite pieces are stereotyped encores, quite irrespective of the style in which they are occasionally given. This I have witnessed on occasions when the music has been wretchedly sung, and the usual encore demanded, to the great disgust of the orchestra and its submissive conductor. Once conceded, even at a first performance, to encore a particular song, duet, or trio, this custom is established. However flattering this may be to a young aspiring vocalist, it becomes eventually irksome to a conscientious artist of established reputation. "Tone for the million, style for the æsthetic few" is but too true; and a few top-notes, delivered with an inflated chest, for a final cadence, *con tutta forza*, are a sure bait to catch applause, and secure an encore. I deeply regret to find, of late, this mode of fishing for encores greatly on the increase among a class of vocalists who have no need of such resources to sustain their popularity.

The above substitution of a loud termination, instead of the original with the traditional shake on the dominant chord,* commanded the most deafening shouts for encore. This happened at the Crystal Palace in 1853, and I was mortified to hear a very great foreign musical authority exclaim—"Voilà le gout des Anglais!" I witnessed the very same effect in the present season, 1868.

Sensuous effects of mere tone thus produced always excite the feelings of the least educated of a mixed audience. In the lowest theatres of Italy a roaring cadence drives the excitable Italians crazy, and an encore is sure to follow.

In oratorios of long duration, it rarely happens that some favourite singer escapes an encore. If this happen in the early part of a work, the other vocalists are most likely to obtain a similar favour, through the persistent calls of their partisans. Tenor singers, with tender throats, suffer most in complying with these indiscreet demands upon their exertions. It is related of the famous Dragonetti, that after performing a most fatiguing solo on the double-bass, he obstinately refused to obey the call for an encore. The public in vain insisted upon the solo being repeated. After considerable delay, the Venetian patriarch of the contra-basso explained to the manager, in his own peculiar cosmopolitan language —"Das *I play encora*, mais si paga encora? per Bacco!" (*Anglicè*—"Well, I play *encore*, but you pay *encore*"); and ten guineas was the penalty which this encore cost the manager. If popular singers, annoyed with the public appetite for encores, were to adopt the same system, managers would soon take means to suppress the nuisance, or else singers would become millionaires.

NATIONAL ANTHEMS.

"RULE BRITANNIA" and "See, the Conquering Hero" are attributed to their rightful paternity, Arne and Handel; but the composers of "God save the Queen," "Non nobis Domine," and the music to

"Macbeth," are unknown, although severally supposed to be Dr. Bull, Byrde, and Locke. During the twenty-seven years I was a member of the Italian Opera Band, the National Anthem was seldom creditably sung—often out of tune and time, and with a most inappropriate cadenza tacked on to the end. Clara Novello threw the people into frantic ecstasy at the opening of the Crystal Palace, Sydenham, in 1854, by the following bit of *ad libitum in alt*:—

The traditional syllabic termination, and the most consistent is this.* The received version is †.

I wish there was a musical censor to punish ladies working their fancy *broderie* on the plain surface of this simple majestic melody. Costa deserves abundance of thanks for suppressing the nuisance of vainglorious impromptu cadenzas, by having arranged the melody to be sung as a quartet or chorus, with the second stanza in the dominant. This arrangement relieves the ear from the monotony of tonic harmony, and also produces an effective contrast of timbre with the contralto voices giving out the melody of the second stanza.

Apart from all these vagaries of the melodic form, the disturbance of the natural harmony of the anthem is equally censurable.

The pupils of the Royal Academy of Music, being honoured by the presence of King William IV. at one of their opera performances, got up the anthem with studious care. The second verse was so completely disguised by crude and elaborate harmonies, expressly done for the occasion, that His Majesty thus addressed General Sir Andrew Barnard, one of the committee: "Barnard, what's that, what's that, what is it they are singing *now?*"

Simplicity of structure and natural harmony are the necessary elements of a popular patriotic melody. The twelfth bar of the Marseillaise Hymn quits the tonal harmony, and none but a French patriot could easily seize hold of this melody. Ex.:*

The words and music of this hymn were composed by J. Rouget de Lisle (born 1760), and dedicated to "la jeunesse française," 27th, 28th, and 29th July, 1830.

Our National Hymn, as is pretty generally known, is adopted in Prussia, but in its simple garb, without the *broderie* of English singers.

Haydn's Melody, from his quartet No. 77, known

as "God preserve the Emperor," adapted to sacred words, and occasionally sung in our English places of public worship, I have only heard played by military bands in Austria. On one occasion, of historical interest to Englishmen, I witnessed, October 1852, a parade of 20,000 soldiers on the glacis of Vienna; a most imposing picturesque ceremony, in honour of a deceased marshal of the empire—the late Duke of Wellington. As each regiment defiled before the Emperor, the cannon boomed on the rampart, whilst the band played, in a spirited majestic style, the National Melody. Every note was expressed *con-tutta forza*, and the effect was very impressive. If our National Melody, *when played*, were given in the same spirited style, the effect would be an improvement on the ordinary *tempo* of its delivery.

The National Portuguese Hymn is a simple strain of no very marked character. The modern National Anthems of Russia and France, though less majestic and pompous in effect than those of England and Austria, are original, pleasing, and appropriate.

The patriotic hymn-tunes of Italy, some original, and others adapted from operas, are not very impressive.

When "Italian unity" becomes *un fait accompli*, we may naturally expect to hear a National Anthem worthy of the event. What I lately heard in Italy was not strikingly expressive of a noble patriot's aspirations.

THE EXHIBITION, 1851.

"THE gathering of genius and science in the forthcoming year is anticipated with feelings of lively interest. Whether it realise the hopes of its sanguine projector or not, the object is noble, the enterprise magnificent; and the attempt so laudably persevered in by Prince Albert, entitles his Royal Highness to the gratitude of every well-wisher to the advancement of knowledge and social economy. Apart from a commercial view of this Exposition, it is satisfactory to contemplate the moral influence of distinguished men of various nations socially brought together to admire the products of human invention.

"Meeting in Switzerland with the great Mendelssohn, and hesitating whether to journey to Vienna or to Rome, he advised me to prefer the latter. 'You will not return home a better musician,' said the composer of 'Elijah,' 'but you will become a *superior artist.*' In this point of view I look upon the results of this Exhibition to vast numbers who will visit it—'they may not become wiser, but *better* men;' and many will become wiser and better too, who are endowed with the capacity to comprehend as well as enjoy the fruits of science and genius therein displayed. 'In solids and utilities,' said the French ambassador to the Lord Mayor, 'England will maintain her supremacy.' If we find that the foreigner excels us in artistic workmanship of articles of ornament, then it behoves the mechanic to do what the musicians have always been forced to adopt—*imitate the best examples of foreign taste.* I shall hail the presence of men of genius and scientific renown—not boors of science that lack refinement—but men who are ennobled by their talents and polished in manners, to whom civilisation owes much, and to whom I shall do all in my power to make their visit agreeable at the Musical Union."—*Record*, 1850.

When these sentiments were published, many of my readers were opposed to the scheme altogether, and no doubt blamed me for indulging in the wish for its accomplishment. Comparing small things with great, both addressing themselves to the anticipations of an active imagination, the beginning of the Musical Union may be likened to the fate of the Exhibition, I found least support where I expected most. The leviathan of the daily press for three long years preserved strict silence, and one weekly journal predicted, to our great surprise, that the Musical Union would ultimately prove the Musical Ruin. One amateur declined to be on the committee because I preferred the advice of another—the noble chairman—on a question which was of vital importance to the undertaking, and has proved to be an essential element of success (the printing of the analytical programmes and biographical notices of the artists engaged). "These programmes," says the author of "Music and Morals," "are models of what such programmes ought to be, and the liberality with which they are distributed, gratis, contrasts forcibly with the fine of sixpence or a shilling, usually inflicted upon concert-goers who desire to know what is piped and what is harped." A noble duke, a staunch patron of music, expressed to me by letter a doubt whether there was sufficient taste among English amateurs to support an institution exclusively devoted to intellectual art. Some thought, and still think, the subscription too low; others considered that I ought to conform to the invidious and ridiculous custom of accommodating subscriptions by following the exploded fashion of rating people according to the class to which they belong, "nobility, gentry, and public."

"Les beaux arts en Angleterre ne consistent que de choses visibles," said a foreigner at a very dull reunion of fine arts. This satire has awakened the attention of an intelligent, active, and liberal gentleman connected with the arts, and I have some hope of seeing one part of my design of a Musical Institute being united with the interests of "les arts visibles," and England spared the reproach of having no library, reading-room, or social rendezvous for educated men of musical genius, whose knowledge of languages, of men and manners of different countries, peculiarly qualify them, apart from the obliging exercise of their art, to give spirit and zest to the monotonous routine of English reunions. On addressing the late President of the Royal Society, and pointing out to the noble marquis the invidious distinction of excluding musicians of European fame from participating in his social gatherings of artists and men of science, I received the following reply :—

"With respect to the contents of your letter, I must acknowledge that there is much truth in what you say; and if I had received it at an earlier period than this, the evening before my last conversazione, I would have endeavoured to remedy the deficiency which you point out; for I should feel no difficulty in admitting the right of a Handel to stand in the same line with a Raphael or a Titian, or a Mozart to rank with a Wren or an Inigo Jones.

"NORTHAMPTON.

"*March* 27, 1847."

"Reverting to the Exhibition, the vast expanse and beauty of its interior naturally create surprise; the dazzling objects of manufacture on all sides bewilder the spectator, and the machinery excites his wonder; but when retracing his steps, with a confused mass of material objects still rioting in his mind, the senses are next awakened by the solemn peal of the distant organ, and the all-absorbing loveliness of Italy's sculpture, to the religious supremacy of art—the ideal takes possession of the soul, wafts it to regions of divine contemplation, and no man that has a heart to feel, and a mind "to take in the spirit of God's gifts," can quit the Crystal Palace without having become *wiser* and *better* for the visit."—*Record*, 1851.

MUSIC AND THE SOCIETY OF ARTS.

CONSIDERING the attractive element of the Great Exhibition in 1851, also in 1862, when thousands assembled daily to gratify the sense with "sounds that delight and hurt not," it is but just that music should claim to be recognised as one of the arts that participate in some way or other in the spoils of those events. I have a vivid remembrance of a very well-meant social entertainment given in 1851 by the Society of Arts, at their rooms in the Adelphi, to foreign artists and men of science. The rooms were hot and inconveniently crowded, the company moved about with difficulty, silently gazing at each other. There was nothing to hear, and no personal introduction for social intercourse. In short, it was one of those dull, stupid entertainments, which, under the title of "at homes," "receptions," and "conversaziones," are peculiar to this country, where persons may be seen jammed together in a silent crowd, nor will "any air of music touch their ears." On quitting the Adelphi gathering, in company with the late Fiorentino, a representative of French art literature, the absence of music from this temple of the arts elicited from him the oft-quoted irony—"*Les beaux Arts en Angleterre ne consistent que des choses visibles.*"

Whether provoked by jealousy of foreigners taking

away the chief prizes for musical instruments in 1851, or by the sarcasms of the foreign critics on our musical wants, and the humiliating reflections of the learned commissioners on the absence of a National Academy of Music, I am unable to state; but a commission is now appointed, with a Royal president, to obtain statistical particulars of conservatories of music in the chief cities on the Continent, with the probable intention of recognising the claims of music in England to share in the advantages now so satisfactorily awarded to the sister arts of design at South Kensington.

Of late years, however, the Adelphi Arts Society has not been altogether unmindful of the claims of music to rank with the sister arts. Musicians and amateurs were once convoked to hear a paper on musical education, written by Mr. Chorley, musical critic of the *Athenæum*, containing some very useful hints; but the discussion that followed was by no means encouraging. One gentleman, a painter, repudiated the idea of invoking the aid of Government, and insinuated that musicians and rich votaries of the muse ought to come forward and provide funds. So think many others, not painters; but we are daily reminded that both rich and poor "have left undone those things which they *ought* to have done." In reply to this opponent of national aid, another painter stood forth and confessed that he had received *gratuitous* instruction in painting at the Royal Academy, and he considered it very hard that poor musicians should not enjoy those advantages which had laid the foundation of his success in the sister art.

This candid acknowledgment of the gratuitously educated painter called forth from another, rejoicing in the honourable distinction of R.A., an observation which both astonished and shocked every reasonable person present—viz., that he did not consider music an *art!* After this explosion from a votary of an art that is *not* a muse, most persons, like ourselves, quitted the Adelphi Rooms with the perfect conviction that this Royal Academician "had no music in his soul." "Let no such man be trusted."

I would strongly recommend to this R.A. an hour's perusal of a very small volume by Fetis, entitled "*La Musique mise à la portée de tout le monde,*" in which he would find that music is more distinctly both an art and a science than any other of the fine arts. It has even been stated in an English print, that music is not a science! England is the country of liberty, where persons totally ignorant of music anonymously write any amount of nonsense; but in France, Germany, or Italy the arts are better understood, and people are not so easily gulled on such matters.

A second gathering of artists at the Adelphi Rooms took place in 1859, to consider the policy of having a fixed standard for a national musical pitch. Finding much time wasted by irrelevant discussion, and knowing the care and trouble bestowed on the subject in Paris, it was suggested that a committee be formed to inquire into the expediency of adopting the pitch established in France by order of the Institute. Opinions in France, at one time, were divided between lowering the pitch *half a note*, or retaining the pitch then established in Paris and now continued in the orchestras of London. The result of the inquiry at the Adelphi, in my opinion, was worse than useless, the pitch recommended by the Society of Arts being absurdly fixed between those in use in Paris and in London; the effect of which would be, if the one recommended were universally adopted, that any of the thousand instruments annually imported from France and countries which have adopted the lower pitch of the French Institute, would be absolutely unavailable for our English orchestras, even by transposition. With few exceptions, the French diapason is universally adopted throughout Europe (1868), half a note below the concert pitch of London.* I earnestly hope that the results of the present committee, composed entirely of amateurs unbiassed by professional interests, will be more successful, and lead to some practical benefit to music and musicians. In no country are musical publications, classical works of the great masters—sacred and secular, instrumental and vocal —*so cheap* as in England, and in no other country is good musical instruction *so dear!* A modern edition of the "Messiah," the whole of Beethoven's and Mozart's Sonatas, Mendelssohn's "Songs without Words," Bishop's Glees, and a thick volume of hymns and chorales cost less money than a pianoforte lesson

* *Vide* p. 160.

by a first-rate master! In fact, there are lessons given in London at high prices, by second and third rate pianists, who, in Vienna, Milan, Stuttgard, Berlin, Brussels, Munich, and Paris, would be extremely fortunate to obtain half the lowest amount demanded. What is wanted to meet the increasing appetite for good music and for the instruction of youths whose parents are unable to afford them a *complete* education, is a National Academy, with Government aid, presided over by an experienced professor of independent means and moral influence, on whose judgment reliance can be placed for the appointment of competent masters in each department. Such a man, it is to be hoped, may be found in London. Genius belongs exclusively to no country, but talent may be obtained by educating those who are endowed with a natural disposition for music; and I ardently hope that the learned and artistically sympathetic Chancellor of the Exchequer (Gladstone) will be able to spare a little of the four millions surplus in aid of the cause of music.* A National Academy with one thousand well-educated students would supply us with competent organists, excellent vocalists, and efficient orchestral and military musicians. As the London mechanic justly observed at a recent meeting in the South Kensington Museum, the competition of foreign schools of gratuitous instruction beats us out of the field. Cold temperaments are found in

* The annuity of £500, granted to the Royal Academy of Music in 1865, was withdrawn in 1868.

every country, which neither education nor practice can mould into artistic shape; but a country that has produced poets and dramatists, *nulli secundos*, can assuredly produce musicians? Precocious talents abound in this country, and the reason that these young musicians fail to realise in manhood what they promised in childhood, is simply the want of a cheap and complete education under competent masters, with access to libraries and good practical exhibitions of the art.

What is meant by a complete musical education includes a knowledge of harmony, counterpoint, composition, instrumentation, musical history, structure and nature of instruments, and the elements of acoustics, requiring, at least, six years' studious application. To these acquirements might also be added an acquaintance with modern languages—Italian, French, and German.

SCIENCE AND ART.

THE rapidity of communication between the Capitals of Europe, by means of electricity and steam, continues to produce important changes in the interests of music and musicians. Engagements are contracted in a few minutes; artists are conveyed from city to city in a few hours; and both in the theatre and concert-room directors are often relieved from the painful necessity of appealing to the indulgence of their subscribers. The application of the electric wire to the organ by Mr. Baker's patented manual could admit of a performer being seated in his manufactory at Paris and playing a voluntary on the organ in St. Paul's Cathedral, London. Nay, more, it is said that by means of telegraphic wires musical intervals can be transmitted, and a melody sung or played in St. Petersburg may be instantly repeated in London.

In company with my master in harmony, the late Attwood, an amateur engineer, the experiment of the screw-propeller on the Thames I heard described as nothing better than a clever invention for small craft in rivers. Upon another occasion, at a reception given by the late Dr. Elliotson, I well remember hearing the late Sir Charles Wheatstone criticised when he mentioned the feasibility of connecting Calais with Dover by a telegraphic wire. The late Mr. Hart Davis also once related to me that he was present at a lecture on gas, when the lecturer was laughed at on prophesying the use of gas to light the streets of London. It would seem that nothing is impossible in science. Whilst, however, science in England is progressing, and the sister art of painting is thriving and located in a temple of her own, with convenience for gratuitous education and public exhibition, I ask, with all humility, is it right for the Government of this enlightened and civilised country to ignore the claims of music?

THE MUSICAL SEASON.

YEAR after year vocalists and instrumentalists of every degree of talent flock to this country in hopes of sharing the golden harvest of a London season. Alas! few succeed; and more than one foreign artist resident in London, with an income *thrice* the amount of the best paid kapellmeister in Germany, has failed to earn enough to pay his expenses the first season of his visit. In Paris the same results, but with this difference, that a reputation gained in that republic of art, and, above all, a *début* at the Conservatoire Concerts, confers a distinction that is prized by the most renowned artists in Europe. Berlioz, in the following humorous description, gives a truthful picture of a season in Paris and London. As was said in the House of Commons in a debate on the salaries of judges, when it is considered how many blanks there are of briefless barristers struggling for fame, the few prizes cannot be grudged an adequate salary, and in the same spirit it may be said the few artists of genius who rise above the crowd of laudable aspirants are never too well paid.

"Il y a un moment de l'année où dans les grandes villes, à Paris et à Londres surtout, on fait beaucoup de musique telle quelle, où les murs sont couverts d'affiches de concerts, où les virtuoses étrangers accourent de tous les coins de l'Europe pour rivaliser avec les nationaux et entre eux, où ces plaideurs d'une espèce nouvelle se ruent sur le pauvre public, le prennent violemment à partie, et paieraient même volontiers des auditeurs, pour les avoir d'abord, et ensuite pour les enlever à leurs rivaux. Mais, comme les temoins, les auditeurs sont chers, et n'en a pas qui veut. Ce terrible moment, dans la langue des artistes musiciens, s'appelle en général *la saison.* La saison! cela explique et justifie toutes sortes de choses que je voudrais pouvoir appeler *fabuleuses,* et qui ne sont que trop vraies.

"Les maîtres de maison soupçonnés d'avoir quelque goût pour la musique sont harcelés par les placeurs de billets, qui, par condescendance pour l'ami du cousin du maître de musique de la petite fille de n'importe qui, se sont engagés à precevoir un peu partout et par tous les moyens l'impôt lyrique. C'est la saison!

"Les critiques sont assaillis par des virtuoses étrangés qui viennent de fort loin faire réputation dans la grande ville, et qui la veulent faire vite, et qui tentent sur eux l'emploi des fromages de Hollande comme moyen de corruption.

"C'est la saison!

"On donne jusqu'à cinq et six concerts chaque jour, à la même heure, et les organisateurs de ces fêtes trouvent fort inconvenant que les pauvres critiques se fassent remarquer à quelques unes par leur absence! Ils écrivent alors aux absens des lettres fort curieuses, remplies de fiel et d'indignation.

"C'est la saison!

"Une foule incroyable de gens qui passent *dans leur endroit* pour avoir du talent viennent ainsi acquérir la preuve qu'ils n'en ont pas hors le leur endroit, ou qu'ils n'ont que celui de rendre fort sérieux le public frivole et frivole le public sérieux. C'est la saison !

"Dans ce grand nombre de musiciens et de musiciennes, marchant sur les talons les uns des autres, se coudoyant, se bousculant, prenant parfois traîtreusement leurs rivaux par les jambes pour les faire tomber, on remarque pourtant par bonheur quelques talens de haute futaie qui s'élèvent au-dessus du peuple des médiocrités, comme les palmiers au-dessus des forets tropicales. Grâce à ces artistes exceptionnels, on peut alors entendre de temps en temps quelques fort belles choses, et se consoler de toutes les choses, détestables qu'on a à subir. C'est la saison !" —Berlioz, 1853.

MUSICIANS IN LONDON.

It would be folly to generalise on individuals of unequal powers of mind, from countries varying in the temperament of their inhabitants; one illiterate, the other well informed, though both endowed by nature to excel in art. But, if there be a needy supplicant for sympathy at a public concert, the musician is the first to answer the appeal; if there be a charitable institution in want of funds, the musician is importuned to lend a helping hand at a musical festival. For his brethren in distress, the musician is ever willing to sing or play. In short, the time devoted to acts of benevolence, one way or other, alone entitles the musician to a generous recognition ; yet, strange to say, in the list of public institutions which largely share in the bequests of deceased millionaires, that of the Royal Society of Musicians, with its fifty widows and children pensioners, seems totally ignored !

The visits of men of genius to England are always welcome; they enable us to judge of the executive art in those countries where the enviable advantages of permanent employment to musicians, stimulate young men of good condition to seek honour and distinction in their profession. To the credit of these foreign visitors, be it said, the list of donors to the Royal Society of Musicians exhibits some of the most illustrious names of musical renown. An English musician once confessed that during twenty years he had played *gratis* at no fewer than two hundred and fifty concerts! Like Timon of Athens, he must have been "born to do benefits."

FOREIGN MUSICIANS IN LONDON.

THE protection given to lyrical productions in Paris is a great encouragement, and nearly every composer of operas, from Glück to Auber, has been in the receipt of considerable annuities from the frequent performance of his works in Paris and the provincial theatres of France. In London, it is no secret that a vocalist is bribed to sing a ballad by a much larger sum than is paid to poet and composer! This species of commerce in art is carried on in a still more extraordinary manner. No wonder that Spohr in 1820, and Jullien in 1859, should satirically allude to the taste of the English for encoring all kinds of ballads. The truth is, that the encores in most cases, like the showers of bouquets at the theatres, are got up and paid for by interested parties. As to incomes of musical teachers, the late Ries,* in addition to supplying, weekly, music-shops with a composition, was known to give sixty guinea lessons in one week; and some established teachers, during the season, give nearly as many. Most of the pianists, getting their guinea per lesson in London, would not receive in Vienna more than six shillings. When a student in Paris in 1827, the highest terms I found were ten francs. Planté, Lubeck, and a few others now in Paris, receive twenty francs. Thalberg had

* Friend and pupil of Beethoven.

one or two pupils in London who gave him two guineas per lesson, and the same amount was refused last season by Rubinstein. It is true that in London the expense of living is greater than in some parts of Germany, but certainly not more so than in Vienna or Paris. I have known a *Maestro di Canto* from Naples obtain a number of pupils on his arrival in London, at one guinea per lesson, who, to my knowledge, in his native city was glad to give seven lessons for the same amount. This maestro is now retired. Foreigners are a long time resident in London before they fall into the habit of living like the English; and when I was told in Vienna by a visitor to the Exhibition, in 1851, that his breakfasts in London usually cost him about one pound sterling, he was angry at my incredulity. However, I discovered that my informant consumed at his morning repast a bottle of the most costly claret, and other delicacies, which English people do not usually indulge in at breakfast.

COMPOSERS AND TEACHERS OF MUSIC AT HOME AND ABROAD.

THE protection of authors' rights in Paris secures to composers of popular works ample remuneration. No such incomes in England have ever been realised by composers as are now enjoyed by Auber, Gounod,

Ambroise Thomas, and Offenbach. In London, however, music teachers generally earn a much larger income than in Paris; but the enjoyment of artistic life in Paris is too seductive to reconcile French musicians, well established in lucrative teaching, to the mechanical existence of the London professor. The high terms given in London for musical instruction, in singing and pianoforte playing, have attracted not only *first-rate* masters from Italy and Germany to reside among us, but a host of uneducated and mediocre professors, who in their own country would barely earn a livelihood. Pianoforte lessons by the best masters cost in Paris 18s.; Brussels, 8s. 4d.; Vienna, 6s.; Prague, 4s.; Stuttgard, 4s.; and Milan, 4s. 2d. Singing masters charge a trifle more to foreigners in general, and English in particular. In Paris, 1827, my lessons were 4s. 2d. for learning counterpoint; and in London half-a-guinea for very inferior instruction. Foreign artists complain of the dear living in London, but I have reason to know that in Vienna, Florence, and Paris, living is not cheap. Foreigners who live in squares and fashionable streets cannot expect to live so cheaply as on flats in their native cities. The artists who come to London during the season and take lodgings in Regent Street or Belgravia must expect to pay more than in the unfashionable *old* streets of Paris. In a *new* street in Paris I have lately visited a very eminent musician, who pays for his *suite* of rooms, of the very smallest dimensions, on the fourth floor, a larger amount than the rent of the entire house I now live in (1868). Besides which, provisions and fuel are not dearer in London than in Vienna, Florence, Milan, or Paris; and good English beer is quite as cheap and wholesome as sham Lafitte and *vin ordinaire.* I admit that distances in this leviathan city of London are great, and time is wasted going from one part to the other to give lessons, but I see no other reason for that general outcry of foreign artists about the dearness of living in London. Florence, in 1842, was the cheapest city in Italy; it is now the dearest. Nevertheless, a singing lesson by first-rate masters is obtained for ten francs, a pianoforte lesson for six francs, and education in every branch of music at the Institute *gratis.* In Paris, as in London, with very few exceptions, where interest sometimes prevails over the claims of true merit, the distinctions conferred on creative and executive musicians are just; and the *social status* which these honours secure to the recipients, induces young men of condition and good families on the Continent to enter the musical profession, in which talent, education, and high moral principles are sure to obtain honourable position, and genius in composition and practical skill, both fame and fortune.

PIANOS, AND MUSICAL INSTRUCTION IN VIENNA.

THE English, says a French reporter of the Paris Exhibition, have no musical instinct. The French, says Fétis, owe the superiority of their lyrical dramas and orchestras to the excellence of their national schools, and not to any natural capacity to excel in the musical art. The Italians have easy access to operas, and live in the midst of song. The Germans, however, for three centuries have had the advantages of musical education in cities, towns, and villages; hence the great number of eminent composers and performers produced in that country, and its just claim to the distinction it enjoys of being the most musical nation of Europe. In Vienna a stall at the best concert and opera-house costs about four shillings and sixpence; the best pianoforte master receives six shillings for a lesson, and a plain grand pianoforte of seven octaves costs forty-five pounds.* I do not recollect seeing any other than a grand pianoforte in all the houses I visited. Upon one occasion, a lady told me that she always had a new instrument every three years, so that the *touch* was always in good condition. "You rich English," she satirically remarked, "lavish a great sum on the exterior of your pianofortes, and keep

* The American iron framework, recently adopted, increases both the brilliancy and cost of the Vienna pianofortes, also their durability.

them as heirlooms after they are unfit to play upon. Our best pianofortes in Vienna are neither so loud nor so strong as yours, but they have a good tone, a good touch, and they are quite powerful enough for our salons; nor do we ruin ourselves by replacing an instrument once in three years." I own there was some truth in what this accomplished lady-pianist stated. I told her that I had a pianoforte in London, an Erard, superior in every respect to all the pianos I have heard in Vienna. "That I believe," said she, "but what did it cost?" I bowed, and was mute.

PIANOFORTES IN VIENNA, LONDON, AND PARIS.

IN 1862 my name was solicited in the direction of a company projected for the importation and sale of foreign musical instruments, at a charge of twenty per cent. less than they are now sold for in London, under the name of foreign patterns, models, etc. In addition to the ten per cent. less cost of musical instruments in Paris than in London, the purchaser is allowed twenty per cent. discount on cash payment, and the professor, or agent, an additional ten per cent. commission. Thus, by direct purchase of a pianoforte at the manufacturer's in Paris, the instrument costs thirty per cent. less than in London, to the amateur. The commission on the sale to agents and artists is excessive. No wonder, therefore, that musical instruments in England cost the amateur more than on the Continent. The manufacturers in England have it in their power to establish a more healthy system of commerce. I never allowed an amateur to pay me the full price charged for an instrument purchased at any of the great houses. One of the leading firms in Vienna (1867) offered to place in my room in London a plain seven-octave grand pianoforte for forty pounds, freight included. Now, as no one can acquire a good touch or style of playing on any but a grand piano, it would be a boon to many families to obtain one direct from the manufacturer, as in Paris and Vienna.

THE ORGAN OF TOUCH.

"The hand is emphatically the organ of touch, not merely because the tips of the fingers, besides being richly endowed with those nerves which confer sensitiveness upon the skin of the whole body, possess in addition an unusual supply of certain minute auxiliary bodies, called 'tactile corpuscles,' but because the arrangement of the thumb and fingers, and the motions of the wrist, elbow, and arm, give the hand the power of accommodating itself to surfaces, which no other part of the body possesses."—GEO. WILSON, M.D., F.R.S.E.

MUSICAL instruments incapable of sustaining and modifying tone, rely chiefly for effect upon the just expression of melody and harmony with accent. In the aggregate resonance of the strings of a pianoforte, a judicious use of the pedals gives semblance of sustained, continued sound. In arpeggio distribution of harmony, Thalberg produced marvellous effects; and upon this speciality of the great Russian pianist, Antoine Rubinstein, a musician of learning and authority, Dr. Gauntlet observes, that a volume of unbroken sound came forth from under his hands that surpassed all the powers of his predecessors!

Czerny admitted that the sensitive touch of a female pianist was often found to invest a pathetic, slow melody, with an indescribable charm "beyond the reach of art." Some pianists are accused of lacking power and passion, but it often happens that a gifted executant of a nervous temperament plays timidly, and is unable to realise what he feels; more especially at a *débût*. Nor is this nervous sensation limited to *débûtants* and young persons. The veteran Lablache more than once told me that he always felt uneasy and nervous the first time of singing a new part. Nor have I ever heard but one musician assert that he *never* experienced the inconvenience of being nervous in playing before a critical audience. This exceptional artist, although not deficient in intellect, be it said, was not of an ardent, sensitive nature. Erskine, in his life of Fox, says, "Intellect alone, however exalted, without strong feelings, without even irritable sensibility, would be only like an immense magazine of gunpowder if there was no such element as fire in the natural world. It is the *heart* which is the spring and fountain of eloquence—a cold-blooded learned man might, for anything I know, compose in his closet an eloquent book; but in public discourse, arising out of sudden occasion, could by no possibility be eloquent."

To expect in any individual executant an equilibrium of all the qualities to constitute a perfect artist would be Utopian. One pianist is accused of coldness, another of over-impulsiveness, both being perfect in mechanism and thorough musicians. Purely emotional music alone distresses the feelings; and those expressive instruments which sustain tone, without the power of accent (the harmonium, for instance), soon cloy the ear and fatigue the mind. Hence it is that the power of imparting pleasure, by varied accents, in every variety of music on the pianoforte, gives to it a preference to all other keyed instruments. How varied in effect are those accents arising from the sense of *touch!* "The organ of touch," says Dr. Wilson, "in many respects, as embodied in the hand is the most wonderful of the senses. The organs of the other senses are passive; the organ of touch alone is active." This sense is a gift; and one so rare that I have no very distinct impression of more than half-a-dozen who have ever *moved* me by the magic spell of an expressive touch! The pianism, in conjunction with the matchless beauty of the music (Beethoven's poetical Concerto in G), that made the deepest impression on my feelings, and which I often recall with the inspired and inspiring visage of the genius executant before me, was Mendelssohn's performance, in presence of the Queen and Prince Consort, at the Philharmonic Concert, the year of his death! Here, intellect, sensibility, power, passion, and poetry were one, indivisible, inseparable! Rubinstein's performance of this Concerto, at Dr. Wylde's Concerts, 1868, was also remarkable for its grandeur of conception, its poetical expression, and wonderful gradations of tone. The effect, altogether, made a deep impression—vividly remembered. The attributes of musical genius in execution are expressed in a few words—instinct, perception, and individuality. Practically developed, these qualities are recognised by the expression, judgment, and phrasing (*distinction*) of the performer. Judging of talents, *testis aurium*, I am rarely deceived, and at once discover the presence or absence of these attributes; and the greatest pianists, Liszt, Thalberg, and Rubinstein, who have developed their gifts at an early age, with the advantage of mental culture, have also realised that which was predicted of them by the most competent critics in Europe.

THE TOUCH.

HINTS TO PERFORMERS ON MUSICAL INSTRUMENTS PLAYED BY THE TOUCH OF THE HAND.—BY LEO KERBUSCH.

THE author of this little work, a resident professor of music in Belfast, has here given an engraving of the bones, muscles, and nerves of the arm, hand, and fingers, with eight short explanatory chapters of useful instruction to pianoforte and violin teachers and pupils. Every well-educated professor has studied the physical formation of the throat and hand, and every tyro, pianist, or violinist, is soon made sensible of the inequality of power in the action of the third finger—the plague of a student's life. It has been repeatedly said that a rich mellow-toned contralto voice is rarely produced from a long narrow throat, nor an expressive touch "*de velours*" from a long bony finger. Dr. Wilson, in his essay on the Hand, explains this clearly in respect to touch—"The tactile susceptibilities of the skin depend on its *plentiful* supply with those wondrous living chords or nerves which place in vital communication with each other all the organs of the body, on the one hand; and that mysterious living centre, the brain (and its adjuncts), on the other." Hence, the successful application of this sense of touch in the performance of the great works of classical writers implies also the possession of mental power to control it. M. Leo

Kerbusch gives directions how to use the arm and hand, and exposes the common faults to which performers are liable.

A painful instance is on record of a pianist, in the zenith of his reputation, some years ago, endeavouring to reach two octaves from the fourth finger to the first, and from the first to the thumb, losing completely, for a time, the sensibility of his touch, and never more appearing in public. Happily, the reputation of this professor had already secured to him plenty of pupils, and by the moral influence of his character and talent combined (a better instructor of the pianoforte I have never known), he has acquired a handsome fortune.

In conclusion, M. Leo Kerbusch merely echoes what was said by Malibran, and has been quoted in the Musical Union *Records*, " C'est l'intelligence qui fait l'artiste." In music, as in painting, for one that excels in the ideal, a hundred excel in the mechanism of art. It is no exaggeration to say that fifty pianists resident in London, can play any composition that has been heard at public concerts during the season. Without disparagement to any other lady pianist, it cannot be denied that the two *debutantes*, this season, at the Musical Union (1866), Mlles. Trautmann and Pacini, possess a touch not common among better known artists. Here I must observe that the French adjudicators of pianoforte prizes justly make a distinction between mere mechanical acquirements and the possession of a cultivated style and touch. I have had occasion to observe in the playing of some youths from Germany, that they play fugues of Bach, and works of the most opposite character, with uniform excellence, and stoical indifference to the charms of style and touch. M. Kerbusch tells his readers that "Touch, like any other sense, may be educated and improved." This is quite true; but, after all, in the language of Shakespeare, "These are gifts which God gives."

On the subject of expressive melody, "Il n'y a pas de logique dans nos émotions," says Reicha, and why one pianist, more than another, invests certain compositions with charms by the fascination of his touch, also defies analysis.

PASSION AND ART.

"Quand un artiste a le malheur d'être plein de la passion qu'il veut exprimer, il ne saurait la peindre: il est la chose même au lieu d'en être l'image. L'art procède du cerveau et non du cœur. Quand votre sujet vous domine, vous en êtes l'esclave et non le maître. Vous êtes comme un roi assiégé par son peuple. Sentir trop vivement au moment où il s'agit d'exécuter, c'est l'insurrection des sens contre la pensée!"—BALZAC.

I HAVE known a pianist so completely the victim of his desire to express his feelings, as unconsciously to use the pedal and destroy the articulation of the most simple ideas. The control of feeling, with power to realise what he aims at, always distinguishes a great artist, and in this particular experienced pianists of the sterner sex, with all their sensibility and nervous temperament, are generally most reliable in playing difficulties, more especially in classical concerted music. On the other hand, the tasteful delivery of a lovely slow movement by a female pianist, gifted with a poetical touch, often realises the *beau ideal* of executive art.

PRACTICAL HARMONY.

It is well known to every teacher that the majority of errors in deciphering chords, in pianoforte music, arises partly in the confused notation of the minor ninth in its inverted positions, the pupil not being able to distinguish the notes forming the interval of the extreme second. I have frequently tried the experiment of making pupils analyse the structure of this chord, and in less time than it occupies to teach them an ordinary piece of music, they have perfectly understood the nature of the interval which so often puzzled them, and never afterwards experienced the slightest difficulty in playing this "terrible discord."

There are few young persons taught in the ordinary mode of pianoforte playing who would be able to answer the questions I have heard put to children in an elementary school of musical education near Vienna. The master chalked on a board several extreme intervals, such as F and G♯; B♭ and C♯; C and D; and interrogated the class assembled as to the root, the key, the structure and inversions of the chord.

The extreme second is found in the inversions of the minor ninths, without the roots.

Derived from Minor Ninths. Full Chords.

To attain only the knowledge of this abstract chord, acquired in half an hour, would save masters many inflictions, and pupils endless blunders in reading harmony. It is a source of pride to see at the Musical Union several of my old pupils, who are quite able to analyse any combinations of harmony, and appreciate their effects.

Now that I am relieved from the custody of the Library of the Musical Institute, recently sent to the Kensington Museum collection of art literature, I intend to arrange a series of lectures, upon practical harmony, and, finally, organise classes of gratuitous instruction in the elements of the science.

*ENHARMONIC TRANSITION—FÉTIS.

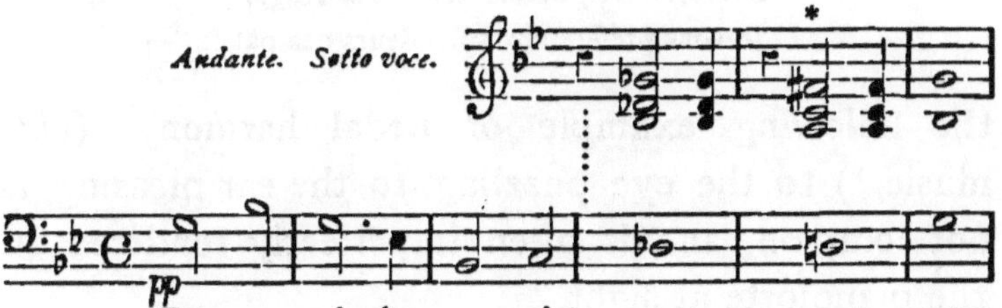
Andante. Sotto voce.
pp
Per se - pul - chra re - gi - o - - - - nam.

THIS extract is taken from a Mass composed, in 1833, for a funeral service in Brussels. It is a novel and an effective example of a consonant-chord, succeeding a unison, and forming a complete cadence, with the enharmonic change to a leading note.

PEDAL AND POETICAL HARMONY.

THE pedal bass, in its normal use, was chiefly the suspension of a prolonged cadence upon the dominant note. Its use, in modern times, offers many novel and striking examples; and the score of "Guillaume Tell" abounds in effects of rare beauty—of rustic melodies, choral pieces, symphonies, and airs upon pedal basses most ingeniously harmonised. The intense colouring of certain expressive melodic phrases is often destroyed by the ignorance and incompetency of the accompanist. There is nothing new of chords in the abstract; but their effects in the orchestra are unlimited.

In the exquisite romance from "Guillaume Tell"—

> "Sombre forêt, desert triste et sauvage,
> Je vous préfère aux splendeurs des palais"—

the following example of pedal harmony, (*vide* music, *) to the eye puzzling, to the ear pleasing, is not common, and is often imperfectly rendered on the pianoforte at sight.

Fétis quotes these chords, with the following analysis of their structure and origin:—

"The piquant harmony at the end of the third bar of this romance may possibly embarrass musicians ignorant of its origin and unaccustomed to analysis. The F♭ in the melody is an alteration of F♮, which provides the accent to express the character of *triste et sauvage.* The primitive note of this melody is F♮, 5th of the dominant chord— 1st inversion, 6-5-3. Ex.  which chord is changed to that of the diminished seventh with C♭. The melodic alteration, therefore, thus—  already mentioned, changes the F♮ to F♭, and produces the harmony of the chord of diminished seventh, with the third altered a semitone—diminished 5th of the Root, B♭.

"This harmony is all the more remarkable, as the discord (B♭ root), after having had momentarily the character of a dominant to a new tonic (E♭), thus—  retakes that of dominant to the original key (A♭). *Ex.*:— 

These harmonic relations upon the pedal (A), the double-bass and violoncello *pizzicato*, with sustained harmony for horns and bassoons, and a pretty Swiss group of notes echoed from viola, clarionet, and violin, form altogether one of the loveliest pictures of expressive, characteristic, and descriptive music that ever emanated from the genius of Rossini. It is seldom sung with appropriate feeling and in pure taste, and very seldom accompanied with delicacy and conception of its poetical character."

Meyerbeer's "Robert le Diable" affords a similar example of intense expression given to a cadence, in the last bars of the romance, *Robert, toi que j'aime,* also by a chromatic alteration of a third* in a discord. I should be sorrow to say how often I have observed this change of harmony omitted by careless accompanists and in arrangements for orchestras. To an unpoetical mind, a mechanic in art, the intense expression given to the supplicating tenderness of the scene by the following harmony may not, perhaps, be fully appreciable. To other minds, it is the finishing master-stroke of genius which crowns this musical gem—this interval so tenderly uttered by the dulcet tone of the horn.

The analysis of this chord proves its source to be the same as the quotation from "Guillaume Tell," 6-5-3. It is here used without a pedal bass.

Source. Substitution. *Alteration.

Fétis, in his *Theory of Harmony,* admits of only one natural discord—the seventh. The ninths are *substitutions* for the octave. Proof—resolve the ninth note, alone. The root of the example in "Guillaume Tell" is B♭; in this from *Robert* it is G♮. Other theorists have different systems, but this is considered simple, logical, and comprehensible; and Fétis has reason to think so, judging by the several translations and editions published of his Treatise on Harmony.

ROBERT LE DIABLE—Meyerbeer.

Coda of Romance "Toi que j'aime." Vide Chord dim. 3rd in the 10th bar.
Horn sustains the note altered—D flat.*
Cadence.
ff
fp
p
pp

GUILLAUME TELL—Rossini.

SCOTCH MUSIC.

NATIVE music is exempt from the restrictive rules of art, and the consecutive harmony of perfect fifths (*vide* p. 126) which constitutes, in the ears of true Highlanders, the charm of the drone-bass to their favourite reel tunes, may be charitably regarded as the national graces beyond the reach of art. In Paris, 1827, whilst studying counterpoint with Fétis, I made the acquaintance of a student in composition, a pupil of Reicha. On one occasion he produced a number of clever melodies, constructed upon the Scotch scale, many of which might pass for airs of native growth. This student, an Alsacian, had never heard a Scotch tune, bagpipe, or known a Scotchman. His rules were simple, viz., to construct melodies with the omission of the fourth and seventh of the scale; to introduce, occasionally, short notes on the accent (snaps), and substitute subdominant harmonies for the ordinary use of dominant. The vulgar notion of concocting a Scotch melody by playing only the black notes of the pianoforte is totally beside the question, and is thus explained. The key of F♯ major, with its scale of black notes only, has no fourth nor seventh; hence, the black notes simply represent those intervals within the rule prescribed to construct a Scotch melody. A more pleasing and effective example could not be adduced than the theme of the scherzo of the Scotch symphony by

Mendelssohn; which said scherzo has suggested the title by which the symphony, No. 3, in A minor, is familiarly known (1). In the first four bars, we have the melody without the fourth and seventh, closing on a short note. The scale of notes represented in this theme, ought, alone, to complete the entire structure of the popular melodies, "Should auld acquaintance be forgot," "The Last Rose," and most of the best traditional tunes—Scotch and Irish. The final cadence of subdominant harmony closes the melody of "Auld Lang Syne" (2); No. 4 exhibits the drone consecutive 5ths.

Another characteristic is shown in the minor melody partaking of the major harmony one note below the tonic. These are the chief features of what are termed Scotch melodies, some of which, says a writer, received from Rizzio the flowing periods of the Italian style. It is also an established fact that the passion for Scotch songs and tunes in Mary's reign induced many unprincipled London musicians to concoct Scotch tunes with surreptitious titles, and despatch them over the Border to sell for tunes of native growth. Mr. William Chappell has explained this kind of traffic in his book on popular music. Out of the materials which are included in the examples 2, 3, and 4, my French fellow-student composed many Scotch songs and dance tunes, very like native growth. It is, therefore, obvious, that by the intrusion of the forbidden intervals, the traditional tunes of Scotland and Ireland lose their native complexion, and sink into the ordinary class of cosmopolitan art.

REHEARSALS AND WEBER.

WEBER is reputed to have said that he preferred a willing and patient musician of ordinary ability, to the greatest artist who shirked rehearsals. It is commonly imagined that artists meet together for the mere practice of the music, whereas, in nine cases out of ten, half the time at rehearsals is often taken up in correcting the errors in the copies, and marking passages with corresponding *nuance*, suggested by the leading artist of the party. In the Pleyel edition of Mozart's and Hadyn's Quartets, the errors and omissions are so numerous, that several important corrections have been made in one composition by artists engaged at the Musical Union.

At the rehearsals of Hummel's Septet for this day's performance (1854), not less than half a dozen misprints in the accompaniments were discovered. Yet these very copies have been played from in public, with all the misprints scrupulously adhered to, for the last ten years. We commend amateurs to procure the Vienna edition. A score of this fine work is recently published in a convenient form.

EDUCATION AND CHARACTER.

> "Learning, if deep, if useful and refined,
> Communicates its polish to the mind."

THE social *status* of a musician in this country is the constant theme of discussion among foreigners, who are apt to form erroneous conclusions from impressions received during the bustle and turmoil of the London season. For my own part, in all the countries I have visited, I find the same courtesies towards artists of genius, education, and character, among well-bred persons. Unfortunately, genius is not necessarily allied to moral principles; and artists of reckless conduct, basking in the sunshine of a temporary success, are not likely to obtain here that permanent respect enjoyed only by men of unblemished character. As our great moralist observes, "Those who, in confidence of superior capacities or attainments, disregard the maxims of life, should be reminded that nothing will supply the want of prudence; and that negligence and irregularity, long continued, will make knowledge useless, wit ridiculous, and genius contemptible." Happily for that branch of the art promoted at the Musical Union, instrumentalists of eminence are for the most part persons of education and character, often gifted with the

> "Creative genius and the power divine
> That warms and melts th' enthusiastic soul."

In those countries where music is more generally cultivated among young men than in England, the artistic relationship with society in general is closer, but not more sincere. This is proved at the benefit concerts during a London season, where much dull music and very inferior performances are tolerated purely out of kindly feeling towards the *bénéficiaire*.

The private practice of chamber music naturally brings artists into social contact with the domestic circles of amateurs; and every day's experience gives occasion to observe that musicians of character and education have no reason to complain of their social position in England. It is quite true that London fashionable music-parties frequently bring persons together who have little taste for the art, and little sympathy for the artist. In those families, however, where music is thoroughly appreciated, both the social and artistic position of the respectable professor is invariably acknowledged, and never more pleasantly than when participating in the domestic hospitality of country life.

THE SOCIAL STATUS OF MUSICIANS IN VIENNA.

THE competition for place among musicians in Germany, as in Paris, is so keen that no artist can expect to hold any prominent and permanent position at Court, or at the national institutions for instruction, without character, education, and acknowledged talent.

That lax principle of *tout est permis chez les artistes* may be tolerated among a certain class of persons in France, but not in well-bred society of Germany; but even in France, owing to a *mésalliance*, a very illustrious musician was long denied a chair at the Institute, which he now, a widower, so worthily occupies. In Vienna particularly, musicians of moral character have much reason to be satisfied with the friendly relations that exist between them and the noble *dilettanti* of Austria. Among the patrons, friends, and connoisseurs of music in Vienna, more or less associated—during the golden period of the immortal triad—with the lives of Haydn, Mozart, and Beethoven, are the well-known names of Prince Esterhazy, Prince Lobkowitz, Prince Radziwil, Prince

Lichnovsky, Prince Rasoumoffsky, Prince Schwarzemberg, Prince Czartoryski, Counts Appony and Erdödy (Hungarians), Archduke Rodolph, etc., etc. The courtesy shown to musical strangers by the press generally is proverbial. No wonder that Mozart and Beethoven, more or less in contact with these princely *dilettanti*, preferred a residence in the Austrian capital. Mozart was offered great temptation to go to Berlin, and Beethoven resisted a salary of 600 golden ducats for life offered by the King of Westphalia. On my first visit to Vienna, in 1845, 1846, after enjoying an admirable performance of quartets, led by the celebrated Mayseder, at the palace of the late venerable Prince Czatoryski, the latter politely gave me an *entrée* to his opera box for the winter season. On one occasion, I observed Thalberg sitting with the Prince Lichtenstein, Berlioz with Prince Metternich, and Parish Alvars (an English harpist and composer, a genius and a thorough musician) with the Princess Esterhazy. The opera, *Fidelio,* was perfectly well given. Opposite to me was an individual making himself unnecessarily conspicuous. "That *imbécile*," said the Prince, "is the nephew of Beethoven. He drives four-in-hand, and will soon spend the 'florins' inherited from his uncle" (*vide* p. 218).

THE SOCIAL STATUS OF MUSICIANS.

"Mores cuique sui fingunt fortunam."

WEBER *fils*, biographer of his father, speaks of monarchs in Germany proud of walking arm in arm with artists—a thing unknown, he rightly observes, in England. I confess that I am not aware of musicians, either in Berlin or Vienna, being on such friendly terms with crowned heads. There is a story told of a *soirée* at the palace of the Emperor Ferdinand of Austria, at which a celebrated pianist was much chagrined at the Emperor's silence on the merits of his music and the reflections made upon his "perspiring" efforts in playing; and, whilst I myself was sitting at a Philharmonic Concert at Vienna, in 1845, with the family of the Prince Czartoryski, this emperor and suite rose from their seats and retired in the middle of the sublime adagio of Beethoven's B♭ Symphony. "Vous voyez, M. Ella, que l'Empéreur aime mieux son diner qu'un adagio de Beethoven," said the venerable prince—the dinner-hour being two P.M.

There are few persons among the noble and wealthy English who delight in artistic social gatherings, such as were so affably and hospitably entertained by that popular nobleman the late Earl of Westmoreland and his accomplished lady. I have witnessed much friendly cordiality between artists and amateurs among the nobility abroad; but here the young rich nobles unfortunately do not cultivate the art of music. The present Emperor of Austria has not, any more than the late Emperor of the French, much knowledge of, or sympathy for, the art. It is a pity that their imperial military proclivities are not softened by its influence.

When Mendelssohn and Meyerbeer visited the Queen of England and the lamented Prince Consort, apart from the usual courtesies so amiably expressed by Her Majesty to all artists honoured with an interview, the knowledge and judicious criticism of the prince both delighted and surprised the two great composers. This I heard, more than once, from their own lips. From philosophers, statesmen, and painters I have also heard similar remarks; and had the life of this prince been mercifully spared, the arts in England would have had an advocate to plead successfully on behalf of their institutions.

The antagonistic spirit and crotchety humours of some English critics greatly tend to damage the social relations of artists, and to create factions where brotherly love should exist. Whatever value an artist may put on honours and distinctions, if he live for his art, and in his art, as Beethoven writes, the good fellowship of his own fraternity is most to be prized. Musicians may be what the poet describes,

"Half-witted, merry, and mad,"

but I never knew a *dull* artist; and those who have

travelled are more or less acquainted with several languages, and bring from foreign courts abundance of pleasant anecdote.

The musical degrees of our English universities are distinctions every musician would covet, were they conferred only upon artists of superior merit. Handel, it is true, disdained the proffered compliment, which Haydn subsequently accepted—Mus. Doc. Oxon. The one English musician whose compositions entitle him to distinction is Sterndale Bennet; not only is our countryman a doctor of music, but professor in the University of Cambridge, with power to confer degrees.

The success of mediocre talents in London often provokes the jealousy of artists of greater merit; but it frequently happens that clever, capricious men, wantonly set at defiance the rules of good breeding, and leave to others of less talent the benefit of having a respectable character and an obliging disposition. Genius without character may bask in the sunshine of public favour, but in no city I have visited does it permanently succeed in obtaining a social *status* in good society.

What is most desirable for the general interests of the arts in England is an Institute like the one in France. Let such an institution be established, composed of the best men in each section of the fine arts; confer honours and distinctions upon its members, and let all matters of national import connected with the arts be confided to their judgment and decision.

We should then require no more æsthetic discussions in the House of Commons about architecture, painting, sculpture, and music. They manage these things well at the Institute in France; and I am credibly informed that the foundation of a similar Institute in England was among the several wise measures contemplated by the Prince Consort. The State, at present, has no care for music, and every musician must care for himself. I have enjoyed the society of princes and ambassadors on the Continent, visited persons of all ranks in my own country, partaken of the luxuries of the wealthy, and the privileges of sport with the highest nobles; but as to social life during the bustle and fatigue of a London season, the artist himself is of necessity unsociable; and the nobles and statesmen are too much absorbed in public duties to seek society out of their own immediate circle. If artists would be content to labour less and promote social intercourse more, with character and talent combined, they would always command in English society that *social status* which is most prized, and secure the lasting friendship of congenial minds and devoted lovers of music. Beethoven had no mean opinion of the English character, and wrote to Ries, 1819, as follows:—"The English are generally very able fellows, with whom I should like to pass some time in their own country." Some foreigners, accustomed to the English climate and society, Germans and Italians, seem to enjoy themselves in this country notwithstanding "*les tristes dimanches*," and our reservedness of manners. One thing is certain, in no city, save St. Petersburgh, do musicians obtain such high terms for lessons, and earn such large incomes, as in London. When piano and singing masters give lessons for eight and ten hours daily during the season, it is obvious that they must be too fatigued to assist at those friendly reunions which make life abroad so pleasant. Hence it is, that few of our eminent instructors, foreign and native, fraternize with the *dilettanti*, and enjoy the social position which is at their command.

In this country the highest honours of the crown and offices of the state are not denied to men of the humblest parentage; whilst supremacy of intellect, with moral influence of character and refinement of manners, command respect, and secure a social status among the best and wisest.

BIOGRAPHICAL MISSTATEMENTS.

> " L'homme est de glace aux véritiés:
> Il est de feu pour le mensonge."
>
> —LAFONTAINE.

THE biography of Weber by his son, translated into English by Mr. Palgrave Simpson, contains the following reflections upon the manners of the English aristocracy towards artists. I am not disposed to question the accuracy of the writer's views on English society in general, but the particular instance referred to in the extract below, and the description given of a custom which *never* existed in any nobleman's mansion, I can authoritatively contradict.

The biographer states that "The most distinguished artists were invited into noble houses—they came and went—the very servants would have turned up their noses at the degradation of presenting them with refreshment. The master and mistress of the house pointed out to them, with lordly condescension, their place, *which was frequently even divided off from the general company by a cord!*" As this stupid story, so frequently repeated by a certain class of disappointed and ill-conditioned musicians in London and on the continent, may possibly prejudice foreigners against the English aristocracy, I will, at once, set the matter at rest by explaining the source of this obnoxious cord. In 1831, I translated the Camp Chorus of Soldiers, opening the second act of Spohr's "Jessonda," and had it well sung and accompanied at the house of Lord Saltoun. The late Sir George Warrender, who was present, requested to have it repeated at one of his concerts under my direction. To keep the company from pressing too near the band and chorus, a silken cord was attached to the pianoforte from the side entrance, *by my orders.* The Duke of Wellington, arriving late, passed through the boudoir, and, as usual, exchanged a few words with the artists therein assembled. On my attempting to put his reserved seat beyond the prescribed boundary of the auditors, His Grace objected to its removal, at the same time directing my attention to the words of the chorus—

> "No song nor sound to a soldier's heart
> Such pleasure is, or does impart."

However, when Mme. Pasta saw this arrangement, and erroneously imagined it purposely made for the reason assigned in the above statement of Weber's son, I immediately had the cord removed. Nor do I know, nor have I ever heard, of any instance of a similar arrangement at a nobleman's house—certainly not for the invidious distinction alluded to by the biographer. Thus, from so trivial a circumstance in 1831 (happening five years *after* the death of Weber), has arisen this libel against the English aristocracy, which I had never seen in print before reading the above biography in 1865.

At the professional and amateur gatherings of Lord Saltoun, which were under my direction for more than twenty years,* the social status of the artist was recognised with the utmost liberality by the most courteous of dukes in the realm. The right hon. Baronet, at whose mansion in Albemarle Street the above story originated, was most affable, generous, and hospitable, and annually expended £1000 in private concerts. To his country residence, Cliefden House (now the property of the Duchess Dowager of Sutherland), I have had *carte blanche*

* Of some thirty amateurs who originally played at these parties, three only survive, viz., The Baron J. B. Heath, General Stephens, and General the Hon. A. Legge.

to invite any number of distinguished artists to luncheon, dinner, and visit the grounds, with carriages provided to and from the railroad station. I trust, after this explanation, German biographers will refrain from calumniating the English aristocracy, and publishing statements repugnant to good taste and common sense.

Musical parties, in London, are frequently given by what the *Times* describes as " men of wealth, who have all the faults of the old aristocracy, without their grace," and who have neither knowledge of, nor sympathy for, the art ; but, talent is always safe in the company of well-bred persons, says Burke, and it is admitted that the English aristocracy, having a genial taste for literature, science, and the fine arts, are most courteous in all their relations with artists.

In a country where music is scarcely recognised as an important element in the accomplishments of young men of condition, and its encouragement is dependent chiefly on the female sex and the clergy, the musician naturally finds fewer of the sterner sex able to appreciate his art in England than on the continent. Without knowledge there is little genuine sympathy, and since the death of the Prince Consort and the Earl of Westmoreland, the arts in general, and music in particular, have lost their best friends and protectors in this country.

THE DUKE OF WELLINGTON AND ROSSINI.

NO sooner was Rossini arrived in London than he was invited by the King to the Pavilion at Brighton. All sorts of incredible stories were circulated about his reception by George the Fourth. In the diary of a dilettante, December 1st, 1829, the true version of an oft-repeated story is thus given: "The newspapers too often get incorrect versions of fashionable anecdotes; one proof whereof is in the following manner of relating a story which has some foundation in truth. When Rossini," says the *Atlas*, "was at the Palace at Brighton, he is reported to have congratulated a certain lady of quality, who moved between him and the Duke of Wellington, that she stood between the two greatest men in Europe." It ought to have been thus told: "The Countess —— in passing to her own refreshment-room, took the arm of the Duke of Wellington, and likewise that of Signor Rossini, remarking to both that she was then conducted by the two greatest men, etc. The fact is, that whatever may be Rossini's opinion of himself, and of his rank in the eyes of the world, he never acts with impropriety; but in society invariably shows a well-bred deference to all present, accompanied by a demeanour which, though manly and independent, is anything rather than vain and assuming." This is a fair estimate of the character of Rossini. A more independent and thoroughly well-bred gentleman, witty and amusing, I have never known.

FEMALE CHORISTERS.

DURING the early part of my professional employment in the orchestra of the King's Concerts of Ancient Music, the principal female choristers were brought from Lancashire. These ladies, who were supposed to have finer voices and a more intimate acquaintance with the *chefs d'œuvre* of the sacred composers than the theatrical choristers in London, were adequately remunerated to remain the whole season in town to sing exclusively at twelve concerts, and were familiarly called "The Lancashire Witches." Choral societies are now increased to such an extent, that if it were required to bring together in London a thousand good treble voices and choristers, I do not apprehend there would be the slightest difficulty. Education, then, in one branch of the art, has removed a prejudice long entertained, that musical intelligence, treble voices, and female choristers were peculiar to the soil of Lancashire. The following allusion to the Rheinische Musik-Schule, in Cologne, perfectly agrees with the opinions I have often expressed on the subject of musical education in England :—

"We have had great poets, painters, and sculptors, why not great musicians? The truth is, that in England the expense of obtaining a thorough course of musical instruction is so large, that the greater number of those that devote themselves to the art must necessarily dispense with their instructors when they are but half educated, and are, consequently, not fairly entitled to call themselves 'Professors.' . . . The Rheinische Musik-Schule was founded in 1850, and is under the able and intelligent direction of Herr Ferdinand Hiller. Its object is to provide musical students of both sexes, with a thorough education in every branch of the art, under the superintendence of the best masters, and at an unprecedently small cost. . . . Pupils are received in April and October in each year, and the yearly charge made for each is £13."

GREEK TRAGEDY AND THE LYRICAL DRAMA.

WITH all my admiration for the genius and learning of the great musical illustrator of Sophocles, Mendelssohn, I have ever felt deeply impressed with the impossibility of investing the ancient tragedies with sufficient musical interest by the united effects of orchestral aid and *male* voices, to suit the taste of the age we now live in. In Berlin the experiment failed to obtain the sympathies of its enlightened public, and the Prussian monarch withdrew the representation of them to Potsdam for his own personal gratification. In Paris, the fashion of the day applauded "Antigone" for a season; but in London, with the advantage of scenic representation and action, and admirably performed at St. James's Theatre in all its musical details, the spirited entrepreneur suffered a considerable pecuniary loss by the speculation. Subsequently, a less perfect attempt was made at the Royal Italian Opera, with Mr. Bartley reciting portions of Œdipus; a most monotonous and unsatisfactory exhibition. Apposite to the subject, some observations of Schlegel will probably be perused with interest—

"The ancient tragedy has been frequently compared with the opera, because it was accompanied with music and dancing. But this betrays the most complete ignorance of the spirit of classical antiquity. Their dancing and music had nothing in common with ours but the name. In tragedy the chief object was the poetry, and every other thing was strictly subordinate to it. But in the opera the poetry is merely an accessory, the means of connecting the different parts together; and it is almost buried under its associates. The best prescription for the composition of the text of an opera is to give a poetical sketch, which may be afterwards filled up and coloured by the other arts. This anarchy of the arts, where music, dancing, and decoration endeavour to surpass each other by the most profuse display of dazzling charms, constitutes the very essence of the opera. What sort of opera music would it be, where the words should receive a mere rythmical accompaniment of the simplest modulations? The fantastic magic of the opera consists altogether in the luxurious competition of the different means, and in the perplexity of an overpowering superfluity. This would at once be destroyed by an approximation to the severity of the ancient taste in every one point—even in that of the costume, for the contrast would render the variety in all the other departments quite insupportable. The costume of the opera ought to be dazzling and overladen with ornaments; and hence many things that have been censured as unnatural, such as exhibiting hereos warbling and trilling in the excess of despondency, are perfectly justifiable. This fairy world is not peopled by real men, but by a particular kind of singing creatures. Neither is it any disadvantage to us that the opera is conveyed in a language which is not generally understood; the text is altogether lost in the music, and the language the most harmonious and musical, and which contains the greatest number of open vowels and distinct accents for recitative, is therefore the best. It would be as absurd to attempt to give to the opera the simplicity of the Grecian tragedy, as it is to declare that there is any resemblance between them."

Reflecting on the immense labour bestowed upon the choral illustrations of these Greek tragedies, I have always regretted that Mendelssohn had not devoted his genius to the production of works more genial to his nature, and thus increased our scanty store of his orchestral and chamber music, at a time when he so successfully produced his Italian and Scotch symphonies and his splendid Trio in C minor.

EUPHONY OF LANGUAGE.

DURING my first visit to Berlin, in 1846, the late Earl of Westmoreland gave me the *entrée* to the large box at the Royal Opera House, occupied jointly by the English and French ambassadors. Mdlle. Lind was then in vogue, and on one occasion, whilst playing the *rôle* of Norma, in the last scene with Pollione, she, with much intensity of feeling and energy of expression, had no sooner delivered the opening melodic phrase, "Du bist in meinen Händen," than the Duc de Dalmatie exclaimed, "O mon Dieu! quelle langue pour la musique!—'*Du bist! du bist!*'" Addressing me, he inquired what were the words in Italian to that fine melody, to which I answered, "In mia man alfin tu sei." "A la bonheur!" exclaimed his Excellency, "*voilà la langue pour la musique!*" I confess that, having been so many years accustomed to the Italian, "*du bist*" grated harshly on my ears; and although, in common with every musician, I appreciate the fine lyrical works of the German school, I can never admit that the German language is a whit better for music than the English.

Allegro moderato. "Norma." BELLINI.

The suppression of the first note of this dignified melody robs it of that stately expression so truthfully adapted to the scene, and renders the German text, in a musical sense, abrupt.

I have long come to the conclusion, that the delivery of the voice and method of vocalising are materially influenced by the nature of a language. The Germans have guttural, and the French nasal voices, and in neither country have singers attained any great eminence without instruction in Italian. Glück declared that, for dramatic expression, the French language was in some respects preferable to the Italian and German. One thing is quite certain, that a drama in any language, truthfully adapted to the music, never produces so good an effect when translated into any other.

One very apt illustration occurs in the following

spirited opening chorus of "Robert le Diable," with the piquant melody joined to the syllabic poetry of the French. I have heard this opera in Berlin and Padua, and however adroitly expressed in German and Italian, the melody loses half its effect.

Allegro. Bachique. Introduction to "Robert le Diable." MEYERBEER.

Le vin, le jeu, le vin, le jeu, les
belles, voi - là voi - là, voi - là mes seuls a - mours.

TIME AND TEMPERAMENT.

FIRST impressions in music are not easily effaced, and often prejudice the hearer against a fine performance, differing in *tempo* and style, to that which his memory retains of the first hearing of a composition by an inferior player. I have observed that quick music, played by a pianist of a cold temperament, and by another of an opposite nature, though taken at the *same pace*, produces an effect so different as to lead to the conclusion that the one played faster than the other. This difference arises entirely from the absence or presence of that attribute which, as Fétis justly observes, distinguishes the mechanical and poetical organisation of a player—viz., rhythmical accent.

Beethoven, once interrogated as to the just time of a certain composition, replied with a gesture—pointing to his heart and head—implying, of course, that it was a matter of feeling and judgment. Mendelssohn, in my presence, once said much the same thing, adding, that as to a shade faster or slower, when he played, all depended on the humour he was in. Amateurs are rarely taught quick music at the pace which professors perform in public; and seldom have I heard Mendelssohn's quick music played so fast by a professor as by the composer himself. Much enjoyment is lost where persons are carping about the precise degree of *tempo*, instead of listening to the true spirit in which the composition is expressed by a great and conscientious artist. The critic of a daily journal, some years ago, condemned the pace at which the overture of Weber's "Euryanthe" was played under Costa's direction at the Philharmonic Concerts, and alluded to the traditional *tempo* of the Dresden Opera Band. It so chanced that, within a few months of this carping about *tempo*, I heard Reissiger conduct the overture at Dresden much quicker than the pace which so offended the English critic.

SACRED MUSIC IN LONDON, PARIS, AND BERLIN.

IN the spring of 1865 Mendelssohn's "Elijah" was performed in Paris with no success. The critics candidly admitted that this kind of entertainment, of serious dramatic music, sung by persons holding the music before them, would never satisfy a public accustomed to the action of sacred dramas in a theatre.

The prevalent religious sentiment of the English middle classes conduces much to the increase of vocal societies and choral performances in London, supported by a numerons class of persons who never enter a theatre. In Paris, there are several institutions for cheap, popular, and gratuitous vocal instruction to children and adults. The Wilhelm, Chevé, and Mainzer systems have each partisans; but mechanising art-knowledge, by any other symbol than the actual notation, is burthensome to the memory. Stern, master of the Berlin Singing Academy, when asked if he adopted the Wilhelm system, curtly replied, "No; it does very well for the French, who have no ears, and"—— for the English he perhaps would have said; but his good taste in speaking to an Englishman cut his reply short of its sting. The use of figures for notes, in the Chevé system, is said to be the quickest and cheapest mode of teaching and printing concerted vocal music, and great efforts are made to induce government to adopt this system for the people and army. The objection to this musical stenography, as a national system of education, was discovered some time ago in Prussia, and an edict issued against its use in public schools. The youths joining the *liedertafel* (singing club) at the universities, unable to read the ordinary notation, were obliged to recommence their musical studies. The same objection applies to all new systems of notation lately invented, many of which have merit. It is hopeless, however, to expect a thorough change in a language so universally understood and adopted throughout the world, as the ordinary notation of music.

POPULAR MUSIC IN BERLIN, 1852.

AFTER a luxurious repast at the Hôtel de Russie, where, for the moderate sum of four shillings, a dinner is served that would not disgrace the patrician *cuisine* of the Clarendon Hotel, London, the question was mooted, Where shall we go for coffee and to hear good music? It was soon decided, after a glance at the journals, that the following programme was too irresistible for true lovers of the art:—

Overture, "Ruy Blas"	*Mendelssohn.*
Andante, from the "Jupiter Symphony"	*Mozart.*
Overture to "King Stephen"	*Beethoven.*
Symphony in G	*Haydn.*
Symphony, No. 1, in C	*Beethoven.*

The band, which consisted of about twenty-six musicians, was conducted by C. Liebig, evidently an intelligent musician, judging by his indication of time and expression of the music, and the effect of his scoring the above pieces for his little band. In summer this entertainment is given in the open air, as in most German places of gambling and relaxation. Professor Martin and I found the orchestra at the extremity of a capacious room, crowded with men taking lengthy libations of very innocent beer; their wives and daughters knitting or stitching, with a cup of coffee for their beverage. It was with difficulty I could distinguish, through the dense smoke of pipes and cigars, the faces of the executants. No sooner did the baton announce the commencement of each piece of music than suddenly the babel of some two or three hundred voices ceased, and Beethoven's symphony was listened to with much more genuine satisfaction, and each movement more enthusiastically applauded than I have often witnessed by the captious young gentlemen who are even prone to find fault with much better performances of the same works under Costa's energetic and masterly direction, at the Philharmonic Concerts in London. The band was not first-rate, but the *ensemble* was good enough to make me enjoy the music. The whole entertainment lasted about two hours. The cost was about 2½d.

There are several similar entertainments in Berlin, in very beautiful rooms. Kroll's Garden, outside the

Barrier, has recently been rebuilt, since its conflagration, on a scale of great magnificence. The entire suite of rooms, for dinners, suppers, smoking, promenade, and music, covers a large area. The music-room, most elegantly decorated, is said to be one of the largest in Europe. The admission to the concert is tenpence. There are two bands. Strauss, from Vienna, plays the dance-music, whilst the band belonging to the establishment performs solos and classical works. Ice, coffee, and beer are served in the music-room, but no smoking is allowed. I have always thought that were rooms constructed in London, of similar dimensions, equally well furnished, offering the same variety of entertainment for mind and body, and conducted with the same decorum and attention to comfort, as at Kroll's establishment, a fortune might be realised by the *entrepreneur.* It is notorious that at the present moment large fortunes are being rapidly acquired in the music halls of London (where instrumental and vocal music, frequently of the lowest grade in art, is heard), to which few persons of the middle classes would have the courage to take their wives and families.

DANCE MUSIC IN VIENNA.

AT one of the principal hotels in Vienna, 1845, a waiter occupied his leisure in composing waltzes for violin and pianoforte, the proceeds of which furnished him with clothing and pocket-money. I frequently examined his MSS., and better waltzes are not heard in London. I suspect these lucubrations of the waiter were published under another name, a custom not unknown to English musicsellers. The *cornet-à-piston* tunes, called waltzes, so popular in London, would not suit the taste of the Viennese; none but the piquant mixed accents of $\frac{2}{4}$ in $\frac{3}{4}$ measure, with light and shade in the execution, clever instrumentation, and spirited rhythmical expression, would satisfy the visitors of the Volks-garten, or dancing-saloons. Even the popular Strauss, engaged to furnish new dance music at the annual grand ball of certain public societies, assembles his patrons to a rehearsal. The favourite new waltz, polka, or mazurka, if strikingly original, is encored, and Strauss cheered to the echo by his admiring friends. If displeased with the music, the *Gemüthlichkeit* of the auditors is changed, and a chorus of sibillations assails the ears of the unfortunate composer.

ITINERANT MUSIC ABROAD AND AT HOME.

THE pleasant city of Vienna is undoubtedly the terrestrial paradise of musicians, where organ-grinders and wandering minstrels are forbidden to exercise their calling in the public streets. In Milan, the police have orders to remove all organ-grinders, whose instruments are not perfectly in tune. What a boon to Londoners if Sir R. Mayne and the alphabetical divisions of police were authorised to exercise a similar authority in this leviathan city! In Paris, a very limited number of itinerant musicians have licence to perform in certain places allotted to them by the police. In this land of liberty, the refuge of the patriot and artist, victims of political convulsions, Neapolitan bagpipers, nigger buffoon banjo artists, the German brass bands (good and bad), and hordes of barrel-organ grinders from the "sweet south," are allowed, in all places and at all hours, to exercise their calling for the amusement of the people, the delight of little children, the advantage of the street pickpocket, to the great annoyance of persons of mental pursuits in general, and of musicians in particular. No wonder that the great triumvirate of composers flourished most in their creative productions, at Vienna, and that the Viennese imbibe a good taste from hearing music only in public places where it is usually well performed. It is to be regretted that so few opportunities are afforded Londoners to hear good military bands. In Paris, during half the year, not fewer than four military bands may be heard in public places and gardens, in which for a few sous every one is entitled to a programme and a seat to hear an hour's selection of well-arranged and original compositions. Although I frequently experience annoyance in London from street music near my residence, the enjoyment of the poor children in by-streets dancing to the strains of the poor Savoyard's organ, disarms all opposition. In England the supply of good music and good native musicians is not equal to the demand. There is much love but little taste among the English lower orders for music, and as amusements are dear, lessons not cheap, and no national academy affords the poor apt musician a liberal education, we must rely on foreign aid to amuse the wealthy and middle classes, and tolerate street music, as it is, for the delectation of the poor.

LONDON STREET MUSIC.

ALTHOUGH the itinerate music of the streets may charm both sculptor and painter at their work, it is an insufferable annoyance in London to musicians.

In the little square where I now reside, recommended to me for quiet and study, I am favoured, morning and evening, with the performances of a German band. The music, well scored, would be agreeable if the *ensemble* were not damaged by the false intonation of worn-out bass horns. In Milan, the police would take special note of this playing out of tune on bass horns as well as on barrel-organs (vide p. 154); "*sous le drapeau de la liberté, en Angleterre, tout est permis.*" I regret to say that this reflection is but too true. In addition to the above voluntary serenades, I have to endure, from 10 A.M. to 10 P.M. (!), the intolerable pest of seven or eight Italian brigands playing organs, one worse than the rest, with drone basses, which none but Scotchmen could possibly listen to without pain. (*Sic*).

Added to this diurnal programme, we are favoured with an Italian and his monkey, a *ruffiano* who swallows burning hemp to the beating of a big drum, and a minstrel who sings to the accompaniment of that odious nasal instrument—the concertina! The arbitrary mandate of early shop closing releases a youth from behind the counter, who, on Saturday afternoons, favours us with a sickening *cornet-à-piston* waltz (vide p. 153). If

Vienna be *il paradiso* of musicians and composers, exempt from the above inflictions, London is nought else than *l'inferno.* If I could but once in the day-time catch a glimpse of the police, I would avail myself of the merciful law of Mr. Bass, M.P., and for a while put a stop to the above nuisances. In Victoria Square it seems that our police-rate only secures us guardians who, like the witches of "Macbeth," "fly by night."—1868.

MILITARY BANDS.

DURING a friendly repast in Paris, when Meyerbeer, Berlioz, Sax, and Chorley were my guests, a discussion arose on the comparative merits of French and German military bands. Meyerbeer awarded the palm to Prussia, Berlioz to Austria, but Sax claimed for *Les Guides* * at Paris a superiority for finish and refinement of execution. To this Meyerbeer replied, "I quite agree with you, my friend, Sax; but do not forget that *Les Guides* include artists of the Conservatoire, holding a high position elsewhere. What I mean is, regimental bands, composed of men taken from the ranks." Since this discussion took place, an important step has been taken to induce first-class artists to join

* All the French cavalry bands are now suppressed, the *Guides* included.

French bands. The masters have now officers' rank, pay, and pension; and military students from different regiments are annually sent to receive instruction at the National Conservatoire. Of late years, I have observed a striking improvement in the military bands stationed at Paris. The Municipal Guard Band is, at the present time, a very efficient corps of musicians. The saxophones, treble, tenor, and bass, are judiciously mixed with a complete set of other instruments, producing a magnificent effect. At the morning parade, as in London, the bands accompany their respective regiments. From four to five o'clock, eight months in the year, a band plays in the Garden of the Tuileries, where a comfortable seat, within a circle set apart, may be obtained, with a programme, for a few sous. From five to six a second band plays in the gardens of the Palais Royal, and a third in the Place Vendôme, to the great delight of persons fond of good military bands. In London, during the half-hour of relief parade, at St. James's Palace, a good military band may be heard, much improved of late years. Why our bands, six of them in London, composed of soldiers, are not permitted to amuse the people, as in all other countries, at stated periods, in public places, I could never understand.

From what source our military musicians are chiefly obtained I am unable to say. The late Godfrey rose from the ranks, and by his probity and assiduity brought the Coldstream band to great perfection, and supplied more than one of our best wind instrumentalists of the London orchestras. During a residence of forty years in London, I do not recollect ever having had the opportunity of enjoying a thorough good performance of a *complete* military band *in the open air*, as in Paris, Berlin, Pesth, Vienna, Venice, Milan, Naples, and recently at Florence. Not many years ago I was tempted to accompany a friend to a flower-show at Salisbury to hear "The Grenadier Guards' Band from London." In a very large open space, I beheld a draft of some dozen red coats in full array, perched in a temporary orchestra, placarded "Her Majesty's Grenadier Guards' Band." The solo cornist, Levy, monopolised all the honours, and was greatly and deservedly applauded.

The colonel of a French regiment has too much *amour propre* to hazard the reputation of his band in the manner I have thus described. In a room, a well balanced combination of thirty or forty wood and brass instruments is sufficiently powerful; but, in the open air, I have rarely heard a band less numerous than the best in Prussia and Austria (averaging sixty performers) produce a very grand imposing effect! The only English military band to be matched *in number* with those of Germany, is that belonging to the Royal Artillery stationed at Woolwich, under the control of its intelligent master, Smythe.

Kästner's "Manual and History of Military Music" contains the following judicious remarks:—

"Il ne suffit pas pour un régiment d'avoir un bon répertoire de productions musicales, ni même de posséder une musique parfaitement organisée; il faut, pour que de bels avantages ne soient point perdus, que cette dernière soit bien dirigée; en un mot, il faut qu'un régiment ait un bon chef de musique."

THE ENGLISH AND FRENCH DIAPASON.

London	273	455	546.
Society of Arts	264	440	528.
French	261	435	522.

THE difference of the London and French diapason is about half a tone. That the Society of Arts should issue a fork differing only three vibrations, appears to me a very great mistake; since, with the single exception of Italy, the French diapason is pretty generally adopted on the Continent. The expense of lowering our large organs to an interval less than a half tone would be enormous.

PART II.

CORELLI,

BORN 1653; DIED 1713.

CORELLI.

[Extract from a Diary kept at Rome in 1697, by a young Scotch Gentleman, an ancestor of the late Right Hon. Sir George Clerk, Bart., Penicuick, N.B.]

"I CANNOT mention here Corelli, without adding a little more about him. He was the chief violinist as well as the chief componist of the age, and perhaps carried both these talents a greater length than ever they had been known before. His manner on the violin is charming, and exceeds what can be well imagined possible on that instrument. His arcade (bowing) is inimitable both for softness and strength, for at the same time he forces out a sound that is like to tear the ear in pieces; nothing can be imagined more great or so strong; one would think that by degrees he raises a sound to the height of a trumpet, and softens it down again to the breathing of a zephyr. This is his manner in adagios, to which he adds innumerable graces, not crowded in confusion, as some do, but gentle, easy, and sliding, and suited withal to the composition of the other parts, which no man but he who has his taste and knowledge in composition can perform. In his allegros, he plays even, clear, quick, and distinct. In his compositions, he is exact and curious to the last degree. He gains a great deal of money, and loves it for the sake of laying it all out in pictures, and, indeed, few private men in the world have such a noble collection of the best originals, from Raphael down to Carolo Marotti. He seldom teaches anybody, yet because he was pleased to observe me so much taken with him, he allowed me three lessons a week during all the time I stayed in Rome. When I saw him first, he was beginning to compose his first work, a violin solo, and he completed it while I stayed with him. He was a good, well-natured man, and on many accounts deserved the epithet which all the Italians gave him of the *divino archangelo.*"

The writer was under twenty years of age. The alleged parsimony of Corelli is amiably explained in this Diary.

HANDEL,

BORN 1685; DIED 1759.

—o—

HANDEL AT OXFORD.

[Extract from the Diary of Thomas Hearn, M.A., of Edmund Hall, Oxford, 1733.]

"*July 5th.*—One Handel, a foreigner (who they say was born in Hanover), being desired to come to Oxford to perform in music in this act, in which he hath great skill, is come down, the Vice-Chancellor (Dr. Holmes) having requested him so to do, and, as an encouragement, to allow him the benefit of the theatre both before the act begins and after it. Accordingly, he hath published papers for a performance to-day at five shillings a ticket. This performance began a little after five o'clock this evening. This is an innovation. The players might as well be permitted to come and act. The Vice-Chancellor is much blamed for it. In this, however, he is to be commended, for reviving our acts, which ought to be annual, which might easily be brought about, provided the statutes were strictly followed, and all such innovations (which exhaust gentlemen's pockets, and are incentives to ————) were hindered.

"*July 6th.*—The players being denied coming to Oxford by the Vice-Chancellor, and that very rightly, though they might as well have been here as Mr. Handel and (*his* ——— *crew*) a great number of foreign fiddlers. They went to Abbington, and yesterday began to act there, at which were present many gownsmen from Oxford.

"*July 8th.*—Half an hour after five o'clock yesterday, in the afternoon, was another performance at five shillings a ticket, in the theatre, by Mr. Handel, for his own benefit, continuing till about eight o'clock.

"*N.B.*—His book (not worth 1d.) he sells for 1s.

"*July 12th.*—Yesterday morning, from nine o'clock in the morning till eleven, Handel and his company performed their music, &c., in Christ Church Hall, at three shillings a ticket.

"In the evening of the same day, at half hour after five, Handel and his crew performed again in the theatre, at five shillings a ticket. This was the fourth time of his performing there."

HARMONIOUS BLACKSMITH.

"AIR AND VARIATIONS BY HANDEL."

IN one of the programmes of the Musical Union *matinées*, I published the *historiette* of this melody. Its popular title is a pure fiction. It is not known by whom the air was composed, although Dr. Crotch attributes it to Wagenseil; this is a gross mistake. I have seen two editions of the original French song, printed before Wagenseil was born. At the Concerts of Ancient Music, this air and variations were the stock-piece of every season, arranged for a full orchestra. The charming poetry of Marot to this air requires a repetition of the first four bars for the first four lines. The original key is F♮.

HAYDN,

BORN 1732; DIED 1809.

HAYDN IN ENGLAND, 1791.

"*Emigravit* is the inscription on the tombstone where he lies;
Dead he is not, but departed, for the artist never dies."

MORE than half a century has elapsed since the founder of Quartets came to London, and composed for Solomon's concerts twelve grand Symphonies. Notwithstanding the alleged influence of our damp and foggy atmosphere operating unfavourably on the faculties of musical genius in this country, these said Symphonies, in originality of ideas, freshness of melodic counterpoint, and beauty of instrumentation, were not surpassed, if equalled, by any of Haydn's previous or subsequent works, written under the supposed more genial influence of a southern sky. As repeatedly observed, climate does not change the organisation of the individual; a cold, sluggish temperament does not change its nature, though its perceptions become more keen by education. The enthusiastic reception of the Andante, in Haydn's Quartet, No. 82, in F, performed at the seventh *matinée* (1868), afforded a pleasant contrast to the taste of the English, as recorded by Bombet in one of his letters dated Salzburg 1809:—

"When Haydn was in England, he perceived that the English, who were very fond of his instrumental compositions when the movement was lively and allegro, generally fell asleep during the andantes or adagios, in spite of all the beauties he could accumulate. He therefore wrote an andante, full of sweetness, and of the most tranquil movement;—all the instruments seemed gradually to die away, but, in the middle of the softest *pianissimo*, striking up all at once, and reinforced by a stroke on the kettle-drum, they made the slumbering audience start." The andante here alluded to is known by the name of "The Surprise," in the third of the twelve Symphonies.

HAYDN'S SKULL.

ONE incident of historical interest, neither published nor much known, I must relate concerning Haydn. On removing the body of the deceased composer from Gumpendorf to its present abiding place in Vienna, it was found *minus* the skull! Medical men, it seems, had noticed some ailment of the great master. Without entering into particulars, I will merely state that, during my last visit to Vienna, in November 1873, I had the honour of dining with the Baron Rokitanzky, the chief director of the great hospitals. After dinner, the Baron took me into his studio, and carefully placed in my hands a well-preserved relic—the missing skull of Papa Haydn.

The fact becoming known that the missing skull of Haydn was in the possession of a medical man, a strong feeling manifested itself in Vienna to have the bodies of Beethoven and Schubert exhumed. In the "Life of Beethoven," edited by Moscheles, it is stated that a few days after the funeral of this composer a considerable sum of money had been offered to the custodian of the cemetery at Wahring if he would bring the head of Beethoven to a place specified in Vienna. On this account the grave was watched every night for some time. In 1863 (thirty-six years after his burial), a committee was formed, and in presence of my friend Hellmesberger, students of the

Conservatoire, and other persons—in all thirty-two—the graves of these inspired musicians, side by side, were opened, and the bodies found intact. A most minute description was published of the actual appearance of the remains, afterwards reinterred in metal coffins beneath suitable monuments. Around the tombs of these illustrious deceased is now an iron railing, upon which I have, on All Saints' Day, more than thrice hung immortelles.

THE RISING SUN.

QUARTET, B FLAT. NO. 78. HAYDN.

THE accidental publication of this Quartet, with an old title-page representing the rising sun, has given to it a fictitious title. The calm expression of the opening theme, and the sublime effect of the glowing rays of the morning sun, have no affinity with one another, and the title is now becoming obsolete.

HAYDN, BEETHOVEN, SCHUBERT, AND MOZART.

THE city in which resided these illustrious musicians is pregnant of delightful associations. My landlady in Vienna, 1845, whose granddaughter, twelve years old, played sonatas of the above composers, was personally acquainted with Joseph Haydn, and witnessed that touching scene at the performance of his oratorio, "The Creation," when prostrate with age and illness, seated in a chair, the quasi-octogenarian was present, and moved to tears. I also dined with Sedlazek in the house occupied by Haydn, when in the service of Prince Esterhazy. At the tombs of Beethoven and Schubert I have knelt, paying homage to their immortal genius, and in the very room in which Mozart penned some of his best music in "Zauberflöte," I have silently drunk to his memory, in company of genial souls (*vide* p. 178.)

MOZART,

BORN 1756; DIED 1791.

PORTRAIT OF MOZART.

A BEAUTIFUL portrait of this divine composer, life-sized bust, painted in oil by Pompeo Batoni, 1770, is now in my possession. Mozart was then in the fifteenth year of his age, and attracted much notice by his having written down, during the services in the Sistine chapel, the "Miserere" of Allegri. "The difficulty of putting down in notes the music performed by a double choir, abounding in imitation and traditional effects, of which one of the chief is characterised by the absence of perceptible rhythm, is scarcely conceivable. Hence the wonder at the unexampled *theft.* Mozart drew out a sketch on the first hearing, and attended the performance a second time on Good Friday, having his MS. in his hat for correction and completion. It was soon known at Rome that the 'Miserere' had been taken down, and he was obliged to produce what he had written at a large musical party, where the musico Christoferi, who had sung in it, confirmed its correctness. The generous Italians," says his biographer Holmes, "were so much delighted, that they forgot to call upon the Pope to excommunicate the culprit." This event made Master Wolfgang the object of great notoriety during his short stay in Rome, and his portrait is said to have been painted on commission by the popular artist of the day, Pompeo Batoni. Another portrait of the young musician, during his Italian tour, was painted in Verona, and is now in the possession of Dr. Sonnleithner at Vienna. This portrait, engraved and bound up in the fourth volume of Jahn's life, exhibits the Salzburg genius with a tight-fitting wig, a laced coat, and an expression of rather a serious cast.* The life-sized front face of Mozart by Batoni presents a more cheerful and

* I am informed that when a child of seven years old, his natural hair was powdered and worn like a wig, with a pig-tail behind, at Court, and on all public occasions.

congenial expression, with dishevelled hair, and an attitude at once *degagé* and inviting, with a roll of paper grasped in his right hand. As most of the known prints of Mozart are simply profiles when an adult, this oil portrait of the boy, partly idealised by the eminent painter, is doubly interesting.

"Pompeo Batoni of Lucca," says Lanzi, "must be considered the restorer of the Roman school, in which he lived until his seventy-ninth year, and educated many pupils in his profession. He came young to Rome, and did not frequent any particular school, but studied and copied Raffaello and the old masters with unceasing assiduity; thus he learned the great secret of copying nature with truth and judgment. He took from Nature the first ideas, copied from her every part of the figure, and adopted the drapery and folds from models. He afterwards embellished and perfected his work with a natural tone, and enlivened all with a style of colour peculiarly his own—clear, lucid, and preserving, after the lapse of many years, all its original freshness. Batoni possessed an extraordinary talent for portrait painting, and for some time painted miniatures, and transferred that care and precision which is essential in that branch to the larger productions without attenuating his style by hardness. If it were ever said with truth of any artist that he was born a painter, this distinction must be allowed to Batoni."

The portrait of Mozart possesses all those qualities, in the fold of costume, pleasing expression of face, and freshness of colour, described in the above extract. This picture has been in England upwards of fifty years; once belonging to a Mr. Haydon, from whom I received instructions on the pianoforte forty-five years ago. I purchased it of an amateur painter and musician, who had the portrait photographed and shown to persons in Berlin, by whom the likeness was recognised.—1868.*

PRESENTATION OF ENGRAVING TO ROSSINI, AUBER, AND GOUNOD.

AN engraving of this beautiful painting of Mozart, when only fourteen years old, I had the satisfaction of presenting in 1867 to Rossini, Auber, and Gounod. The composer of "Il Barbiere" was delighted with the gift, and declared that I could not have given him a more welcome present, since it completed his collection of known prints of his favourite composer—"Oui, voilà l'homme qui va au cœur avec sa musique!" Within half an hour after this, I was with the gallant and venerable Auber, eighty-five years old, who was equally gratified with the possession of the engraving of the illustrious Mozart. After discussing matters musical in a friendly spirit, we parted on the most affectionate terms. Next I saw Gounod; he also was delighted

* See Frontispiece.

and enthusiastic in his encomiums on Mozart. In all discussions I have had with illustrious musicians of all nations, I have ever found the same adoration for the genius and learning of the divine Mozart. Poor Mozart! he died in debt, whilst the three great living masters, recipients of this engraving, are in the full enjoyment of the golden rewards of modern appreciation.—1868.

LATENT HOMAGE TO MOZART.

POSTERITY seems willing to pay homage to neglected genius, and throughout Europe one hears of monuments and statues to the memory of poets, painters, and musicians. The Viennese have just realised, in one concert only, £200 for a statue of Mozart. In 1842, Mendelssohn inaugurated the statue of Mozart at Salzburg, and gave me a description of the ceremony at a friendly repast in Lucerne. This statue in the market-place is said to be a good likeness. Thrice have I visited the birthplace of Mozart and the cathedral for which he wrote masses, the house in which he lived in Vienna, and the room on the Kahlenberg, where the overture of "Zauberflöte" was composed, a few weeks before his death. The first opera I heard in my youth was "Don Juan," and at the funeral of Weber, I assisted in the performance of Mozart's "Requiem." I need not say that the lovely portrait in my possession perpetually recalls mixed emotions—sorrow for the domestic grief of Mozart whilst living, and pleasure in remembrance of the various beautiful works I have heard and played of this immortal musician.

At Prague, November 4th, 1787, Mozart writes—"My opera, 'Don Giovanni,' was given here on the 29th of October, with the most brilliant success." At Vienna, August 1788, Mozart alludes to the language used in the announcement of his Prague opera, "Don Giovanni," with the title of his appointment yielding 800 gulden per annum, which sum (£80), he said, "is too much for what I do, and too little for what I could do." The paragraph runs thus—"The music is by Herr Mozart, *capellmeister, in the service of His Imperial Majesty.*"

The greatest composers and theorists I have known have all expressed their unbounded admiration of Mozart as a composer. Mendelssohn adored him; Novello, *père*, well read in all the works of the great Italian and German masters, idolised him; Chopin considered him *le poéte par excellence;* and the learned Fétis worships him. Perhaps no greater homage to his genius could be paid than the performance of his *chef d'œuvre*, "Don Giovanni," at the three principal lyrical theatres this season in Paris (1866).

Mozart and Weber both died just as the world had become sensible of the power of their genius. Had these masters survived a few years more to witness the universal influence of their works, riches and honours would assuredly have been their reward from an admiring and grateful public. Alas! fate decreed otherwise. Mozart died December 5th, 1791, aged 35, one year older than Schubert, three years younger than Mendelssohn, and five years younger than Weber.

MOZART'S SUMMER RESIDENCE, 1791.

IN the neighbourhood of Vienna, overlooking the city, the Danube, and the vast plain towards Styria, rises a small chain of hills, on the summit of which formerly stood a large convent. Murray's "Hand-book to Southern Germany" gives an excellent description of the locality; and as no visitor to the imperial capital of Austria should omit to explore the heights and recesses of these wooded mountains, both historically and musically interesting, I will here insert an extract from the above work.

"The Leopoldsberg, 824 feet high, is the last eminence of the chain of the Wiener Wald (Mons Cetius), which, branching off from the Alps of Styria, and embracing one side of the plain on which Vienna stands, stretches out like a cape or promontory, and descends abruptly towards the Danube. On a projecting ledge, about half-way up the hill, a wooden summer-house, called the Belvedere, has been erected, overhanging the river. It commands a very fine and most extensive view. The towers of Presburg, forty miles off, and even the foremost eminences of the more distant Carpathians, are discernible, it is said, in clear weather. Vienna is seen to great advantage. The majestic spire of St. Stephen's, rising against the sky, is a beautiful object; but the striking feature of the view is the Danube, the monarch of European rivers, which even here is larger than any in Britain, and rolls its rapid and mighty stream at your feet, hurrying along vast floats of wood and heavy-laden barges on its broad bosom. A little below Nussdorf it is split into various small streams by a number of wooded islands, and is crossed by the wooden bridges over which runs the high road from Vienna to Prague. Its windings may be traced for a short distance. It is then partly concealed by the dense mass of foliage which covers the islands, and only appears here and there, in flashes or sheets, among the forests, wherever a bend in its course exposes a reach to view. The battles of Asperne, Essling, and Wagram were fought among, or near, these islands. The vast expanse of the river above Nussdorf, and the rapidity with which its current sweeps onward, are very striking; but it is very shallow, and, being spread out over so wide a surface, often leaves bare, large unsightly banks of gravel.

"Looking up the stream, the town and monastery of Kloster Neuburg are seen to advantage; and nearer, on the opposite side of the river, is the Hill of Bisamberg, which produces one of the best

Austrian wines. The Leopoldsberg receives its name from the Austrian Markgrave, who built a castle on its summit, which has now disappeared. A small church and rude tavern occupy its site.

"Those who desire a continuation of the same prospect may ascend the loftier top of the adjoining Kahlenberg; though more extensive, it can hardly be considered more striking than that from the Leopoldsberg. It was on the slopes of the Kahlenberg that John Sobieski encamped with the army of brave Poles, whom he led to succour Vienna from the Turks. On the morning of the 12th September 1684, the Christian banners were descried from the walls of the straightened city, floating on the heights of the Kahlenberg. That very day the Turks were attacked and routed.

"The inhabitants of Vienna repair in flocks to the Kahlenberg on Sundays, and ascend its heights in order to enjoy the prospect and fresh air. The building on the summit was originally a convent, founded by Ferdinand II., suppressed by Joseph II., afterwards a summer residence of the Prince de Ligne, who died and is buried here. Mozart composed part of the 'Zauberflöte' in the inn (Casino)."

In a small room, at one end of this casino, situated on the verge of the mountain, Mozart, four months previous to his death, resided for a short time, in hopes of recruiting his strength; and in this modest rural retreat, he is said to have composed the memorable overture and the priests' march of "Zauberflöte." The visit to this casino, in 1845, I have always remembered, as one of the most interesting of my musical rambles on the Continent. In company with my late countryman and brother artist, Parish Alvers, the celebrated harpist, I ascended the Kahlenberg, and as we rode through the vineyards, we could perceive groups of happy, merry citizens, threading their way through the winding footpaths, taking advantage of the lovely day to enjoy a "picnic" and the charming scenery. Immediately on our arrival at the summit of the mountain, we hastened to the room once occupied by Mozart, and on the door of which had been carved in large letters, "Das Zimmer des virtuosen Mozart." The day previous to our visit, a young musical student had made his pilgrimage to this "sacred spot," and defaced the word "*virtuosen.*" When remonstrated with, for such an act of wanton mischief, the fanatical youth excused himself by saying, that it was a downright insult to call Mozart "*virtuosen,*" more especially to write it on the door of an apartment in which was produced an overture that had immortalised him as a composer! With this explanation, the youth escaped punishment.

Alvars enjoyed the anecdote vastly, and to the great astonishment of mine host applauded the discriminating taste of the *fanatico*, telling him, at the same time, that the erasion of the word "*virtuosen*" would rather tend to increase than diminish the number of musical pilgrims to the Casino. Mine host, like the late proprietor of Shakespeare's birthplace, cared little for the immediate object of musical visitors to this hallowed temple of the muse, and was quite satisfied with the prospect of increased consumption of viands and other cheer that enriched his store of wealth. The Italian word, "virtuoso," in English literature, is used to signify "a lover of the liberal arts;" the precise signification of it, as used among German musicians, implies "an executant of ability." The terms applied to musicians by the Germans are various. "*Tondichter*" (the poet of sounds) was the appellation given to Beethoven, instead of the ordinary name "*Tonkünstler*" (the scientific musician). The creative faculty in art should ever command the greatest honours, however gifted may be the executive powers of a player on any instrument. When the English admirers of Kean insisted on a public funeral in St. Paul's for this tragedian, the "Times," in one of its usual powerful articles, significantly pointed to the modest niche in Poet's Corner to the memory of him whose genius created actors! Posterity has crowned the memory of poor Mozart by a just appreciation of his genius, and although his grave remained for years a neglected spot, by the individual exertions of Madame Hasselt-Barthe, the prima donna of the Court theatre, a suitable monument is now placed over his remains This latent homage to Mozart, and the above incident, are proofs of the idol-worship inspired by the creative genius of this composer among those best qualified to appreciate his works, and I never listen to that *chef-d'œuvre*, the overture to "Zauberflöte," without calling to mind the mingled emotions I experienced on visiting "Das Zimmer des virtuosen Mozart" on the Kahlenberg, in 1845.

MOZART IN ENGLAND, 1764.

THE father's account of his visit to London with his gifted son and daughter is thus recorded in Holme's Biography :—

"On the 27th of April, five days after our arrival, we were with their Majesties from six to nine o'clock. The present we received on leaving the royal apartments was twenty-four guineas only; but the condescension of both the exalted personages is indescribable. Such were their friendly manners, that we could not believe ourselves in the presence of the King and Queen of England. What we have here experienced surpasses everything. A week afterwards, we were walking in St. James's Park, when the king and queen came driving by, and, although we were all differently dressed, they knew and saluted us; the king, in particular, threw open the carriage window, and put out his head, and laughing, greeted us with head and hands, particularly our Master Wolfgang. . . . On the 19th May we were again with their Majesties from six o'clock to ten. Nobody was present but the two princes, the brother of the king, and the brother of the queen. Twenty-four guineas again on going away."

The benefit concert of the family on the 5th of June was most fashionably patronised, and very profitable. The father records, with due honour to the profession, that "most of the musicians would take nothing for their assistance." However, as time wore on, the family began to feel the usual influences of declining novelty. The receipts of these concerts gradually diminished, while an outlay of £300, which their first year in London had cost, did not tempt them to try a second. Having rejected some proposal, and lost money, the father suddenly becomes censorious on the subject of English manners, and continues: "After deep consideration, and many sleepless nights, I am determined not to bring up my children in so dangerous a place as London, where people, for the most part, have no religion, and there are scarcely any but bad examples before the eyes. You would be astonished," writes the father, "to see how children are brought up here, to say nothing of religion." The locality where he lodged, at Chelsea, near the Thames, was not exactly the neighbourhood to find congenial associates for his gifted son and daughter. On the subject of remuneration to musicians playing at the English court, it should be mentioned that the number of artists annually migrating to this country, with letters to our Royal Family from continental sovereigns and princes, has caused a fixed sum to be given—

irrespectively, to all soloists—a trifle less than the *honorarium* given to Master and Miss Mozart by George III.

After his first performance in public, May 9th, 1764, little Wolfgang is thus announced in the programme of Graziani's benefit concert, May 17th :—

"Concerto on the harpsichord by Master Mozart, who is a real prodigy of Nature; he is but seven years of age, plays anything at first sight, and composes amazingly well. He has had the honour of exhibiting before their Majesties greatly to their satisfaction."

THE MOZARTEUM, SALZBURG, 1867.

By the courtesy of the founder of this Institution, Doctor F. E. von Hilleprandt, I had an opportunity in September 1868 of inspecting the interesting relics of Mozart in the library of the Mozarteum. Amongst these relics, were autographs, musical and epistolary, many portraits of himself and family, a massive gold ring, his pianoforte, and spinet. One of the miscellaneous objects that attracted my especial notice was a small packet thus inscribed, in German, by his wife: "*Wolfgang Amade Mozart brought this with him from England.*" (This was in 1765, when he was eight years old.) Imagining some valuable trinket concealed within, I cautiously removed the cover, and found a large silk pocket-book, with the initials "B. P. L." tastefully worked upon a satin ground. In one of the pockets was an envelope, and my readers may well imagine the disappointment I experienced on seeing printed upon it, in capital letters, "*The Genuine Court Plaister, London!*"

A still more interesting relic was found, said to have been Mozart's earliest declaration of love, "Music and Words," addressed to a young lady, prior to his passion for Constance Weber, who ultimately became his wife. In Dr. Von Köchel's thematic Catalogue, this unpublished love-song, numbered 147, at page 146, is thus inserted:—LIED, "Wie unglücklich bin ich nit," fur eine Singstimme mit Clavier begleitung, componirt 1772 (aus früher Zeit, O. Jahn, vol. 3, p. 147). This lied I present to my readers, with a free translation of the original:—

MOZART'S "LOVE-SONG."

(*Written when thirteen years of age.*)

(ANDANTE.)
Wie un - glück-lich bin ich nit, wie schmach - tend sind
What sad cares op - press my heart, when I from my
CEMBALO.

mei - ne Tritt, wenn ich mich nach dir len - - ke nur die Seuf - zer
love must part; with fal - t'ring steps I go - - - - Sighs a - lone can
trö - sten mich; al - le Schmer - zen hau - fen sich wen ich auf dich ge - den-
bring re - lief; Thou a - lone canst soothe my grief, for bound - less is my woe
ge, wenn ich auf dich ge - den - ke.
- - - For bound - less is my woe. - -

MOZART AND THE EDITOR.

MOZART répondit à un éditeur qui lui recommandait d'être plus populaire : "*Nun so verdien' ich nichts und hungere und scheer' mich doch den Teufel d'rum !*" —ce désintéressement n'existe plus.—LENZ.

DI SCRIVERMI, OGNI GIORNO GIURAMI, VITA MIA.

THIS exquisite composition, a Quintet in "Cosi fan tutte," one of the lovliest inspirations of Mozart, an especial favourite of the lamented Prince Consort, was included in the programmes of the State Concerts, at Buckingham Palace, generally once every year. Its dramatic situation is admirably expressed, with detached notes, uttered by the ladies, supplicating, with sighs and tears, a letter every day from their departing lovers.

It appears that the music of the above opera has recently been adapted to scenes from Shakespeare's "Love's Labour's Lost," at the Théâtre Lyrique in Paris. In allusion to the transposition of the above Quintet, the critic justly remarks—"Il commence par des notes separées par des silences, comme il convient à la situation de deux femmes éplorées dont les soupirs coupent la respiration, dont les sanglots arrêtent la voix. Ce même quintette se trouve au *second* acte, de 'Peines d'amour' (it is in the first scene of the *Italian libretto*), mais dans une situation calme où personne ne pleure. Qu'en reste-t-il ? Une mélodie charmante sans aucun doute, et un admirable tissu harmonique. Mais le sens dramatique n'y étant plus, l'impression qu'en reçoit le spectateur est presque nulle : *verba et voces, prætereaque nihil.*"

The most perfect music, unsuited to the action of the Drama, will ever fail in effect on a theatrical audience ; but, introduced as a detached, complete *morceau* in a drawing-room, this short Quintet, sung with delicacy and expression, must always be listened to with satisfaction.

In spite of the frivolous story of the original *libretto*, the excellent performance of the music has made "Cosi fan tutte" a stock piece at the Italian Opera in Paris during the past winter (1867). *En passant*, we may observe that Rossini has constructed the opening bars of his Trio, "L'usato ardir," on the model of Mozart's Quintet "Di scrivermi."

"CLEMENZA DI TITO" AND IL "DON GIOVANNI."

No more beautiful examples of simple melodious counterpoint can be found than in the latest productions of Mozart. The first quotation is taken from the last movement of an aria in "Clemenza di Tito," which Malibran, in her time, made popular at the London Classical Concerts; a composition too much neglected by contralto singers at the present day. The second quotation, one of the most lovely inspirations in "Don Giovanni," presents an inner rising figure for viola and violoncello upon a pedal note, with two melodic parts in descent, that is the admiration of all musicians, and has been adopted by most composers. Well might it be said of Mozart that he thought contrapuntally. The original MS. of "Don Giovanni," I have examined at the residence of its envied possessor, Madame Viardot, at Baden-Baden, and the erasures and changes throughout this *chef d'œuvre*, are very few indeed. I may here mention that I had in 1866 a secret mission to purchase the autograph of "Don Giovanni;" but Madame Viardot, with commendable pride, refused to part with it. The Austrian Government has been anxious to purchase it for the National Library in Vienna. It was first offered to the British Museum for a much smaller amount than I was authorised to give Madame Viardot for it. To the surprise and regret of all English musicians, Signor Panizzi, the late librarian, allowed the precious MS. of Mozart's finest lyrical work, of universal interest, to go out of England into private hands. In justice to Madame Viardot, I must add, that she is generous enough to allow artists, on personal introduction, to inspect the autograph. Each number of the opera is carefully bound in separate covers, and the examination of the entire score, in company with the owner's brother, Garcia, afforded me infinite delight.

MOZART AND BEETHOVEN IN VIENNA.

THE persistent reflection of foreign musicians and critics upon the alleged neglect of the above composers by the Viennese, is justly complained of by the present generation. A little inquiry into the habits, manners, and character of the above inspired masters, during their residence in the Austrian capital, would set matters in a true light. That Beethoven imagined himself friendless and a pauper was no fault of the thousands of Viennese who attended his funeral; and that Mozart, like the once idolised J. B. Cramer, in London, died in poverty, and was buried amidst a very small circle of admiring friends, was not attributed to the want of due appreciation of his genius. On fixing his abode in Vienna, 1781, Wolfgang thus addresses his father: "I have here the *best* and most *useful* acquaintance in the world; I am *beloved* and *esteemed* by the highest families; I am treated with every possible consideration, and *well paid* into the bargain." A handsome monument has been placed over his grave, a tablet on the façade of the house in which he resided at Vienna, and during the summer months musical pilgrims may be seen, on festive occasions, wending their way to a picnic on the summit of the Kahlenberg, to quaff a bumper to the pious memory of the divine Mozart, seated in the very room where the immortal overture to "Zauberflöte" was conceived and written, September 28, ten weeks before his decease, December 5th, 1791.

CHERUBINI,

BORN 1760; DIED 1842.

CHERUBINI.

THIS learned maestro, more renowned for his wit than for his sensibility, on meeting Tulou the flautist returning from the funeral of the oboe-player, Brod, was thus addressed: "Ah! maestro, we have lost our dear friend, Brod." Cherubini, who was deaf, exclaimed, "What! what!! what!!!" Tulou repeated with a loud voice, "Brod is dead!" "Ah!" said the stoic Cherubini, turning away, "*Petit son, petit son*"—little tone. (His tone was not loud, but his taste and intelligence placed him in the highest rank of executants.)

BEETHOVEN,

BORN 1770; DIED 1827.

BEETHOVEN AND MOZART.

WHEN first introduced to Mozart in 1786, in his sixteenth year, Beethoven had already gained celebrity by his improvisations. Mozart, sceptical of the power attributed to young Beethoven, gave him for improvisation the subject of a fugue-chromatique, which contained the counter-subject of a double fugue, treating the youth *un peu en bagatelle.* Beethoven accomplished his task wonderfully well, inverting the subject and converting it into a double-fugue according to rule. Mozart then turned to the musicians near him, and said, "You, gentlemen, will live to witness great things of this boy." This anecdote was told Lenz by the venerable Abbé Stadler, who was present at this interesting scene. Mozart, in the fulness of his heart, prophesied the truth. Nine years later, in 1795, Beethoven composed his Op. 1, three Trios for pianoforte, violin, and violincello.* When first performed in the presence of Haydn, the latter advised Beethoven not to publish the Trio in C minor, No. 3, it being, in his opinion, —to use the jargon of the present day—" music of

* *Vide* page 205.

the future"—not suited for the taste of the musical public of that time. As every one now admits, the Trio in C minor is a *chef d'œuvre* of originality, beauty, symmetry, and poetical imagery, simple and easy of execution, and, perhaps, the most popular of all his trios among amateurs and artists.

BEETHOVEN AND THE PAINTER DANHAUSER.

THE genial painter of *tableaux de genre*, who died in the bloom of life, 1845, at Vienna, had a profound admiration for the genius of Beethoven, and the latter, pleased with the unsophisticated manners and engaging demeanour of the gifted youth, allowed him free access to his residence. Danhauser, seizing a favourable opportunity, expressed his desire to hand down to posterity a model of the great poet of sounds. Beethoven, who considered portrait painting and sculpture as one and the same thing, tried hard to excuse himself, and confessed that he had no ambition to see himself portrayed, and that he cherished ease and comfort too much to sit to any artist. Danhauser persisted, and persuading Beethoven that he ought to leave a faithful representation of himself to posterity, the latter at last gave way, and a day was fixed for his visit to the painter's studio.

We should add, that besides painting in oil, Danhauser devoted much of his time to modelling. Should the reader be unacquainted with the process of modelling from nature, I will briefly mention that the face of the model is covered over with a tepid liquid mass of clay or plaster, which in cooling becomes hard, and forms a solid crust, and when taken off presents a correct impression of the face, and from which a cast is subsequently taken. It is easily understood that this operation is one of extreme discomfort to the sitter, the face being entirely walled in; sufficient air for breathing can only be admitted through a quill or tube inserted in the mouth, and the plaster in drying produces a disagreeable sensation to the skin. Removing the clay from the face is also a matter of difficulty, and accompanied by some pain to the sitter, as each individual hair adheres to the mould; and is extracted perforce with it on its removal. All this the artist had not communicated to Beethoven, fearing that such explanations might defer the execution of his project. The unsuspicious model, therefore, had not the least idea of what he had to encounter.

After anxiously waiting Beethoven's arrival at the hour appointed, the musician at last entered the studio, and preparations were commenced. Beet hoven was first bidden to remove his neckcloth and coat, and then take a seat. "You will not decapitate me?" said he, much astonished at all the proceedings. Danhauser tried to pacify the composer, and promised to shorten the uncomfortable operation as much as lay in his power. To the great amazement of Beethoven, he now began to cover his eyebrows with thin slips of paper, and the hairy part of his face with an oily liquid; finally, to smother the whole with plaster of Paris, having first begged him to take a quill in his mouth, and to shut his eyes firmly.

Beethoven appeared dismayed; but when the coat of plaster gradually began to thicken, and the glow of the drying matter began disagreeably to affect his face and forehead, he became horrified and enraged, and suddenly jumping up, with hair standing on end, he tried to disengage himself from the plaster, and exclaimed, "Sir, you are a garotter—a bandit—a monster!"

"For Heaven's sake, my most honoured Kapellmeister," stuttered the confounded artist. But Beethoven interrupted him violently—

"A rogue—a cannibal!"

"But, permit that I"——

"Away!" roared Beethoven. Smashing to atoms the chair upon which he had been sitting, he snatched his hat and coat and rushed out of the room, forgetting to put either of these garments on.

Danhauser hastened after the raving man, and tried to pacify him; but Beethoven, extricating himself from his grasp, exclaimed, "Go back, you cunning assassin! Do not attempt to approach me, or I'll throttle you." After these words he ran out of

Danhauser's house, slamming the door behind him, the face still covered with plaster, and deadly pale, like the ghost in "Don Juan," spluttering and bubbling, leaving the poor artist frustrated in his most beautiful intentions. Down all the staircases he continued to hear the curses and imprecations of the flying man. All intercourse between Beethoven and Danhauser ceased from that moment, though they occasionally met. Yet, each time he caught sight of Danhauser the old rage returned, and when perceiving him occasionally at a distance, he took care that the length of a street should divide them.

It was destined, however, that Danhauser should triumph, and crown his most ardent wishes; for, after a certain lapse of time, he succeeded in obtaining a faithful impression of Beethoven's face. The painful proceeding this time did not transform the old Titan of music into an exasperated madman—his face smiling peaceably all the while the artist manipulated at his ease. The triumph, however, was a sad one, for the spirit of harmony had passed away.

A little appendix might be added to the comico-tragic event just related, which occurred at the time of the modelling.

Danhauser, having obtained from the Hofrath Von Breuning and Kapellmeister Schindler, friends of Beethoven, the permission to model the deceased, went with his colleague to the house of the defunct on the Glacis. After having made a portrait in pencil, Danhauser began the necessary preparations for moulding. An unforeseen obstacle presented itself. The beard of the deceased, which had not been touched during all the period of his illness, had to be removed. Danhauser sent for a barber, who, of course, was willing to take the impending element away from chin and cheek, but demanded a ducat for his services. A ducat was more than the young artists possessed between them at that time; they, therefore, had to send this unwilling Figaro away and undertake the operation themselves. Rauft hastened to fetch his razor, and to sharpen the blade for the occasion. Danhauser applied the soap, and Rauft cut the bristly beard, after which Danhauser began his work. The sculptor Dietrich finished the bust of Beethoven from the mask taken by Danhauser, the only faithful portrait in existence. Unfortunately the mould broke at the thirteenth cast. It is said that the original mask of the deceased remains till this day in the possession of the painter, Cramolini, in Vienna.

The above particulars are compressed from the original, published at Vienna, in 1867, by Dr. J. N. Vogl, with a wood engraving of the interior of the artist's studio, and the portrait of Beethoven standing erect, looking like a maniac.

BEETHOVEN, MEYERBEER, MOZART.

Born 1770; died 1827. Born 1791; died 1864. Born 1756; died 1791.

That Beethoven and Meyerbeer, unlike Mozart, were fastidious in shaping their melodic inspirations for print, after first jotting them down on paper, I can speak from personal knowledge. The original theme of the finale to the Quartet in G, Op. 18, underwent two changes before the one published (No. 3) was finally adopted. The autograph, in pencil, I examined in Vienna, 1845, and, to the best of my memory, the three versions were as follows:—

The fac-simile of the original jottings of "Adelaide," in my possession, differs from the printed version. Meyerbeer invariably had with him a musical pocket-book, which he once showed me during one of our rambles together, at Spa, in 1852. It contained several pages of closely-ruled music-paper pretty well covered with his pencilled jottings. Mozart, on the contrary, committed at once his ideas to paper, and made fewer changes in his first copies than most composers. In the complete development of the theme of a fugue, *accompanied*, occupying three pages, in four parts, there is not a single erasure! (*Vide* "Dr. Von Köchell's Chronological Catalogue," printed in Leipzig, 1862.) The original autograph of this sketch, now in my possession, I purchased of the late celebrated collector of musical autographs, Herr Fuchs, in Vienna. The recently deceased learned Kapellmeister and contrapuntist, Sechter, completed the fugue, and scored it for a full band, and, by desire of the late Prince Consort, it was played at one of Philharmonic Concerts in London. (*Vide* Music.)

The simple development of the fugal theme quoted is followed by a second short figure, the autograph ending abruptly at the 44th bar. Sechter, in completing the entire movement in full score, has added 242 bars, with a few more instruments than originally indicated in my autograph copy.

How difficult it is to construct a theme with a figure of accompaniment, susceptible of involutions and contrasts, in the rigorous style of scholastic music, no one can better appreciate than musicians who have had their probationary experience in theory and counterpoint. Fétis once truly observed that Mozart, like Bach and Handel, *thought* contrapuntally; in other words, their creations were not only beautiful in themselves, but equally so in their adaptations for the purposes of inversion and other innumerable contrivances which constitute the great merit in a classical work of art. "Sto pingendo" was the reply of a painter accused of idleness; and when I read of the tardiness of *great* musicians in completing their labours, it always calls to mind the beautiful description given by Disraeli of the struggles of literary characters. "It is in revolving the subject that the whole mind becomes gradually agitated; as a summer landscape, at the break of day, is wrapt in mist; at first the sun strikes on a single object, but the light and warmth increasing,

FUGATO. MOZART, COMP. 1777.

AUTOGRAPH, IM BESIT VON MR. ELLA IN LONDON, 1845.

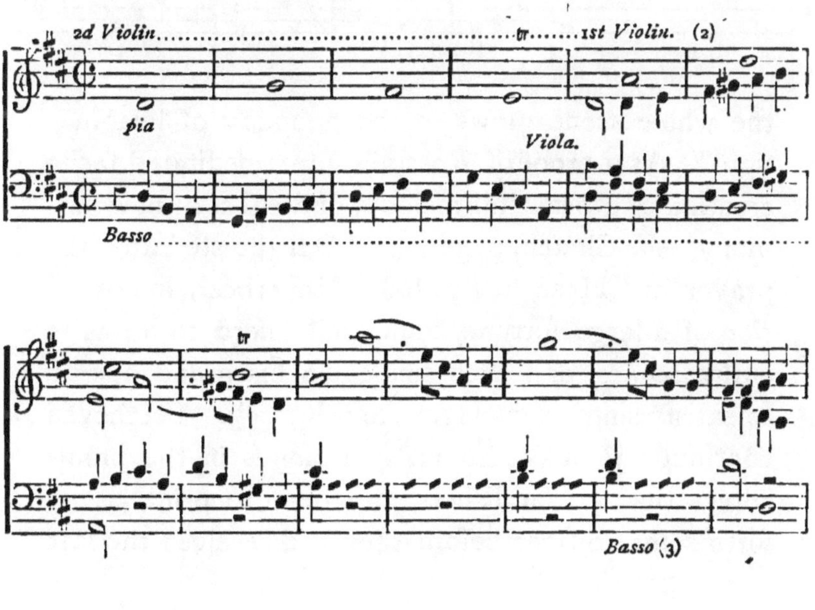

the whole scene glows in the noonday of imagination." As a proof of Rossini's unpremeditated facile creation of a beautiful melody, and effect of new harmony, *vide* Sketch, page 236, " Dal tuo stellato," the prayer in " Mosé in Egitto." Meyerbeer, in possession of a large fortune, could well afford to re-write entire scenes, and even finales to his grand operas, to satisfy singers, managers, and himself. Beethoven continued to make so many changes in the proof-copies that his publishers, impatient to print, issued forth some editions before they had received the last finishing stroke of the fickle master; hence the discrepancies that are found in the various early copies of Beethoven's Pianoforte Sonatas. Of Mozart's manner of conceiving ideas and committing them to paper, no more interesting account was ever given than in his own confessions, with which I shall conclude this sketch. "When I am, as it were, completely myself, entirely alone, and of good cheer—say travelling in a carriage, or walking after a good meal, or during the night, when I cannot sleep,—it is on such occasions that my ideas flow best and most abundantly. Whence and how they come, I know not; nor can I force them. Those ideas that please me I retain in memory, and am accustomed, as I have been told, to hum them to myself. If I continue in this way, it soon occurs to me how I may turn this or that morsel to account, so as to make a good dish of it—that is to say, agreeable to the rules of counterpoint, to the peculiarities of the various instruments, &c. All this fires my soul, and, provided I am not disturbed, my subject enlarges itself, becomes methodised and defined, and the whole, though it be long, stands almost complete and finished in my mind, so that I can survey it, like a fine picture or a beautiful statue, at a glance. Nor do I hear in my imagination the parts successively, but I hear them, as it were, all at once (*gleich alles zusammen*). What a delight this is, I cannot tell! All this inventing, this producing, takes place in a pleasing, lively, dream. Still the actual hearing of the *tout ensemble* is, after all, the best. What has been thus produced I do not easily forget, and this is perhaps the best gift I have my Divine Maker to thank for. When I proceed to write down my ideas, I take out of the bag of my memory, if I may use that phrase, what has previously been collected into it in the way I have mentioned. For this purpose the committing to paper is done quickly enough, for everything is, as I said before, already finished; and it rarely differs on paper from what it was in my imagination. At this occupation I can, therefore, suffer myself to be disturbed; for, whatever may be going on around me, I write and even talk, but only of fowls and geese, or of Gretel or Bärbel, or some such matters. But why my productions take from my hand that particular form and style that makes them Mozartish, and different from the works of other composers, is probably owing to the same cause which renders my nose so large, or so aquiline, or, in short, makes it Mozart's, and different from those of other people. For I really do not study or aim at any originality: I should, in fact, not be able to describe in what mine consists, though I think it quite natural that persons who have really an individual appearance of their own are also differently organised from others, both externally and internally. At least, I know that I have not constituted myself either one way or the other."

BEETHOVEN EN PROMENADE, AT VIENNA.

LIKE Czerny and other resident musicians, Beethoven took his daily stroll before dinner, and on his way home was in the habit of calling at the music-shops. Here be it observed, the usual dinner-hour in Vienna is two o'clock, and at the principal music-sellers, German, Italian, and French musical journals are regularly filed and read by professional visitors. Being offended with a certain editor, who complained of his writing too difficult music (*vide* following Sketch), Beethoven, *en passant*, would open the door, and, without entering the shop, call out, "Gut morgen, dumm; dumm, gut morgen"—"Good morning, stupid; stupid, good morning." On a cold, windy day, in total abstraction, the illustrious musician has been seen on the ramparts pacing slowly along, humming to himself with his hat in hand, and his dishevelled hair "streaming like a meteor in the troubled air." On these occasions, rude youths would shout, "Now, stupid, why don't you put on your hat?" On another occasion, passing through the narrow entrance from St. Stephen's Platz to the Graben (the narrow street is now much wider, 1868), Beethoven was seen to stop suddenly, and jot down something on paper in hand. A waggoner with his team cracked his whip, which Beethoven, being deaf, heeded not; but, fortunately, a person to whom Beethoven was known, prevented the inspired master being disturbed. On the authority of the late Alvars and Kapellmeister Reuling, of the Imperial Opera, the subject of the C minor Symphony was thus first committed to paper. If this is true, the story of Fate knocking at the door, with other alleged influences, suggesting this theme, is mere twaddle and rhodomontade.

That Beethoven, in one of his very last laboured Quartets, constructed a movement in a capricious mood out of a few intervals, neither very melodious nor effective, is accredited; but a Grand Symphony produced in the best period of his poetical life, with such a theme as the one quoted, though instantaneous in conception, is worked out with such lovely rhythmical melodic phrases, it is hard to believe the rhapsodic nonsense which some writers have indulged in their description of it.

BEETHOVEN AND THE PUBLISHER.

I WAS told, in Vienna, that a publisher having ventured to reprove the great musician for writing music too difficult, Beethoven pettishly replied, "I write for minds, not for merchants."—"Ich schreibe für Gemüther, nicht für Kaufleute."

BEETHOVEN'S THREE PIANOFORTE TRIOS.

OPUS I.

"DURING a period of ten or twelve years, it was at Prince Lichnowsky's musical parties that almost all Beethoven's works were first tried, and the refined taste of the Prince, as well as his solid musical acquirements, commanded such respect from Beethoven that he readily followed his advice in regard to the alteration and improvement of this or that of his compositions—a point on which he was extremely self-willed.* At the house of this Prince the three Trios, Opus I, were first played in the presence of Haydn and most of the amateurs and artists of Vienna. On this occasion Haydn expressed himself

* Moscheles' Life of Beethoven.

delighted, but advised deferring the publication of the trio in C minor, which Beethoven very justly considered the best. This advice gave offence, and was attributed by Beethoven to envy and jealousy on the part of Haydn. Fétis shrewdly observes that one of the most striking characteristics of Beethoven's genius, and that which distinguishes his works from those of all other composers, is the spontaneity of the *episodes*, "par lesquels il suspend l'intérêt qu'il a fait naître, pour lui en substituer un autre aussi vif qu'inattendu. Cet art lui est particulier. Etrangers en apparence à la pensée première, ces épisodes occupent d'abord l'attention par leur orginalité, puis, quand l'effet de la surprise commence à s'affaiblir, Beethoven sait les rattacher à l'unité de son plan, et fait voir que dans l'ensemble de sa composition la variété est dépendante de l'unité." No critical analyst has better explained the effect of this prolific creative faculty than the above learned theorist. The amateur will find in these Trios abundant melodic phrases and episodes, scattered throughout in pleasing contrast to the two principal motivi, and treated with the most consummate art. In the extenuated and somewhat laboured movements of certain works of his latter life, this spontaneity of bright and melodic episodes is not so remarkable. In one of 243 letters of Beethoven,* lately published by Longmans and Co., the com-

* In English, by Lady Maxwell Wallace (Hon. Member of Musical Union).

poser states that, on principle, he never published a work within the year of its completion.

The Trios, Op. 1, were the first publications of importance of Beethoven, although not his first compositions. They first appeared in 1795, the third year of his residence in Vienna, and in the twenty-fifth year of his age.

The figure of the Finale in the Trio, No. 2, is formed upon one note (G) grouped in semiquavers. This figure, repeated by the piano, takes an additional note (semitone below). "Without doubt," says the critic, "this was owing to the imperfect mechanism of the clavecin, which did not permit the repetition of the same note with rapidity and distinctness." Towards the end of the Finale the response of the piano is inverted, and the appoggiatura (legato) is given to the violin. The repetition touch in modern pianos makes the figure, as originally conceived, easy of execution. Czerny was of opinion that the original figure on one note is preferable; since, according to the division of vibrations included in the octave, the leading note in the pianoforte is a shade too flat and the effect of the imitation unsatisfactory.

The figure, also, on one note, in Rossini's overture to "Semiramide" is disguised by an appoggiatura in some printed copies for the pianoforte to render the music easy and saleable—an alteration which is most offensive to delicate ears, and quite needless for agile fingers, upon *modern* pianofortes.

"Acting on the suggestion of Czerny, quoted by Mr. Ella, Jaell availed himself of the repetition touch of the pianoforte (at the sixth matinée of the Musical Union), to echo the subject of the violin, thus rendering the response perfect, as Beethoven assuredly would have written it."—*Bell's Messenger*, 1866.

BEETHOVEN'S SONATAS AND FUGUES.

THE delicate texture of some, and the elaboration of others, the miniature character of the early ones, and the fugal structure of the later works, require a special audience, and a suitable *locale*. If we place a delicate work of the sister art too far from sight, its merits are not descernible; and were we to place the pianist at one extremity of St. James's Hall before an audience of six hundred persons, it is possible that the *delicate* features of these Sonatas, however well expressed, would fail to be appreciated by those at a distance from the player. These reflections long ago occupied my serious attention, and determined me to place the executants nearer to the audience; and, as far as my judgment guides me, the position of the central *palco* is good, and every note, in the most delicate trait of the quartet players, *can* be heard. It is quite true that some sonatas, of a less dignified character and smaller proportions than others, played in a concert after one of Beethoven's or Mendelssohn's grand quartets, would be an injudicious choice. Again, some of his later sonatas, of grand design, are best suited for a special coterie of connoisseurs. Op. 106, in B♭, and Op. 110, in A♭, have repeatedly been suggested to me, and as often refused to be played at the Musical Union. Proud as we are of the intelligence of our musical public, there are sonatas better calculated to satisfy a numerous audience of varied tastes and capacities than either of these magnificent creations, with their rigorously constructed fugues—the finale of Op. 106 being a fugue *à tre voci!* Fugues to scholastic musicians are always interesting; but, to those unable to trace the evolutions of each part, most wearisome. Haydn's fugues in his quartets, *à la rigeur* in the elaboration, are always ineffective; whereas Mozart's Quartet in G, and Beethoven's in C, contain fugal finales that are strikingly beautiful, with melodic episodes and contrast of character; and, for the same reason, the overture to "Zauberflöte," and the fugue in the Jupiter Symphony, adorned by the lovely melodic creations of Mozart's genius, contain a thousand additional charms to the strict development of this scholastic species of counterpoint. There is no poetry in an instrumental fugue, however melodic may be the tema for solution. The real effects of fugues can only be *felt* when large bodies of voices or instruments give distinct outlines to the mass of harmony, perceptible in the contrast and variety of *timbre*, taking up the subject. Hence orchestral and choral fugues are listened to with reverence, and sometimes with great delight, by a mixed assembly of persons, who would be bored to death to hear the same fugues played by four instruments, and even much more so on the pianoforte. Do we not hear the organist constantly making use of the conventional *appoggiatura* to give accent to the fugal figures, failing other means to render the *rentrée* intelligible in the elaborated combinations? I have said enough to justify my reluctance to introduce at the Musical Union music best understood in a circle of connoisseurs specially summoned to admire its sublime and occasionally incoherent ideas, such as the posthumous quartets and some of the later sonatas of Beethoven, with which every musician and musical student is, or ought to be, well acquainted.

It is now forty years since I heard in Paris all the known printed chamber-music of Beethoven played by a party specially organised for the purpose; since which, in my private residence, I have passed hours of delight in listening to Beethoven's sonatas, from time to time played by Mendelssohn, Thalberg, Döhler, and many other musicians of less note. It is the fashion to say that Thalberg could only play music of his own coinage; this is a delusion. Every student of music in Germany learns to play Beethoven's sonatas, just as Englishmen are instructed to read Milton and Shakespeare. The grandchild of mine host, when in Vienna, 1845, at twelve years of age, played some of Beethoven's sonatas capitally. The importance attached to this revived passion among enthusiasts for Beethoven's difficult sonatas, has given rise to some pleasantry in the American musical journals on John Bull's affectation for classical music.

Moscheles gives the following wholesome advice: —"The study of Beethoven's sonatas should be earnestly entered upon after the mind has been cultivated by a course of education at once philosophic and elegant; without such a preparation, the study will infallibly be harassing and disagreeable, even to those who possess more than common susceptibility for musical poetry. Music is the offspring of deep feeling, and by deep feeling alone can its genuine beauties be comprehended and enjoyed."

THE MOONLIGHT SONATA.

OP. 27. BEETHOVEN.

AN edition of this Sonata is printed with the frontispiece representing a moon, a lake, a lover, and a lady at the latticed window. This scene is purely the fanciful description of a critic on hearing the opening movement expressively performed. The exquisite pathos and touching simplicity of the music is highly suggestive, and as—

> "Soft stillness and the night
> Become the touches of sweet harmony,"

by no very great stretch of the imagination the truth of the critic's imagery has been universally credited, and the above title adopted as appropriate.

BEETHOVEN'S C MINOR SYMPHONY.

THE following notice of a performance I attended last December in Vienna is from the pen of the accomplished *dilettante*, whose description of a pilgrimage to the tomb of Beethoven is printed in the Musical Union "Record" of 1866.

The rehearsal and performance are described with acumen and truth, and the remarkable abilities of the energetic and instructive Herbeck are in no respect overrated. I shall have occasion to speak of the organisation and discipline of the Vienna Concert Bands in a future sketch; but I wish not to let slip this opportunity of recording the most satisfactory, effective, and impressive execution I have ever heard of the C minor Symphony of Beethoven by a very numerous body of musicians.

"Yesterday I was present at a very interesting performance of classical music in the Redouten Saal, one of the most magnificent halls and concert rooms in Europe. The day before, by the kindness of Meister Hellmesberger—I like the grand old German word much better than the modern title of 'Professor'—I had been permitted to attend the rehearsal of this gigantic performance, Beethoven's Symphony in C minor, by an orchestra of one hundred and fifty accomplished artists, and was filled with wonder and admiration at the patience evinced by the performers in spite of the innumerable checks and stoppages they were subjected to, as well as at the intelligent reading and finished interpretation of the great work manifested by their leader, Kappellmeister Herbeck. Not a salient point was left undeveloped, not a *nuance* of expression undefined: the crescendos and diminuendos were shaded in with that unity of intention and execution which can only be obtained from a body of instrumentalists far enough advanced in the art they illustrate to be capable of utter self-abnegation *ad maiorem magistri gloriam*, and of faithful, affectionate belief in their conductor's inspirations.

The fruit of such training is found in such an inimitable performance as I heard yesterday morning. Inspiration on one side, *appreciation* on the other—who can wonder that an orchestra of distinguished solo players should attain a result approaching perfection? I lay particular stress on the word appreciation, because I have been strongly impressed more than once with the character of the audiences assembled to enjoy the frequent musical banquets prepared for the Viennese public. In the body of the hall, on Sunday morning, might be perceived venerable artists and critics, contemporaries of Beethoven—ancient captains of the craft, whose mere presence acts as a stimulus upon their disciples on the platform. In this city, near which his bones lie buried, the *tempi* and colouring of Beethoven's works are become an exact science. The Conservatoire in Paris, our own grand Philharmonic Societies have altered the former in many instances, subdued or brightened the latter according to the 'lights' of their successive leaders, but here a great reverence guarantees the integrity of the master's fabric; it is curious to notice the suppressed murmur by which any trifling infringement of the traditions, however artistic, is greeted by the public. To sum up, Beethoven has become a creed, a symphony, a profession of faith; and I wish to state emphatically that there exists in this city a musical public second to none in the world for knowledge, judgment, and appreciation."

Here I cannot omit adding a few words in respect to the ponderous tones and splendid effects of the fourth string (E) of the German double-basses, four notes below the lowest note (A) of the English three-stringed instruments. The dominant pedal note (G) in the above symphony and the tonic (A♭) of the slow movement are the most prevalent intervals employed. In England we lose these impressively grand pedal basses by transposition.

BEETHOVEN'S QUARTET IN E MINOR.

(No. 8. Op. 59.)

JUST and sound criticism has long awarded to this composition a high place amongst the chamber works of Beethoven. To trace the different evolutions in the counterpoint of this splendid production, demands extreme attention. Let the amateur reflect that a single idea taken from among any of the movements of this quartet, and analysed, will be found to be intrinsically not less *sublime*, as an emanation of profound thought and extraordinary genius, though heard with but one instrument to a part. Nay, more; we need only remind the novice in art that the sublime effects of monster choirs and bands are derived from the duplication of executants, not from the multiplicity of parts; and that the "Messiah," in its original score, consists of no more real parts than the quartet.

If it were insisted on that the immortal works of the great Italian painters should be withheld from the gaze of the unpractised eye—that a visit to the Vatican should be denied to a novice in sculpture,—

the world at large would be pretty much in the same state of ignorance of the treasures of bygone ages in painting and sculpture as are the great mass of the English people in respect to great productions of Beethoven.

The plaster cast of some forgotten hero had long been my *beau-idéal* of statuary, until I wintered in Rome, where, by repeated visits to the Laocoon and the Apollo Belvedere, I imbibed a taste for the sublimity of sculpture, and ultimately experienced an indescribable sensation of delight in admiring what my Mentor made me feel were the true merits of these art-wonders. The timid and mistrustful amateur should abandon himself to his impressions, bearing in mind that in the more vague parts of this quartet there is nothing that will not become perfectly clear to his comprehension after frequent hearings. The set of three quartets, Op. 59, dedicated to the Prince Rasoumoffsky, are considered, by many professors, Beethoven's grandest of quartets; they are certainly not surpassed in terseness of part-writing, variety of ideas, and clearness of design. They are also totally beyond the skill of ordinary amateurs, and nothing short of a correct execution can render them satisfactorily intelligible. This particular quartet, No. 8, was the especial favourite of Ernst, and, in 1844, he played it at my private reunions, with Mendelssohn at his side, and Master Joachim turning over the leaves. Every one was moved by the intense expression of this poetical violinist in the following strain of pious harmony:—

Molto Adagio.
Si tratta questo pezzo molto di sentimento.
cres.
p
f

BEETHOVEN AND THE PRINCESS LOBKOWITZ.

ONE evening, soon after the publication of his Sonata No. 2, D minor, Op. 31, Beethoven was invited to play it at the residence of the Count Browne. In a passage descending in groups of two notes, Beethoven made a mistake, and inadvertently played to each crotchet three and four notes. The Princess Lobkowitz tapped Beethoven smartly on the head with her hand, saying, "If you strike a pupil with one finger for only one wrong note, it is only fair that the master receive chastisement with the whole hand for making several." (Beethoven had struck Ries with his finger for playing a wrong note at a previous party.) Beethoven was not a man to enjoy practical jokes, but to this rebuke he submitted with good grace.

BEETHOVEN'S NEPHEW.

DURING the performance of "Fidelio," at the old Opera-house, in Vienna, 1845, the venerable Prince Czartoryski called my attention to a conspicuous individual opposite. "That imbecile," said the Prince, "is the nephew of Beethoven. He is a chemist, and drives four-in-hand. I expect he will soon spend the florins he inherited from the illustrious Beethoven." Strange to say, before my departure for Vienna in October 1873, a paragraph went the round of the English Press, stating that the widow of this nephew was in distress, and some annuity was provided for her by the State. Upon inquiring of Herr Pohl, the librarian of the Vienna Conservatoire, and editor of the "Life of Beethoven," I was assured that there was no truth in such a statement. Two daughters of the widow were well married, and the mother well cared for. It is a constant source of annoyance to the Vienna *dilettanti* that so frequent mention is made of the alleged neglect and poverty of Beethoven. The gift of £100 by the Philharmonic Society, however well meant, was returned to the donors, and sufficient money was inherited by the "troublesome Carl" to enable him to drive, as I have seen, four-in-hand.

TOMBS OF BEETHOVEN AND SCHUBERT.

ON the 19th of November 1845, the late esteemed publisher of music, Signor Mechetti, invited me to accompany him to the cemetery of Währing, a small village on the outskirts of the city. The immediate object of this act of courtesy on the part of Mechetti, to whom I was only known as an occasional contributor to his Musical Journal, was a mystery to me. When we had reached the left extremity of the cemetery, Mechetti suddenly directed my attention to the dazzling grandeur of the scene that presented itself below the eminence where we then stood. The glittering rays of the setting sun behind the gilded spire of St. Stephen's Cathedral, with the fine Kahlenburg on our left, the vast plain of the Danube stretching as far as the eye could discern, and the Styrian mountains in the distance, formed altogether a grand panorama of natural scenery. Whilst gazing at this prospect in silent admiration, and thinking over the lives of the triumvirate of musical genius—Haydn, Mozart, and Beethoven—as they pursued their professional career in the imperial city, Mechetti gently placed his arms about my waist, and turned me round with my face towards the east, saying, "*Ecco! la tomba di Beethoven!*" This unexpected gratification of being on the spot where thousands of musical pilgrims had paid tribute to the genius of the immortal musician at his funeral in 1827, quite overpowered my feelings, and I am not ashamed to say that I kissed the flagstone that covers his remains, and plucked a bunch of fern which grew at the base of the monument—a memento that I still preserve. Whilst preparing to make a sketch of the tomb, a mass of persons, attired in black, gradually approached the spot where Mechetti and I stood. As the procession advanced, we moved a few paces, when we observed a general halt and uncovering of heads close to the tomb of Beethoven. My curiosity became excited to know the meaning of this dumb show, for not a word was uttered during the whole of the ceremony. Mechetti, at first ignorant as myself of the cause of this gathering, suddenly recollected that the 19th of November was the anniversary of the death of Schubert, whose mortal remains lie buried by the side of those of Beethoven. From among the crowd I observed a grave, black-bearded personage step forward, and with bended knees place on the tomb a wreath of laurel, entwined with a blue ribbon, on which was printed in letters of gold, "*The Father of German Song.*" As musical ceremonies are forbidden in Catholic cemeteries, the party retired, as they came, with measured step, and without uttering a word. This silent homage to musical genius threw me into a state of reverie, and I found myself involuntarily following in the train of these worthy votaries of the muse. Mechetti quickly pursued, and bade me return to the spot where the wreath of laurel was deposited. Presently we saw the same party assemble outside the cemetery, immediately behind Schubert's tomb, and a choir of fresh well-chosen voices sang a vocal quartet with such pathos and solemnity of expression as moved every one present to tears. It is utterly impossible for me to describe, and for any English musician that has not visited Germany to comprehend, the religious zeal of such a spontaneous homage to departed genius in that country. Never shall I cease to remember this affecting ceremony, got up, as I afterwards learned, by the members of the Vienna *Liedertafel.* The music of this ceremony I have adapted for two soprani, one tenor, and one bass voice, from the MS. copy furnished me by Mechetti. The simplicity of the harmony and purity of the part-writing produce a fine effect when sung with becoming feeling. The original key for male voices is C major.

On All Saints' Day, 1866, I made a third visit to the above tombs, accompanied by a most excellent amateur pianist, Mr. Kingston, his lady, and lovely daughter. His description and a picture of the tomb are published in the Musical Union "Record" of 1866. I give a short extract of his graphic account of our visit:—

"Arrived at the cemetery, one of my companions, a maestro in the divine art, summoned up the memories of a visit he had paid twenty-one years ago to the grave of the greatest musician the world ever knew; and, taking the lead, guided us straight to a small square inclosure surrounded by a low railing, almost hidden by red and white asters, at the further end of which rises a plain block of grey marble, upon which is inscribed in letters of gold the one word 'Beethoven.' Not without emotion did we contemplate the repository of those sacred remains. The silent, mournful poetry of the spot was enhanced by a tender little incident never to be forgotten by any of those present. The plain white wreath we had brought as a poor tribute of our reverence for the master was confided to the tiny hands of a fairy-like English child, the daughter of one of our party—golden-haired *boöpis*, fresh and fair. Carefully lifted over the railing, she—somewhat awe-stricken, I confess—placed the wreath on the slab covering Beethoven's ashes, and then stood under his graven name, a type of life and beauty. We gathered each a flower from the tomb, as well as from that of Schubert, surmounted by a bust of that romantic melodist, and passed on to Nestroy's resting-place. . . . Many female forms clad in deep mourning did we pass by, bent in silent grief over the cold grey tombstones. Many a child's grave was adorned with fresh flowers, a tiny statue of the Redeemer, and a little pillow, bound in rose-coloured ribbon and surmounted by a nosegay. Green hills with soft round outlines environ God's acre at Währing. A brilliant sun shone over us. Abundant evergreens gave life and colour to the otherwise melancholy scene. Subdued, but not saddened, we left a spot the memory of which will not easily be effaced from my mind."—*Daily Telegraph.*

Elegy, sung at the Tomb of Schubert, near Vienna, in 1845.

Composed by GRAUN.

The above free translation of this elegy may prove acceptable to those who may wish to sing it in English.

HUMMEL,

BORN 1778; DIED 1837.

—o—

"*HONOR ALIT ARTES.*"

THE long-expected news of the death of George the Fourth arrived in London on the day fixed for Hummel to dine at Clarence House with his pupil, the Royal Duchess. As the distinguished composer and pianist was on the eve of quitting England, and the Queen desirous of personally testifying her regard to the Kapellmeister of Weimar, Hummel received a special command on the same day to dine with their Majesties. The party, as might be supposed, was strictly private, limited to persons in immediate attendance upon the King and Queen. Hummel, gratified by the kindness of the Queen's reception, was wont to boast, with just pride, that he was the first guest invited to dine with King William the Fourth and Queen Adelaide.

In my opinion, the man who had the genius to create the Septet in D minor, apart from all Hummel's executive skill as a pianist, was worthy of every personal courtesy which royalty could bestow.

AUBER,

BORN 1782; DIED 1871.

—o—

MY acquaintance with this illustrious musician began in a very singular way. Arriving on one occasion too late for the first *coup d'archet* at the Conservatoire Concert, I entreated the box-keeper, and even offered her a bribe, to let me enter. Madame was inexorable, and, pointing to a venerable-looking gentleman seated in the corridor, added, "*Vous voyez, M. Auber n'entre pas, il est trop tard.*" I respectfully saluted the maestro, and he smilingly observed, "*Il faut se consoler.*" The next day I paid him a visit, and inquired if it was true that he was once a clerk in a merchant's office in London. He replied that he had been in a *banking house*, and at the Peace of Amiens, 1802, left London for Paris. I observed on the pianoforte there was a MS. score. He told me it was an opera. On the production of this new work in 1867, the following lines appeared in a Paris journal:—

> "'*Un jour de bonheur!*'* c'est le nom charmant
> Du vif opéra, plein de badinage,
> Que ta muse, Auber, comme en se jouant,
> Vient de nous donner, harmonieux gage
> Du génie éclos en toi tout enfant.

---

* Name of the Opera, given 1867. Opus, 42.

"Posséder intact et pur un talent
Dont la chaude ardeur triomphe de l'âge,
Fait de chaque jour qui te voit chantant
'Un jour de bonheur.'

"A tes blancs cheveux rendre un noble hommage ;
Te voir là, debout, seul représentant
Du groupe sacré qu'Halévy, qu'Adam,
Qu'Hérold composaient ; ouïr ton ouvrage
Fut pour un public recueilli, fervent,
'Un jour de bonheur.'"

FÉTIS,

BORN 1784 ; DIED 1871.

FÉTIS (FRANÇOIS JOSEPH).

Chevalier de la légion d'honneur, and director of the Brussels Conservatoire since 1833.

TO this learned musician, theorist, composer, historian, and critic—born at Mons, 1784—I chiefly owe what knowledge I possess of music and musical literature. In 1827, Fétis was professor of counterpoint and librarian at the Conservatoire in Paris, also editor of the "La Revue Musicale." The rapid manner in which he glanced over and corrected the most complex exercises of counterpoint greatly astonished me after the prosy examinations of my previous instructor in London. The early numbers of his "Revue," now rare and costly, contain masterly essays; and his "Biographie des Musiciens," the most complete work of its kind, contains a mass of valuable information. There are some inaccuracies in this work as to dates, inevitable in so voluminous a publication. When I reflect upon the vast labour of this veteran's life, I was astonished to find him still, hale in 1869 and hearty, engaged in finishing his long announced "General History of Music." For a list of his works, operas, masses, &c., and notice of his life, *vide* "Record," 1856, with his portrait.

Of the numerous literary productions by Fétis, not one has been more popular than "La Musique mise à la portée de tout le monde," a small volume full of useful instruction, translated in America and London —"Music Made Easy." I recommend amateurs of music to procure this work.

WEBER,

BORN 1786; DIED 1826.

—o—

WEBER'S "OBERON"—THE MERMAID'S SONG.

THIS elaborate opera was produced under the direction of its composer, after sixteen rehearsals, at Covent Garden Theatre, in 1826. Of the few popular melodies in this last work of Weber, the Mermaid's Song may be cited as the one that has been most frequently adapted, arranged, and introduced in various fantasias. Yet it narrowly escaped being omitted, at the suggestion of the stage manager. Little Miss Goward, to whom was assigned this charming song, had a pleasing mezzo-soprano voice. Weber, *fils*, in the lately-published biography of his father, gives the following account of the last rehearsal. Miss Goward, who sang the Mermaid's Song behind the scenes, could not continue to keep time with the band. "Cut that out," cried Fawcett, with impatience. "Cut it out?" shouted Weber, to the surprise of all, as he sprang with one bound over the balustrade into the orchestra, and mounted to the conductor's desk. "What do you mean? I'll soon show you how it will go;" and after pointing out the place where the singer could best be heard, and directing the due tone of the band, he soon showed, indeed, how his wondrous song would, could, and should "go." In after times, the Mermaid, as at present, sings floating on the waves.

The flowing simplicity of the melody, the novel figure of accompaniment for the horn, and the exquisite harmony that gives relief to the tonal colour of this song, cannot be too highly appreciated. Such a lovely creation to be "cut out," one can well imagine, must have raised the indignation of poor Weber, harassed, fatigued, and ill as he was—in the last stage of consumption. That Weber was anxious to have this song delivered with feeling, simplicity, and strictly in time, may be inferred from the following anecdote, the truth of which I had confirmed by Mrs. Keeley, formerly Miss Goward. After the first trial, by the prima donna, the composer folded up the MS., saying, "Tank you, madame." After another trial, by a seconda donna, Weber politely thanked her, and again pocketed the MS. At last Miss Goward was invited to try over the song. Her singing, in tune and time, with natural expression, realised the composer's intentions, and with a smile he stooped and kissed the forehead of the little girl, saying, "Dat vill do; you sall sing de song." It has been churlishly stated that Mendelssohn must have been brooding over this melody when writing his overture to the "Midsummer Night's Dream."

Mermaid's Song. WEBER.

Overture. MENDELSSOHN.

The phrase here quoted * from the Overture, is suggested by Titania's request to her fairies—

"Sing me now asleep."

The exquisite treatment of this fragment of Weber's melody, in its adapted form, never fails to produce sensation. It has been the privilege of all musicians to copy their predecessors in design, and the accident of the greatest composers to have adopted melodic creations similar to those of others. Fuseli's favourite aphorism at once defines the boundary of imitation, in asserting that "Genius *may adopt*, but never steals."

WEBER'S LETTER TO MR. WM. HAWES.

(Dated Dresden, Sept. 18th, 1825.)

"As for the souvenir with which you will honour me, my dear sir, I shall be highly delighted in accepting it as the *first* and *only* mark of remembrance which I have received from among managers in Europe." Mr. Hawes produced the first version, in English, of "Der Freyschütz," and the souvenir consisted of a silver cup valued at fifty guineas. Poor Weber, within a twelvemonth after the above date, was buried at Moorfields, and I assisted in the performance of Mozart's "Requiem" on that melancholy occasion.

MEYERBEER,

BORN 1791 ; DIED 1864.

MEYERBEER AT THE MUSICAL UNION, 1855.

THE illustrious maestro, deeply impressed with the general appearance and musical intelligence of the audience, inquired of me, "D'ou vient ce public sérieux?" I replied, "De leurs chateaux." Two-thirds of the members and visitors are non-residents in London.

TEMPO DI MARCIA.

WALKING with Meyerbeer, in 1852, at Spa, during the performance of the Coronation March in his opera of "Le Prophète," I mentioned that the bands in London played it quicker. "*Pourquoi?*" replied the maestro. The only answer I gave him was, "In England *time is money.*" Fétis, in his letters on Music in London (1829), remarked that the slow movements in the Grand Symphonies were played *too fast*, and the quick movements *too slow.* The authority of Moscheles, however, during his residence in London, established the traditional *tempo* of Beethoven's works which is now generally adopted.

CZERNY,

BORN 1791; DIED 1857.

CZERNY—HIS ARRANGEMENTS AND COMPOSITIONS.

THIS most remarkable pianist and composer, adapter, and critic, the son of a Bohemian professor of music, was the companion and friend of Beethoven, and instructor of Döhler and Liszt.

Before my departure from Vienna, in 1845, Czerny desired me to pay him a visit. Up three flights of stone stairs lived this venerable musician, in a suite of ample-sized rooms, much of the same character as the flats in Edinburgh. No sooner was my name announced than Czerny came to the outer door, and gave me a cordial welcome. As I passed through his library, he begged me to observe his collection of English literature. "You see, I have your Byron, Scott, all complete in that case; and your immortal Shakespeare—your Beethoven, eh?—Gottes lieber Mann, eh?" Our interview lasted some time, in the course of which I inquired "how it was possible he had ever found time to publish so many works?" He replied, "I will surprise you the more when I tell you that I was twenty-eight years of age before

I published my first work, and that I have written more music in my lifetime than any living copyist. You may imagine this when I state that I have written more than one thousand pieces that have never been printed, and have never employed a copyist to prepare any of my publications."

I was curious to know the truth of what had been described, as to his mode of working at four different publications at a time. Czerny smiled at my feeling astonished at his *modus operandi*.

In each corner of his study was a desk with an unfinished score in hand.

"You see, my dear Mr. Ella, that I am working for the English," showing me at the same time a long list of national tunes to be arranged for D'Almaine and Co. At a second desk I found Beethoven's Symphonies *à quatre mains*, half finished, for Cocks and Co. At a third desk he was editing a new edition of Bach's fugues; and at a fourth he was composing a Grand Symphony. After finishing a page of one score, he passed on to another desk; and by the time he had written a page at the fourth desk, he resumed his labours at desk No. 1.* Such, then, was the mechanical labour of this musician's life. No wonder that his own compositions smelt of the lamp. In manners, he was gentle and unaffected; as a teacher,

* In Letter No. 14, vol. i. page 25, of Beethoven's Correspondence, translated by Lady Wallace, Beethoven, excusing his idleness in not writing to his friend, says, "I live wholly in my music, and scarcely is one work finished when another is begun; indeed, *I am often at work on three or four things at the same time.*"

matchless; as a critic, honest and generous. His pupils of both sexes always spoke affectionately of "Papa Czerny." Upon all questions concerning the tempo and style of Beethoven's music, the authority of Czerny's opinion is sacred. He gave me many anecdotes of musical celebrities; and, from the date of this adieu, 1845, to the time of his death, I was honoured by many tokens of his remembrance, and the present of a printed score of one of his own Grand Symphonies.

Exclusive of arrangements of Symphonies, Oratorios, Operas, Overtures, &c., Czerny published some 850 peices for the pianoforte. His MS. works include a Grand Method for the Pianoforte, 24 Masses, and 4 Requiems for full Orchestra, 300 Graduels, Motets, Concertos, Symphonies, Quartets, and Quintets, and Songs with and without Orchestra. Czerny also published at Schott and Co., Mayence, in 4to, "Esquisse de toute l'histoire de la musique," &c. Had not Czerny lived a retired life, he could not have produced such a fabulous number of works. "*Il était bon homme et de bonne compagnie; mais les conditions qu'il s'était imposées pour ses travaux l'avaient obligé à se renfermer en lui-même.*"—FÉTIS.

This *Impromptu*, written in my album, bespeaks the hand of an experienced master.

(The original key, C sharp major.)

CHARLES CZERNY. *Nov.* 21*st*, 1845. *Vienna.*

ROSSINI,

BORN 1792 ; DIED 1868.

DAL TUO STELLATO.

THE novelty of this chromatic progression from F♯ to F♮, so contrary to the established rules of scholastic harmony, once gave rise to the following dialogue in Paris :—

Pedant.—What do you say to this flagrant transgression of that libertine Rossini ?

Cherubini.—What do I say ?—I only wish I had made it.

This beautiful prayer in "Mosè" produced at Naples, 1827, affords a singular example of a successful expediency turning the tide of an equivocal success of a splendid opera. I give its history, as related verbatim from undoubted authority by a writer well acquainted with the incidents of Rossini's life :—

" Voilà le désert et la mer Rouge. Aux premières

représentations à *San Carlo*, le public se montra impitoyable : les Hébreux et les Egyptiens furent maltraités. Il manquait évidemment quelque chose à cette scène qui finissait le drame froidement sur un effet de décoration plus froid encore. Un matin Rossini, entouré de ses amis, causait avec cet amiable abandon, ce naturel railleur qui eurent toujours tant d'attrait pour les élus de son intimité. Par un hasard étrange, la conversation roulait sur le malheureux machiniste qui avait compromis le troisième acte du 'Mosè ;' la mer, au lieu d'être au-dessous du rivage, s'élevait de cinq à six pieds au-dessus, de telle façon que toute la salle voyait les flots s'agiter dans les airs. C'était nouveau, à la vérité, mais le machiniste fut impitoyablement immolé sous le ridicule. Au moment où Rossini et ses amis se débattaient dans le rire au récit de cette scène burlesque, la porte s'entr'ouvrit doucement, et l'on vit à travers une demi-obscurité se dessiner l'ombre d'un homme dont la figure était enfoncée sous un large chapeau. Rossini avait reconnu l'auteur du libretto de 'Mosè' :—

" Que diable veux-tu, Tottola ? tu as l'air d'un conspirateur," lui dit le maëstro.

"Ah ! il y a longtemps que je le cherche, et je l'ai trouvé."

" Eh ! quoi donc, mon brave ami ?"

"Ah ! pour le coup, je réponds du succès, si vous me venez en aide."

" De la musique, encore de la musique, j'en suis certain."

"Oh! ce n'est rien, presque rien, et, si vous le voulez, le troisième acte de 'Mosè' produira un furieux effet."

"Comment cela?"

"J'ai ajouté une prière pour ces infortunés Hébreux avant de leur faire passer la mer à pied sec. Demain on donne l'opéra; il ne tient qu'à vous de faire rester le public jusqu'à la fin."

"Laisse-moi tes vers, mon brave Tottola, et reviens dans une heure."

"Pendant que ses amis continuaient à causer bruyamment, Rossini passa dans un petit cabinet, et en sortit au bout de quelques minutes en s'écriant: 'La chose est faite, Tottola sera content.' Rossini venait tout bonnement d'improviser cette prière sublime, qui suffirait à elle seule pour immortaliser son nom. On annonça qu'elle serait chantée le lendemain pour la première fois. Le public, qui avait pris l'habitude de quitter le théâtre à la fin du second acte, quelquefois même avant le premier, attendit avec impatience jusqu'au dénoûement. Après les premières notes, il y eut un silence de recueillement. A mesure que le chant se développait, une sorte de frissonnement traversait la salle, et lorsque le peuple tout entier unit ses accents pour répéter l'hymne sainte, l'admiration ne connut plus de bornes. Jamais peut-être on ne fut témoin d'une ovation aussi imposante."—ESCUIDER.

ROSSINI FLATTERED BY A LADY.

THE extravagant praises lavished on the maestro by the Parisian ladies soon made him totally indifferent to the "dolce parole" of the fair sex. After a fatiguing rehearsal of "Semiramide," which had already been admired and applauded all over Europe, Rossini was accosted, on leaving the theatre, by a lady, who detained him a full half-hour speaking of the merits of the opera. After every term of flattery in the French vocabulary was exhausted, the impatient maestro, interrupting the stream of her eloquence, sarcastically replied with an air of assumed modesty, "Madame, vous êtes bien aimable de m'encourager."

REISSIGER,

BORN 1798; DIED 1859.

REISSIGER AND "WEBER'S LAST WALTZ."

BY the death of this artist, Germany has to mourn the loss of one of its best musicians, although not a man of remarkable genius. At the age of ten years he distinguished himself as a pianist, under the tuition of his father. After studying music at Leipzig, he commenced a course of theology in the University, but soon abandoned himself to his favourite pursuit, and at the age of seventeen he made his first essays in religious composition.

In his professional travels, he visited Munich, Vienna, Berlin, Italy, and France, where several of his works were produced, and was afterwards invited to the Hague, to assist with his experience in forming a Conservatoire. In 1827, this musician finally took up his residence at Dresden, invested with all the titles and functions of chapel-master enjoyed by his immortal predecessor, Weber. Here, in January 1846, I made his acquaintance. The lyrical and orchestral works of Reissiger were not his happiest efforts in composition; but his religious music placed him high in the esteem of his compatriots, and his numerous pianoforte trios and quartets, brilliant and melodious, have long enjoyed great favour among amateurs in this country. As stated in the "Musical Union Record" of 1846, the elegant bagatelle known as "Weber's Last Waltz," was composed by Reissiger.

BERLIOZ,

BORN 1803; DIED 1869.

HECTOR BERLIOZ.

As it is always interesting to know something concerning the early development of a musician's passion for art, the following extract from the fifth volume of the "Nouvelle Biographie Universelle" will no doubt be acceptable to my readers:—"Berlioz (Hector), musicien compositeur, né le 11 Décembre 1803, à la Côte-Saint-André (Isère.) Son père, qui exerçait la médecine dans le pays, désirait lui voir suivre la même profession. Passionné pour la musique, qu'on lui faisait apprendre pour son agrément, le jeune Berlioz supplia vainement ses parents de permettre qu'il se livrât exclusivement à la culture d'un art pour lequel il se sentit une vocation." After gaining the first prize at the Conservatoire in Paris for composition, in 1830, Berlioz visited Italy, and, on his return, produced those colossal works, romantic, characteristic, and descriptive, which meet with the reception that has been, and ever will be, the fate of every original product of the human mind that differs from the conventional taste of the million—enthusiastic admiration from some, and utter dislike from others. The biogr aher thus remarks with great justice,—"quel que soit la diversité des opinions émises sur les productions de ce compositeur, on ne peut méconnaitre qu'elles ont un style, un cachet d'individualité qui leur sont propres, et qu'elles tendent à aggrandir la sphère de l'art."

No author has had to contend with greater vicissitudes in professional life than Hector Berlioz; none ever received more enthusiastic applause from intelligent communities, more honours and distinctions from societies and courts, and *less* substantial recompense for the product of his genius; yet, nought depressed by his chequered life, Hector Berlioz calmly submits to his fate with the dignified resignation of a true philosopher in advance of his age. "There is no celebrity for the artist," said Gesner, "if the love of his own art does not become a vehement passion; if the hours he employs to cultivate it are not for him the most delicious ones of his life; if study becomes not his true existence and his first happiness; if the society of his brothers in art is not that which most pleases him; if in the morning he flies not to his work, impatient to recommence what he left unfinished. These are the marks of him *who labours for true glory and posterity;* but if he seek only to please the taste of his age, his works will not kindle the desires, nor touch the hearts, of those who love the art and the artists." The enthusiastic artist of Zurich has here graphically anticipated the description of the life of Berlioz recently published.

Since his retirement from the "Débats," in which influential journal Berlioz was engaged as musical critic for several years, he has visited Vienna, St. Petersburgh, and Moscow, to conduct selections from his most admired compositions. In those cities he was received by the *dilettanti* with every mark of respect, and his music with the greatest possible enthusiasm. Of all the eminent musicians I have known, Berlioz is one of the most instructive art companions, and the most devoted and sincere in friendship.

BERLIOZ IN VIENNA.

"Leben athmet der bildene Kunst; Geist fordr'ich von Dichter; Aber die Seele spricht nur Polyhymnia aus."—SCHILLER.

A GENIAL sympathy for all the arts exists in Germany; but music, in the capital of Austria, finds an appreciative public never loth to pay tribute to its gifted disciples.

On two occasions, in 1846 and 1865, I had the good fortune to be present in Vienna at the concerts of Berlioz, and at the banquets given in compliment to his genius and ability as composer and critic. In 1845, Baron Lannoy presided, and with a gold baton in his hand, addressed Berlioz in the following complimentary language:—

"Monsieur, les professeurs et les amateurs de musique Viennois, ici présents, désirent vous donner un gage de la haute estime que vous leur inspirez.

Ils admirent l'originalité, la verve et la savante instrumentation de vos compositions, votre beau talent comme critique et comme théoréticien, et votre direction claire, précise et pleine de feu. C'est en leur nom que je vous prie d'accepter ce bâton de mesure. Puisse-t-il rappeler à votre souvenir la ville où Gluck, Haydn, Mozart, et Beethoven ont vécu, et les amis de l'art musical, qui s'unissent à moi pour crier, Vive Berlioz !"

I subjoin some verses, delivered on the occasion by Castelli, a copy of which I have received in the poet's handwriting; a compliment I greatly prize among the many other gifts of friendship during my visit to this city—the cradle of musical genius.

IMPROMPTU.

Gesprochen beim Festmahle welches BERLIOZ *gegeben wurde.*

Der *Haydn* hat ein Landhaus gebaut,
Das war so lieblich und war so traut,
Der *Mozart* setzt ein Stockwerk darauf,
Da stiegen mit ihm wir so gerne hinauf;
Der *Beethoven* setzte darauf einen Thurm
Dahin konnt' ihm folgen nicht mehr ein Wurm,
Der *Berlioz* suchte zu geben noch weiter
Da fanden sie garnicht dazu mehr die Leiter,
Doch sei gesegnet sein Muth and sein Streben,
Er lebe um seinen Triumph zu erleben.—CASTELLI.

There were present at this ceremony Maestro Nicolai, Strauss, Alvars, Felicien David, Ernst, Mayseder, Czerny, the Directors of the Conservatoire, and the *élite* of vocal and instrumental talent in

Vienna. In 1866, a similar banquet took place, presided over by Prince Constantine Czartoryski, at which I was present.

Homage like this to a French musician on the soil of the triumvirate, Haydn, Mozart, and Beethoven, is creditable to the intelligence and liberality of the Austrian dilettanti and artists.

Here, and in Paris, one hears no talk about neglect of native talent as in London. Der Künstler hat *kein Vaterland;* and this belief acted upon, English, German, French, Italian, Russian, worthy the suffrage of a critical public, are sure to obtain it in the capital of Austria.

COSTA,

BORN 1807.

COSTA—HIS DEBÛT AS VOCALIST.

"Celsâ sedet Æolos arce
Sceptra tenens, mollitque animos, et temperat iras."—ÆNEID.

IT is known to the original members that, until the third year after its birth, the Musical Union gave no decided promise of longevity, and the director's Matinée was therefore an object of vital importance to its very existence. The prosperity that now crowns my labours, in having reared this once fluctuating and precarious offspring to robust health and maturity, does not make me unmindful of the past; and there is no act of professional sympathy which I recollect with more satisfaction and grateful remembrance than the personal attendance of Costa at the Director's Grand Matinée, with his golden tribute at the door in support of the Institution, then in its infancy. Now that I have retired from orchestral service, I can mention this trait of Costa's generosity without being accused of servile adulation; and will also add, that by similar acts of kindly feeling towards those under his *baton*, he has permanently and deservedly secured their affection.

No musician within my recollection, foreign or native, has achieved so much in the improvement of our public musical institutions and orchestras,—no artist, vocalist, or instrumentalist has survived the vicissitudes of public opinion in his laudably ambitious career with greater credit and approbation. Unlike most foreign artists who have acquired a fortune in this country, Costa is too proud of his time-honoured artistic position in England to retire and lead a *dolce far niente* life in the more genial atmosphere of his native city, Naples. In his social relations with those who obey his magic wand, and are subject to his discipline, I know of many deeds that greatly redound to his credit. The poor invalided chorister has felt the helping hand of his tender sympathy, and temporary aid has more than once, to my knowledge, relieved a member of his band in pecuniary difficulties. From the time of his *début*, as a vocalist at the Birmingham Festival in 1829, to the year of my retirement, in 1848, from the band over which he now so ably presides, I always enjoyed his acquaintance. This has now grown into an intimacy of mutual affection: as Cicero truthfully says, "Omninò amicitiæ, corroboratis jam confirmatisque et ingeniis et ætatibus, indicandæ sunt."

COSTA AND ORCHESTRAL DISCIPLINE.

In my early days, members of the Opera Band were neither very patient nor always punctual at rehearsals. During the thirty years of my directorship of the Musical Union I cannot call to mind a single instance of four foreign artists being assembled punctually at a rehearsal. When first Sir M. Costa wielded the baton at Her Majesty's Theatre, absentees at rehearsal were fined; nor until the last grand rehearsal of an opera was there any certainty of a full attendance. Artists with pupils at a guinea per lesson could well afford to pay the fine. At my suggestion Sir. M. Costa suppressed all fines, and obtained the power of engaging and dismissing members of the band. Beginning the following season, Sir Michael thus addressed the musicians of the orchestra:—"Gentlemen, I am happy to tell you that I have abolished *fines* for absentees (*great applause*); BUT,' any one absent at rehearsal without my permission, forfeits his engagement" (*murmurs, sotto voce*). Punctual, Sir Michael ever was, and is; and the complete band attended at all future rehearsals. This good example in the orchestra had its influence on the stage, and I well remember Grisi arriving too late to rehearse her cavattina in "La Gazza Ladra," and being rebuked by the conductor. The result of this discipline was very soon manifested advantageously to all engaged. The six and eight rehearsals were gradually reduced to two and three, and finally the choir and band were so thoroughly well drilled, that the revival of any opera never required more than *one* patient rehearsal. This immense economy of precious time during the London Season, every musician appreciated, and hence the universal favour of Sir M. Costa among the artists submissive to his moral discipline.

BALFE,

BORN 1808; DIED 1870.

"*THE LIGHT OF OTHER DAYS.*"

In the month of May 1836, I called upon Balfe. He had just penned the above ballad. He sang it to me, and predicted for it "*a great hit.*" This very ballad, I am credibly informed, has realised more than six thousand pounds to the publisher. In this country of commerce and speculation, it is not surprising that every tyro, capable of rhyming verses and humming a tune, should compete for such prizes as are obtained by a popular ballad. Many of these effusions are published with the most egregious errors in the accompaniment, by persons evidently ignorant of the simplest elements of harmony.

MENDELSSOHN,

BORN 1809; DIED 1847.

MENDELSSOHN AND HIS PROTÉGÉ.

BY special invitation, I accompanied a literary friend, in April 1844, to the residence of the late Madame Dulcken, Pianist to the Queen, to hear a youth play the violin. M. Dulcken was in doubt whether a boy of the age of Master Joachim, then fourteen, would be allowed to play at the Philharmonic Concerts, and both Sir Henry Bishop and Sir George Smart were sceptical on the matter. On the Tuesday following, the youthful violinist came to my second weekly quartet union, and led Beethoven's Quintet in C. At two other of my private musical gatherings Master Joachim played solos, or led quartets, and ultimately I mustered a notable assembly of musical lions to hear him play Beethoven's Posthumous Quartet in B♭. Royalty and nobility crowded my room, but the most illustrious of the company comprised Mendelssohn, Moscheles, Dragonetti, Ernst, Lablache, Döhler, Offenbach, Benedict, Thalberg, Sainton, Sivori, Sir George Smart, Sir Henry Bishop, and Costa.

The next morning Mendelssohn called to thank me for the very great interest I had taken in the success of his *protégé*, and for the notices which I had published of his playing. Mendelssohn then consented to play at the next reunion; and, in compliment to him, I afterwards wrote suggesting that, in addition to his Trio in D minor, the programme should consist of his music exclusively. I also mentioned that a piano from any of the celebrated makers would be obtained, on his naming the one he preferred. To this letter I received the following reply, so characteristic of the man—his modesty and kindly feeling. It is written as printed, in English, underlined where I give italics:—

"HOBART PLACE, EATON SQUARE,
May 17th, 1844.

"MY DEAR SIR,—Let me thank you in a few words for your kind note and invitation, and I shall be most happy to play my Trio on Tuesday next, and if Ernst will accompany it (as he has often done already at Dublin) I anticipate a *great* treat from it! Any of those pianos you mention will do, of course; but if I *must* make a choice, I would prefer Erard's.

"I have only one favour to ask: do not make the programme out with too much of my music, as you seem to intend doing; and instead of having a Quartet and Trio, have only the latter, and let me have some other Quartet. The hearer will be *as well* pleased (to say the least), and I, for one, much more. But as for the Trio, once more, I shall be most happy to play it.—Always yours very truly,

"FELIX MENDELSSOHN-BARTHOLDY."

Had the art of photography in 1844 been popular, as at the present time, we might have had a pictorial souvenir of this performance of Mendelssohn, and Joachim at his side, with Ernst and Hausmann at the violin and violincello. In the first Allegro, Ernst failing to turn his page in time for the *rentrée* of the violin, Mendelssohn improvised an elegant rhythm of four additional bars of music, which elicited bravos from all present.

A bank director humorously accused Mendelssohn of "putting more notes into circulation than allowed by printed authority." The composer, with joyous spirit, laughed heartily at the success of his improvisation, and Thalberg had his joke upon Ernst, *voltando, non subito.* "It has never been our duty to record a greater musical treat," said the *Morning Post*, "than the effect of the Trio in D minor, and the Elegie for the violin, performed by their respective composers—Mendelssohn and Ernst." The programme also included Beethoven's Quartet in E minor, to which Mendelssohn listened with intense delight.

Six weeks after his first appearance at my parties, Joachim performed Beethoven's Violin Concerto at the Philharmonic Concert, conducted by Mendelssohn. The programme of this concert, May 27th, 1844, is one of historical interest, and worthy a place in this publication—a model programme of the halcyon days of the Society, with a full subscription, and an enthusiastic audience.

PART I.

Symphony, in B♭ (No. 4)	*Beethoven.*
Duet from *Pascal Bruno*	*J. L. Hatton.*
Violin Concerto, Master JOACHIM	*Beethoven.*
Duet, Quintet, and Chorus (*Faust*)	*Spohr.*

PART II.

Overture, and all the Music (first time) of the *Midsummer Night's Dream*	*Mendelssohn.*
Song and Chorus—Vocalist, STAUDIGL (*Fidelio*)	*Beethoven.*
Hunting Chorus (*The Seasons*)	*Haydn.*

"The presence of Mendelssohn," said Ayrton, in the *Examiner*, "infused new spirit into the band; and the music was executed with an ardour that evinced the influence he possesses, and the confidence he inspires, whenever he wields the *bâton.*"

MENDELSSOHN AND BEETHOVEN.

AT a time when so much curiosity is awakened, by the publication of Mendelssohn's letters, to know what this musician thought of the genius and works of the great masters that preceded him, the following extract (from the "Music of the Nineteenth Century," by the late Professor Marx, published by Cocks and Co., London) will be read by every musician and amateur with deep interest. In my opinion, Mendelssohn gives a most satisfactory meaning of a phrase, often misapplied by certain musicians to the works of their favourite master.

"This composer has opened a new road!—Well, I ask, what do they mean by such an assertion? Do they merely intend to say that he has proceeded upon a road which no one else had traversed before him, or does the assertion not rather imply that the composer has opened a track which leads to a new and more charming region of art? For, every one capable of wielding a shovel and moving his legs can open a path for himself; but if they employ the expression in the higher sense, I deny its applicability altogether. *There is no such thing as a new road*, simply because there is no new region of art to which it could lead. They have all been explored long since.—New roads! That artist is sure to be led astray who gives himself up to this cursed demon! No artist has ever opened a new road. At the most, he only did his work a little better than his immediate predecessors. Who is to strike out a new path in art? A genius. Well, has Beethoven shown us a new road entirely different from that in which Mozart walked? Are his symphonies altogether new in form and conception? I say, No. I cannot perceive any extraordinary difference between Beethoven's first Symphony and Mozart's last, either as regards artistic excellence or effect. The one pleases me, and so does the other. To-day, I listen with delight to Beethoven's Symphony in D major; to-morrow, I feel equally happy in listening to that of

Mozart in C major, with the fugue at the end. But the idea of a new road never enters my head. Then, again, take Beethoven's 'Fidelio.' I do not mean to say that I find every passage in it fully to my mind; but I should like an opera named which can produce a deeper effect, or yield a more delightful artistic enjoyment. Will you point out to me a single piece in it in which Beethoven has struck out a new path? I do not find one. On looking into the score, as well as on listening to the performance, I everywhere perceive Cherubini's dramatic style of composition. It is true that Beethoven did not ape that style; but it was before his mind as his most cherished pattern."

"And what about Beethoven's last period?" inquired the writer. "What about his last Quartets, his Ninth Symphony, his Mass (Op. 123)?—Surely no work of any of his predecessors or contemporaries can be likened to them."

"That may be true in a certain sense," continued Mendelssohn, with great animation. "Beethoven's *forms* are *wider* and *broader;* his style is more polyphonic and artistic; his ideas are more gloomy and melancholy, even where they endeavour to assume a cheerful tone; his instrumentation is fuller; —*he has gone a little farther on the road of his predecessors, but by no means struck out into a new path.* And, to be candid, where has he led us to? Has he opened to us a region of art more *beautiful* than those previously known? Does his Ninth Symphony really afford to us, as *artists*, a higher enjoyment than most of his other symphonies? As far as I am concerned, I confess openly that I do not feel it. It is a feast to me to listen to that symphony; but the same, if not a purer, feast is prepared for me in the Symphony in C minor."

The above criticism of Mendelssohn, on the character and forms of Beethoven's later works, accords with opinions frequently expressed by living writers. The Ninth Symphony, with all its manifold beauties, sublime phrases, and novel effects, is too long, and the vocal parts are inconveniently written and seldom satisfactorily sung.

MENDELSSOHN AND INSPIRATION.

"IF I wish to hear Italian music," said Mendelssohn (1831), "I must go to Paris or to England. The Germans, however, take it amiss when you say this, and persist, *per force*, in singing, playing, and acquiring new ideas here, declaring this is the land of inspiration; while I maintain *that inspiration is peculiar to no country, but floats in the air.*"

This statement is borne out by the fact of so many *chefs-d'œuvre* being produced neither in any particular country, nor yet in the fatherland of their composers. Handel, a Prussian, composed the "Messiah" at Gopsall Hall, Leicestershire; Rossini, Spontini, and Cherubini, Italians, their greatest lyrical and sacred works in Paris; Haydn, an Austrian, wrote his best symphonies in London; and Mendelssohn his best symphony in Rome!

WAGNER,

BORN 1813.

THE PILGRIMS' CHORUS.

WHATEVER difference of opinion exists on the merits of the entire opera of "Tannhauser," no one denies Wagner the credit of having produced in it a choral melody and march of singular beauty and originality. As for the choral march, I know nothing finer in modern art; and the solemn majesty of the Pilgrims' Chorus, with its climax (explained below), is most impressively grand. This chorus, which forms the leading theme of the introduction and coda of the overture to the opera (*too* frequently repeated) is admired for its novel and expressive transitions of chromatic harmony (see music *). As noticed in my sketch of Music in Paris 1867–78, after the performance of this overture, at one of the Pasdeloup's Concerts, with a band of one hundred performers, three rounds of applause followed, with a summons for the conductor. When given at the Philharmonic Concerts in 1867, it was neither understood nor effective, partly owing to the instrumentation being too powerful for Hanover Square Rooms. The music quoted embodies the complete melody sung by the Pilgrims, and for the more easy comprehension of the chromatic transitions of harmony in the second division of the chorus, it is transposed from E♭ to G major. With the violin accompaniment to the final verse, supported by the full power of the band in stately measure of $\frac{9}{12}$ and the vocal melody strengthened by the trombones, the *tout-ensemble*, in a theatre or a spacious music-room produces a most overpowering effect (*vide* music †). Having heard "Tannhauser" in Vienna and elsewhere, I am inclined to think it is not calculated to please an English audience. However, I should be very sorry not to have witnessed both "Tannhauser" and "Lohengrin." History tells us that Euripides, having presented Socrates with the writings of Heraclitus, a philosopher famed for involution and obscurity, inquired afterwards his opinion of their merit. "What I understand," said Socrates, "I find to be excellent; and therefore believe that to be of equal value which I cannot understand." Under shelter of this wisdom of the Athenian moralist and philosopher, I reserve my opinion of the merits of Wagner's declamatory treatment of the lyrical drama.—1859.

THE PI

TANHAUSER.

To face p. 258.

RUBINSTEIN,

BORN 1829.

PRECOCIOUS TALENT.—LONDON, 1842.

"Les talens précoses sont une exception à la marche lente et graduée de la nature."—BALLIOT.

THE Musical Diary of the late Mr. Ayrton, now in my possession, contains an interesting description of "The young Rubinstein," published in the *Examiner* newspaper in 1842. The writer speaks of the youth's talent, after hearing him at the late Mr. Alsager's, one of the proprietors of the *Times*, and a well-known patron of music. On the margin of the published notice, the writer adds, *This is a real prodigy;* and by all who have listened to Rubinstein, in the various works performed by him, with equal success, at the Musical Union, any particulars of the early development of his genius will be perused with interest.

"*A musical wonder.*—A Russian boy, named Antoine Rubinstein, a native of Moldavia, who has not yet completed his twelfth year, is, and has been during the last few weeks, in London under the care of his teacher, M. Villoing, with a view to exhibit his extraordinary talents in this metropolis, though we believe that he has not yet performed in public.

In private parties he has displayed his powers as a performer on the pianoforte, and excited the astonishment, not only of those who are easily and willingly surprised by youthful genius, but of professors who judge of a performance by its own ability. This lad—who is small for his age, and very slenderly made, though his head is of large dimensions—executes with his little hands the very same music in which Thalberg excels, and to perform which, it has been jocosely said, this celebrated artist has been furnished with five fingers and two thumbs to each hand, put in motion by steam power. We have heard Rubinstein play some of those pieces, and can answer for the unimpeachable correctness of his performance; and what is still more remarkable, for the force which, by some almost unparalleled gift of nature, he is enabled to exert a degree of muscular strength which his general conformation, and especially that of his arms and hands, would have induced us to suppose he could not possibly possess. To gratify those whose taste leads them to prefer fashionable music, he plays the *fantasias* of Liszt, Thalberg, Herz, &c.; but when exhibiting before real connoisseurs, he chooses for his purpose the elaborate compositions of the old German school—the learned and difficult fugues of Sebastian Bach and Handel, all which he executes with an ease as well as a precision, which very few masters are able to attain; and, to add to the wonder, he plays everything from memory, this faculty being, apparently, as fully developed in him, as it is now and then, though rarely, in adults, who have perfected it by long practice.

"We recommend this prodigy—for such he is—not only to the amateur of music, but to physiologists, or psychologists, who by their inquiries may perhaps enlarge their knowledge of the human mind, and throw some light on that obscure but interesting and, too often, melancholy subject, premature genius, combined, as it is in this instance, with partial premature strength."—*Examiner.*

It is as well to inform the readers of this glowing description of "a *real* prodigy," that the writer, Mr. Ayrton, was a sound musician, a scholar, and an independent critic, who had neither pupils nor *protégées.* His diary contains all his articles on music that appeared in the *Examiner* newspaper from the year 1847 to 1856, with annotations, and descriptions of certain London critics in other journals. Of Rubinstein, in the 28th year of his age, the following notice, in 1857, is fully borne out by a more intimate acquaintance with his talent:—"His ardent temperament is at once recognised, both in the character of his compositions and in the vigorous expression of his playing. To those who prefer the passive, inanimate style of running over the keys, without emphasis and *chiaro-scuro,* Rubinstein's power of execution will give cause for alarm. The amateur is simply directed to this fact, in respect to tone and touch; any amount of force from the *wrist* only can never strain the action of the pianoforte beyond the resistance of its mechanism. On the other hand, it is very easy, by contraction of the muscles from the shoulder, to break a string with the single blow of a finger. The touch of Rubinstein is delicate and *souple* in the extreme, where the character of the music demands delicacy and elegance of expression (as instanced in his poetical version of Chopin's "Berceuse" in 1857, encored); and in music of impassioned colouring, his youthful, ardent nature yields to the impulse of the moment. His mechanism, at eleven years of age, was equal to the performance of the most complicated fugues of Bach, and brilliant *tours de force* of Thalberg's fantasias, and the ease with which he now plays the most difficult music is perfectly astounding! Whatever excess of passion may be observed in his occasional bursts of expression, age will ultimately sober down; but where the absence of this passion is perceptible in the temperament of an artist, nor age, nor clime, nor study, can supply the want."—1859.

In a tour throughout England, Scotland, and Ireland, and in a series of pianoforte recitals in London, 1877, Rubinstein realized in three months £12,000! No such amount was ever obtained by vocalist or actor in England in the same space of time.

HERBECK,

BORN 1831; DIED 1877.

KAPELLMEISTER HERBECK AS CONDUCTOR.

TO appreciate the technical knowledge and practical skill of the conductor of an orchestra, to judge fairly of his system of discipline in obtaining from the executants the scrupulous observance of details in *nuance*, one must be present at rehearsals of a fine work, under the absolute control of the directing mind. I am spared any description of Herbeck's mode of conducting a Symphony of Beethoven, by quoting that of an accomplished amateur, whose description of a pilgrimage to the tomb of Beethoven is printed in the "Musical Union Record" of 1866.

The rehearsal and performance are described with acumen and truth, and the remarkable abilities of the energetic and instructive Herbeck are in no respect overrated. I wish not to let slip this opportunity of giving some account of this remarkable musician, a short extract translated from the *Volks-Zeitung* of Vienna, 1866:—

"Johann Franz Herbeck, born in Vienna, December 25, 1831, is the son of a poor tailor. Having shown an aptitude for music in his infancy, he was early instructed in singing. At the age of ten years his beautiful voice and musical intelligence procured him an engagement as choir-boy at the Monastery of the Holy Cross.

"His voice, a high and brilliant soprano, and his method of singing, having attracted the notice of the cognoscenti of Vienna, the Prelate sent him to study harmony with the Imperial Kapellmeister Notter. On completing his education in music and philosophy in 1856, he became Director of the Wiener-Männer-Gesang-Verein (male choir), the most popular of all singing unions in Vienna and known throughout Germany. The reputation of this union is entirely owing to the transcendent abilities of Herbeck, who has devoted ten years of his life to its progress and perfection. In 1858 he was appointed Choir-Master and Professor at the Conservatoire; in 1859 he was elected Conductor of the grand concerts of the Music Society of Vienna, given in the Redouten Salon; and, finally, in 1866, he was nominated Imperial Chapel-Master." Under his able direction, I have heard masses performed to perfection.

"As a composer, in various branches of the art, Herbeck has obtained great reputation. Besides overtures, choruses, and songs, he has produced three grand symphonies, two instrumental quartets, three grand masses, and other classical works, frequently exhibiting a thorough independence of treatment in form and instrumentation.

"The name of Herbeck stands, however, in another sense, prominently before the public, associated with that of the Austrian 'melodious Crœsus,' Franz Schubert. It was Herbeck who saved from destruction and oblivion the works of Schubert. Having collected them, he presented them in a new form to the musical world. More than ten years did Herbeck devote in gathering together the despised and hidden treasures, in trying them, and in bringing them into some order for publication. Truly may he be called the preserver of Schubert's works. The result of his labours is shown in the long list of Schubert's compositions that have been published and performed, some of which, under Herbeck's direction, have afforded the amateurs of Vienna infinite delight at their orchestral concerts. If Schubert's fertility be a matter of wonder, the indefatigable zeal and self-sacrifice of his apostle is no less so, for he has dedicated the work of a lifetime to the exhumation of these productions, and only a man born with equal genius could have brought light into such a chaos.

"The many orchestral *chefs-d'œuvre* produced under his baton leave nothing to desire by the most rigorous critics. For intelligence, *élan*, reverence for the author, inspiration, and truthful expression, Herbeck, as Director, is without a rival. Foreign countries have bestowed upon Herbeck diplomas, and the Emperor of Austria has acknowledged his merit by a decoration. Equally noble in his private as in his public character, he shows in the one a strong artistic individuality, in the other "ein deutsches gemüth."

From my intimate acquaintance with this eminent musician—the Costa of Vienna—I can endorse the truth of the above biographical sketch. In the hands of such a man the art is safe from profanation—is a faith, a religion!

Frequently at Herbeck's and other classical concerts, I found myself sitting next to persons so thoroughly conversant with "high art," that I mistook them for learned and experienced musicians. One proved to be the gallant and wealthy Bohemian, Count de Wilczek; another, Dr. Müller, the custodian of a Royal Gallery of pictures; and a third, an intimate friend of Beethoven, Dr. Leopold von Sonnleithner. This amateur had formerly conducted orchestral performances of Beethoven's Symphonies, and gave me the "*tempo giusto*" of certain movements which had been explained to him by the composer. A musical audience composed of such accomplished dilettanti as the above is satisfied with nothing short of perfect execution.

Wherever there is knowledge there is sympathy; and at the subscription concerts in Vienna the companionship of genial natures among the audience greatly enhances the pleasure of enjoying a fine performance of classical music. On all occasions I observed that the best works were most admired, and the merits of new compositions and executants always liberally appreciated. Concerts of *bénéficiaires*, vocalists, instrumentalists, and composers, in Vienna as in other cities, are attended by mixed audiences. The *bénéficiaire*, however, is the chief actor *en scène*, and the entertainment upon no occasion exceeds two hours in duration. What a boon to musicians if this custom existed in London!

ADAM,

BORN 1803; DIED 1856.

ADOLPH ADAM.

THIS accomplished musician, and composer of "Le Chalet" and "Le Postillon de Longjumeau," died in Paris, after a short illness. His lyrical works were numerous, but in England the name of Adam is associated with the ballet of "Giselle," the music to which is admired for the originality of its melodies, beautiful effects of its instrumentation, and dramatic truth of its expression.

TRIBULATIONS D'UN MUSICIEN.

A story is related of Cherubini venting his rage against the parents of precocious children, when presently appeared, by appointment, a lady describing her little companion as a wonderful genius—"a perfect child of Nature." "Madame," said the maestro, "leave him with us; we will adopt him." "Quel bonheur de trouver un enfant *de la Nature*, tombé sur la terre, sans père, sans mère, sans sœur, sans frère."

THE following souvenir, from the pen of the late gifted composer of many charming operas and that most exquisite ballet music, "La Giselle," Adolphe Adam, truthfully depicts scenes we are constantly doomed to witness:—

"Il y a un proverbe qui dit, qu'il n'y a rien de plus à redouter qu'un dîner d'amis et un concert d'amateurs. Les proverbes sont la sagesse des nations, et rien n'est en effet plus sage et plus véridique que la maxime que nous venons de citer. L'on doit s'estimer bien heureux lorsqu'on n'est pas frappé de ces deux fléaux à la fois; mais il est bien rare qu'après avoir té forcé d'avaler le dîner d'ami, composé, pour l'orédinaire, du classique pot-au-feu, suivi de quelqu'un de ces bienfaisants légumes qui vous rappellent les beaux jours et les succulents repas du lyceé; il est bien rare, dis-je, qu'après ce maussade festin, vous ne soyez pas encore régalé d'un petit concert, impromptu après le dessert. C'est la petite fille de huit ans qui va vous faire juger de ses progrès. On ouvre le piano, à qui il ne manque qu'une demi-douzaine de cordes, vu qu'il n'a pas été accordé depuis la dernière soirée on l'on a dansé au piano, et l'enfant chéri est prié de jouer quelque chose pour faire plaisir à l'ami de la maison. Mais l'enfant chéri, qui prend ordinairement sa récréation après le dîner, ne trouve pas de tout amusant de donner un échantillon de ses talents à une pareille heure, et fait une moue longue d'une aune. 'Allons, fais donc voir à Monsieur que tu es une grande demoiselle à présent,' dit le papa en traînant sa fille du côté du piano. L'enfant résiste, le père se fâche, et la virtuose en herbe se met à pleurer. La maman se met alors de la partie: 'Pourquoi la brutaliser ainsi,' dit-elle à son mari: 'tu sais combien elle est timide, elle n'osera plus jouer, à présent. Allons, mon enfant, sois raisonnable, et si tu joues bien ton morceau, tu iras embrasser le monsieur qui aime beaucoup les petites filles qui sont bien sages.' Douce perspective!

"Vous croyiez en être quittes pour entendre un peu de mauvaise musique, vous serez obligé, bon gré, mal gré, d'aller embrasser cette charmante petite fille qui, à l'aide du mouchoir de son père, est occupée dans un coin á sécher ses larmes. Il faut bien vous résigner; après bien des façons, vous avez le bonheur d'entendre: *Ah! vous dirai-je, maman! Je suis Lindor*, *Triste Raison*, et autres petits airs de cette fraîcheur, exécutés sans mesure, et avec un accompagnement obligé de fausses notes. Après ce charmant concert, vous êtes forcé de subir l'embrassade promise, et de mêler vos compliments à ceux de la famille enchantée. N'est-ce pas qu'elle est vraiment étonnante? dit le père; oh! elle est organisée pour la musique comme on ne l'est pas. Elle retient tous les airs qu'elle entend. . . . Elle n'a que deux ans de leçons. C'est sa mère qui lui montre. Elle est excellente musicienne. Est-ce que vous n'avez jamais entendu chanter ma femme? Elle a une voix magnifique. Dis-donc, bonne amie, il faut chanter quelque chose à Monsieur. Allons, ne vas-tu pas faire l'enfant, à présent? Il faut encore joindre vos instances à celle du mari, qui est allé décrocher une vieille guitare qu'il met un quart-d'heure à accorder. Puis, mêlant sa voix à celle de sa moitié, il vous refraîchit les oreilles de *Fleuve du Tage* ou de *Dormez donc, mes chères amours*, à deux voix. Ordinairement on prend son chapeau après le dernier couplet, et on se retire en remerciant le couple aimable de la délicieuse soirée qu'il vous a procurée, et l'on ne remet plus les pieds dans la maison."—*Souvenirs d'un Musicien.*—*Adolphe Adam.*

BEGREZ,

BORN 1784; DIED 1863.

BEGREZ AND CHERUBINI.

"C'est l'intelligence qui fait l'artiste."—MALIBRAN.

THE subject of this memoir was born at Namur, in Belgium, and educated at the Conservatoire of Music in Paris. After obtaining the violin prize, and making considerable progress in harmony and composition, Begrez eventually became the first tenor singer at Her Majesty's Theatre, under the management of Ebers, and for many seasons his name figured in the programmes of most public and private concerts in London. I have always advocated a knowledge of the elements of musical science to qualify a vocalist to become both useful and efficient, and the accidental circumstance which influenced the destiny of this Belgian musician is worthy of record.

By his fellow-students Begrez was much respected for his musical intelligence, and known to possess a pleasing tenor voice of considerable compass. Cherubini having composed an Offertorium for a grand religious public festival, was informed on the eve of its performance of the sudden illness of the principal tenor vocalist. Early next morning, the invalid's part was sent to young Begrez with a request that he would study the music and sing it, before noon, at the place appointed. In vain did violinist and amateur vocalist plead inability; Cherubini was peremptory, and assured the *debûtant* that he had the greatest confidence in his musical intelligence. At the performance, the admirable singing of Begrez produced a deep impression, and at the end of the service the illustrious Cherubini rushed to the front of the choir and cordially embraced him in the presence of the whole congregation. After this unexpected event, Begrez, by the advice of a fellow-student, Auber, now the successor of Cherubini, determined to lay aside the violin and become vocalist. After residing in this, his adopted country, upwards of half a century, contributing freely to private and public charities, he bequeathed a handsome sum to his foreign relatives, and, at my suggestion as one of his executors, *one thousand pounds* to the Royal Society of Musicians.

BEGREZ AND TOM COOKE.

THE late Irish composer and vocalist, Tom Cooke, being complimented on his appointment to sing at the Bavarian chapel, Warwick Street, with Begrez, replied, "Faith, and I never came so near *beggary* before!"

BOS,

BORN 1670; DIED 1742.

JEAN-BAPTISTE DU BOS ON MUSIC, POETRY, AND PAINTING.

IT may interest my musical readers to know something of this remarkable man of polite learning, whose writings were quoted by Gibbon and other historians, and translated into English and other modern languages. I own to have largely profited in my art-education by the perusal of his "Critical Reflections on Poetry, Painting, and Music; with an Inquiry into the Rise and Progress of the *Theatrical Entertainments* of the Ancients."

The Abbé du Bos was born at Beauvais in 1670. He entered the Foreign Office under Torcy, and was afterwards *chargé d'affaires* with important missions to Germany, England, &c. He died at Paris in 1742, perpetual secretary of the French Academy.

Voltaire (*Siècle de Louis XIV.*) says of Abbé du Bos:—"Tous les artistes lisent avec fruit ses réflexions sur la poésie, la peinture, et la musique. Il ne savait pourtant pas la musique, il n'avait jamais pu faire de vers, et n'avait pas un tableau. Mais il avait beaucoup lu, vu, entendu et réflechi."

Speaking of particular works decried by critics,

the Abbé remarks:—"It was Molière's comedies that put us out of conceit with Scarron and other poets that preceded him; and not the books that were written in order to detect the defects of those pieces. In case we should be entertained hereafter with better performances than those which are already in the hands of the public, there will be no occasion for critics to come and advise us to quit good for better. Those who have a mind to diminish the admiration which the public entertains for Virgil, and to deprive him of his readers, must favour us first with a better poem than the Æneid."

Of painting, he says, the effect which painting produces on men surpasses that of poetry, and quotes Horace in support of his opinion:—

> "Segnius irritant animos demissa per aurem,
> Quam quæ sunt oculis subjecta fidelibus."
>
> —*Hor. de Arte.*

> "Things only told, though of the same degree,
> Do raise our passions less than what we see;
> For the spectator takes in every part,
> The eye's the faithfullest servant to the heart."
>
> —*Creech.*

The Abbé says that "the sight has a much greater empire over the soul than any of the other senses," and gives an example of the comparative sensation of hearing the cries of a wounded man, and the sight of his bleeding wounds; metaphorically speaking, he says, "that the eye is nearer to the soul than the ear." I may here venture to remark, in respect to the senses, that the reason of the lyrical art being so universally popular in all countries where it is well represented, is owing to the union of arts appealing to both the sight and ear, together with incidents in the drama to satisfy the understanding.

"Our French music," says l'Abbé, "has within these fourscore years met with a fate not unlike that of Roman declamation in the time of Cicero. About a hundred and twenty years ago, neither singers nor players on instruments were capable of executing more difficult music than a series of long notes—*du gros Fa*. Dancing was much the same, for the movement of all the ballet airs was quite slow, and when Lulli wrote quick airs requiring greater rapidity of movement, people complained that the right taste for dancing had degenerated into a vulgar entertainment" (*vide* Patrician Art, (Vestris) p. 334). The condition of the musical, terpsichorean, and other arts in France, thanks to an enlightened and liberal policy, under the present government (1868), is most satisfactory.

The Abbé du Bos seems to have had religious faith in his theory of climate exercising its influence on creative genius in art. We are told that the Greeks borrowed their arts from the Egyptians and carried them to Etruria, and that the Romans were at first shocked with the violent gesticulation of the Greek actors. From Italy the arts travelled north; and, in proportion to the amount of education afforded to the people possessing an aptitude together with encouragement to cultivate music and painting, other countries have produced eminent artists.

The Abbé offers some useful hints on the abuse of musical word-painting, a prevailing vice in modern song-writers. "If a musician pays some regard to the expression of *a word*, he ought to do it without losing sight of the general purport of *the phrase* which he has set to music."

It has been observed, in reference to certain vocalists and performers of modern times, that they are prone to *paint notes* instead of *colouring phrases*, thus enervating the expression of a flowing, poetical melody. In support of his views, disapproving of excess of florid passages, Du Bos quotes the Abbate Gravini. "Vocal music," says this critic, "ought to imitate the natural language of the human passions, rather than the singing of canary birds, which our music (Italian, eighteenth century) affects so vastly to mimic with its quaverings and boasted cadences."

The Abbé remarks again :—"The first principles of music are the same as those of poetry and painting. Music, like those two arts, is imitative; and, like those arts, it must conform to the general rules with respect to the choice of the subject, the probability, and several other points, as Cicero observes :—'Omnes artes quæ ad humanitatem pertinent, habent quoddam commune vinculum, et quasi cognatione quadam inter se continentur.'"

The Abbé offers some useful hints to modern composers, and the work throughout abounds in valuable information.

COLL,

BORN 1811.

—o—

M. ARISTIDE CAVAILLE-COLL AS ORGAN BUILDER.

THE above eminent organ builder is a thoroughly practical man, learned in the science of acoustics, and the inventor of important principles for the production of sound by equal pressure, and the novel formation of tubes to secure perfect intonation. It is also due to this organ builder that the invention of Mr. Barker, of Bath, of the pneumatic lever, facilitating the touch of large organs, was first appreciated and adopted by him in the fine instruments of St. Denis and the Madelaine. The great importance of this pneumatic lever did not escape the attention of the Juries at the Paris Exposition, 1855, and the decoration of the Legion d'Honneur was conferred on Mr. Barker, the inventor. This improvement of the organ-touch by an Englishman was rejected and opposed by the makers in his native country. Such is not the uncommon fate of genius! Another equally important novelty by Mr. Barker, I hear, is likely to become generally in use—viz., an ingenious application of magnetic power to open the stops, and thus relieve the organist from the labour of using his hands; also the application of the electric wires to the organ pipes, enabling the player, with the manuals, to be seated at any convenient distance from the instrument. This is patented in London.

DR. DEHN,

BORN 1796; DIED 1858.

DR. DEHN, THEORIST, AT BERLIN.

THIS learned musician, instructor of Rubinstein and *custode* of the magnificent National Musical Library in Berlin, died in the sixty-second year of his age. I enjoyed the honour of his acquaintance, and have passed many profitable hours with him, in the library under his charge, at Berlin. In a friendly discussion (1846) on Prejudice and Patriotism in Art, Dr. Dehn assured me, that an overture, supposed to be Bach's, was soundly hissed at the Theatre in Leipzig; but, on being known to be the composition of Mendelssohn, it was afterwards admired!

DRAGONETTI,

BORN 1753; DIED 1846.

DRAGONETTI AND HIS DOG "CARLO" AT THE OPERA.

THE Venetian patriarch of the contrabasso, at the age of fourscore and ten, had few attachments he valued more than that of his faithful dog Carlo. At the opera during the performances Carlo usually slept at his master's feet, close to my seat in the orchestra. Upon one occasion Carlo dreamed aloud and accompanied the long sustained note (Fa) of "Casta Diva" with a most melancholy "whine." Grisi looked daggers, and muttered a few angry words to Costa; the latter bit his lip and said nothing; the Druids, on the stage, stared at each other; the musicians in the orchestra were convulsed with laughter (*sotto voce*), the occupants of the stalls were indignant, the Prince Consort looked amazed, and Dragonetti, trembling for the fate of Carlo, actually shed tears. This outrage on the feelings of *la prima donna assoluta* deprived Carlo of his free admission.

Early in the following year, 1846, the veteran contrabassist showed signs of rapid decay, took to his bed, and died in the 93d year of his age.

Lablache, within a few hours of his death, was soothed by the melody of "Sweet Home," and Dragonetti, the last few days of his life, listened with tender emotion to the Quartets of Haydn, Mozart, and Beethoven. In grateful remembrance of kindness shown him in his youth, Dragonetti bequeathed a considerable sum of money to the poor of Venice.

DRAGONETTI AND ERNST—THEIR OPPOSITE CHARACTERS.

> "Homo qui errante comiter monstrat viam,
> Quasi lumen de suo, lumine accendat, facit,
> Nihilominus ipsi luceat, cum illi accenderit."

THE Venetian patriarch of the double-bass, with all his wondrous skill and many social good qualities, was a painful example of selfishness in refusing instruction to young professional students on his own instrument. Ernst, made of kindlier stuff, would part with his last coin to do a generous act; nor was he unwilling to "light another man's candle by his own." The one died rich, lamented; the other died poor, beloved.

DRAGONETTI AND THE OPERA MANAGER.

THE latter, complaining of the expense of the band, Dragonetti quaintly observed that "it was the only perfect thing in the theatre." "How so?" inquired Laporte. "Because it has never a sore throat, nor a sprained ankle."

ERNST,

BORN 1814; DIED 1865.

ERNST AND DELOFFRE.

THE late *chef d'orchestra* at the Opera Comique, in Paris, was principal second violin, for several seasons, at the Musical Union. On quitting London for his present appointment, Ernst justly remarked that I had lost an excellent second, a most conscientious musician, and a thorough artist. To which I added, "and a safe one, who never played a wrong note nor made a mistake." Ernst humorously replied, "I should be sorry were you to pay *me* such a compliment." The impulsive genius of Ernst occasionally led him to a daring flight,

> "Which, without passing thro' the judgment, gains
> The heart, and all its end at once attains."

GASPERINI,

DIED 1868.

—·—o——

GASPERINI AT STUTTGARD, 1866.

FRENCH musical literature, by the recent death of this musician in the prime of life, has lost one of its ablest critics and most brilliant writers. Gasperini was a staunch partisan of the idealists in art—Berlioz, Schumann, and Wagner—and author of the most elaborate favourable review of the works of Rubinstein in the "Figaro" of Paris. My acquaintance with this excellent man and conscientious writer commenced at Stuttgard, in the autumn of 1866. It was at a banquet I attended in this town, after a fine performance of Abert's opera, "Astorga," Gasperini, in his jocular manner, inquired if it was the custom in London *to take a nightcap and a sandwich* when going to a benefit concert, beginning at one and never ending till seven. Like Berlioz, this musician was originally destined for the medical profession. M. Pasdeloup pronounced a few words at the tomb of poor Gasperini, most significantly true:—"Médecin, critique, orateur, poète et musicien, notre excellent ami avait toutes les facultés. Il n'attendait pas que les hommes de génie vinssent à lui, il allait à cux, il les devinait." Emile de Giradin thus concluded his funeral oration :—"Il était exclusif, mais toujours conscientieux. C'est une grande perte que fait la critique musicale." He was a warm-hearted friend to a conscientious artist, and an inveterate foe to charlatanism.

GRISI AND ALBONI,

BORN 1812; DIED 1869.—BORN 1823.

—o—

GRISI AND ALBONI IN "LA GAZZA LADRA."

LISTENING, a few nights ago (1868), to the duet in "La Gazza Ladra," so apathetically received by the audience, I was reminded of a very different scene that occurred in 1848 at the Royal Italian Opera, exhibiting the vulgar taste of an insensate inconsiderate public towards a favourite prima donna. This popular duet expresses the agony of Ninetta in prison, wrongly accused of theft, and the sympathy of her fellow-servant. Both singers, Grisi and Alboni, delivered their solos with true expression, the contralto in the dominant, a fourth below. The *timbre* of Alboni's contralto voice in this pathetic melody told wonderfully on the audience. When called to sing her part a *third* time, the sensitive nature of the insulted soprano was painfully hurt, and for a while Grisi left the stage. The selfishness and thoughtless distinction of a mixed public, in their excessive transports of delight from mere sensual effects, are a constant source of annoyance to an intellectual artist. In this particular duet, however, I recollect the handsome Mdlle. Brambilla being encored in her solo, when Grisi was yet young and lovely, and her voice in its best condition. La prima donna, then, had absolute power, and at her bidding the duet was afterwards omitted. In the other instance, with Alboni, the opera itself was not repeated. How perfectly sung and acted was "La Gazza Ladra" with Grisi, Brambilla, Rubini, Tamburini, Lablache, and really efficient *Italians* in the subordinate *rôles*, all in their prime, I am painfully reminded in listening to the cosmopolitan *troupe* of vocalists now on the Italian stage. The union of the two voices of Grisi and Alboni in the following slight embellishment of the sequences of the original arpeggio,* for the *contralto*, invariably produced a marked sensation.

DUET—"LA GAZZA LADRA."—ROSSINI.

CADENZA.

AT THE CLOSE OF THE ROMANCE À DEUX VOIX, IN MEYERBEER'S "PROPHÈTE."

THE original cadenza is totally beyond the ordinary range and capability of amateur vocalists. The one here given has been frequently sung, and involves no risk of a *fiasco* at the conclusion of a very pretty duet in the first scene of the opera.

CADENZA SUNG BY PERSIANI AND ALBONI.

IN "TANCREDI," AND COMPOSED BY COSTA, 1848.

THE true art of cultivating the voice seems greatly neglected, and modern declamatory music gives little hope of hearing such accomplished feats of vocalisation as in the above cadenza twenty years ago. Notwithstanding her thin-toned voice, Madame Persiani, in phrasing with taste and expression, florid and graceful melody, was the most perfect mistress of her art that has appeared at the Italian Opera to my recollection. The following cadenza, sung at the close of the romance, "Sombre forêt," in "Guillaume Tell," is novel and characteristic, with its Swiss-like forms, and was exquisitely sung by Madame Persiani. For the convenience of voices of ordinary compass, it is here transposed a fourth below the original key.

ARIA, "AH! NON GIUNGE"— "SONNAMBULA."

THE above *broderie,* when sung by Madame Persiani, was immensely effective. La Patti, more recently, introduces very surprising *fioriture* in the same aria, totally beyond the ability of any amateurs. The passage I now print is gracefully conceived, and, by transposition, may be repeated by any skilful vocalist.

MDLLE. ALBONI.

THE following *cadenza*, sung by this accomplished vocalist in the air "In si barbara," in "Semiramide," will give amateurs an idea of the compass and flexibility of her beautiful voice. The contralto register extends from B♭ down to G, powerful and sympathetic in quality; the upper tones being delicious in *timbre*, and connected with the chest-notes without any sensible inequality of power—a rare property in voices of this species. I do not hesitate to say that I have *never* witnessed an audience so moved by the pathetic delivery of a simple cantabile, as in the above air sung by Mdlle. Alboni at the Royal Italian Opera in 1847.

HELLMESBERGER,

BORN 1829.

HELLMESBERGER, CONCERT-MASTER, VIENNA.

WERE I desired to afford my readers an example of a thoroughly well-educated and an accomplished German musician, practical and theoretical, I should not hesitate to name the above *chef* of the Court Theatre, Chapel, and Concert Orchestra, professor and a director of the Conservatoire in which he was educated, at Vienna. He is a first-rate violinist in every sense, and a good pianist, endowed with the faculty of remembering and playing all kinds of music—the most complicated and original—after one or two hearings. He is also a linguist; talks and writes Italian, French, and English. His wife, too, a charming lady, mother of a numerous family, is the daughter of a celebrated actor. The hours passed at rehearsals of varied and new chamber-music, at Hellmesberger's, are among the pleasing reminiscences of my visit to Vienna, 1866. In 1847 this artist and a brother now deceased played at the Musical Union. The position Joseph now holds in Vienna, both artistically and socially, is well earned.

HOLMES,

DIED 1859.

EDWARD HOLMES, CRITIC AND HISTORIAN.

THE death of this musician and critic, which took place on the 4th September 1859, is chronicled in Novello's "Musical Times" of October, with a just tribute to his memory.

Every one acquainted with the deceased and his writings will lament the loss of so accomplished a musician and honest a critic. The moral influence of his "good name," and the merits of his contributions in various journals, give an impetus and dignity to musical commentary that was acknowledged throughout the profession. Of late years he chiefly occupied his pen with the masterly and lucid analyses of the Masses of Haydn, Mozart, and Beethoven, published in Novello's "Musical Times," and perused with delight and instruction by thousands in England and America. His "Ramble among the Musicians in Germany" and "Life of Mozart," two interesting works, are in every musician's library. Holmes was not merely a refined judge of music, but so devout a worshipper of the science, that he never could be induced to compromise its true interests for any worldly advantage. Musical literature in this country can ill spare so conscientious a man, so upright a critic, and one so imbued with true devotion to his art as the lamented Edward Holmes.

LABLACHE,

BORN 1794; DIED 1858.

LABLACHE ENGAGED TO TEACH SINGING.

THE great Neapolitan basso vocalist, who commenced his professional career as a contrabassist, was a most accomplished musician. Fond of literature and the sister arts, and a man of acute observation, his fund of anecdotes, so racily told, was inexhaustible. It is related that a stranger once visited Lablache in London, and with extreme politeness asked his terms for a singing lesson. Lablache replied—*Two guineas.* The stranger then placed on the table a bank-note, and made an appointment to see Lablache the same evening. The latter, on arriving at the appointed address, was announced and introduced by the valet in a magnificent saloon, brilliantly lighted up, where several ladies in splendid toilette were presented to him, and an animated conversation ensued. At last, embarrassed and impatient, Lablache inquired to whom he was to give a singing-lesson? "We do not want a lesson," said the lady of the house, "we only wished to enjoy your conversation, *vous êtes si drôle.*" "Il y avait deux choses—disait Lablache—me fâcher et rendre l'argent—le garder et rire de l'aventure.—Ma foi, j'en ai ri."

LABLACHE AT NAPLES, 1846.

LABLACHE, on the threshold of his pretty villa at Naples, in the month of November, with a bright sun in the azure sky, and the picturesque bay below, thus feelingly apostrophised his native country: "Si questa terra fosse benedetta da una costituzione Inglese, sarrebbe troppo vicino al cielo per l'abitazione degli uomini."

LABLACHE AND HIS SNUFF BOXES.

AT one of the crowded weekly receptions given by Lablache, during the Carnival in Paris, I arrived late, and was unable to penetrate beyond the anteroom. Here I placed myself on a tabouret, and was amused in examining an immense collection of snuff-boxes, arranged in admired disorder in an elegant cabinet. In 1858, the year of his death, these snuff-boxes were sold in Paris by auction. They amounted to hundreds, from imperial, royal, princely, ducal, and literary donors, brilliant in diamond, pearl, malachite, lapiş-lazuli, or humble horn. The Queen Victoria having once inquired of Lablache, if it was true that he had a large collection of snuff-boxes, he replied, "Yes, your Majesty, I have one for every day in the year—three hundred and sixty-five." The Queen most graciously observed that the collection was not complete, and presented Lablache with another—for Leap Year.

MALIBRAN.

BORN 1808; DIED 1836.

MALIBRAN, PAER, AND RIES.

IN company with Lablache and Ivanhoff, I visited Malibran a few days only before she died, at Manchester, 1836. During our interview, at intervals she was cheerful and witty in conversation, and I well remember Lablache saying with emotion as he left the room, "*Ah! Il y a trop d'esprit pour ce petit corps.*" Soon after Malibran's death, I went to Paris, and here, for the first time since I assisted at his farewell concert in London, 1824, I met Ries, friend and pupil of Beethoven. Dining with him and his English wife, in company of the Maestro Paer, composer of "Agnese" and some eighty other works, I related to them the fatal accident which led to the illness and speedy death of Malibran, viz., her fall from a horse, and being dragged a considerable distance on the ground, in Hyde Park, some weeks previous to her arrival at Manchester.

"Poor Malibran!" said Ries; "many a slap in the face did she receive from her father when at fault in singing part-music with her family." "Ah! but those slaps in the face," said Paer, "made Malibran what she was—the best vocalist and *reader* of music that ever lived. She had a natural antipathy to singing-masters, which I can vouch for from personal and painful experience."

"How so?" inquired Ries.

"I remember," said Paer, "once dining with the family of Garcia, and having little Marie on my right. During the repast, I constantly experienced a piquant sensation and strongly suspected my tricksy neighbour. The little gipsy looked so demure and serious that I was loth to incur the displeasure of her father by complaining. In the evening, however, I discovered that the mischievous minx had tattooed me with a pin like a red Indian."

Poor Malibran! I saw much of her when in London. She was impulsive; at times her singing was the *beau ideal* of pure art, at others she was capricious, unequal. "Au degré d'élévation où vous êtes parvenue, vous devez imposer votre sentiment au public, non subir le sien." To this reflection of Fétis, she replied, "Il y a à peine deux ou trois connoisseurs dans une grande salle où je chante; ce ne sont pas eux qui font les succès, et sont des succès que je veux. Quand je chanterai pour vous seul, je ferai autre chose." Malibran made her *début* at London in the "Barbiere," June 7th, 1825, and died at the age of 28, September 23rd, 1836, at Manchester.

There are always vocalists, I fear, who sacrifice their art for the *vox populi*. They are to blame.

MOLIQUE.

BORN 1802; DIED 1869.

MOLIQUE—REFUGE IN LONDON, 1848.

THIS eminent composer and violinist died at Cannstadt, near Stuttgard, aged sixty-seven. As a violinist he was more remarkable for his mechanical powers than for poetical expression, and the passive sensibility of his temperament was evident in the general character of his numerous compositions. Although written with classical purity, satisfactory to the understanding and pleasing to the ear of a musician, the music of Molique rarely produced a deep impression on the general public. He was deservedly esteemed for his talent, and much beloved by all who enjoyed his friendship. Driven to England by the political crisis of 1848, he remained, with his family, a resident in London, until his retirement in 1866. Molique first played at the Musical Union, May 2d, 1848, and Mdlle. Anna Molique made her *débût* April 21st, 1857, in a trio, Op. 52, the composition of her father.

MOORE,

BORN 1779; DIED 1852.

THOMAS MOORE, THE IRISH POET.

NO person was ever gifted with a more sensitive organisation for music than the deceased Irish bard. Had he received a thoroughly sound musical education, it is difficult to say whether he might not have produced some great composition as gorgeous in melody and harmony as the Eastern imagery of his "Lalla-Rookh." He had a genuine sympathy for the music of Haydn and Mozart; but confessed that the fine, solemn music of our best cathedral writers was beyond his comprehension, saying that, if he had been educated to their style, he should have enjoyed it. Education, custom, and manners exercise a much greater influence on art and artists than some persons are willing to believe. There was a time when England surpassed all other nations in church and madrigal music. The climate has not changed; but the remains of Puritanism sufficiently explain to us why music is less understood now than in the Elizabethan age.

NADAUD,

DIED 1864.

NADAUD AND THE "PAS DE QUATRE."

"Music is to the dance what words are to music—that is, in other terms, the music for the dance is, or ought to be, the words of the poem itself; by which the action of the dancer is fixed and determined."—NOVERRE, *Essay on Ballet Dancing.*

IN my younger days the ballet was not only the most costly part of the entertainment, but frequently the chief attraction at Her Majesty's Theatre. *On a changé tout cela.* Nevertheless, the grand histrionic ballets of yore, and others founded upon mythological subjects and faëry legends, afforded great scope to the imaginative faculty of composers, and excellent practice, without restraint, in instrumentation. Our English composer, Bishop, gained his first laurels in ballet music, and the music of "Giselle," by Adolphe Adam, and other ballets of the French repertoire, are *chefs-d'œuvre* of their kind.

During the performance of the opera, the musicians of the orchestra were generally attentive, zealous, and well disciplined under the control of the conductor's authority; but the prospect of two hours of ballet music, after three acts of a long opera, was not popular with the band. The interruption, too, of partisans encoring their favourite dancers, and the delay in gathering up the bouquets from Covent Garden Market, thrown on the stage chiefly by relatives of the rival dancers, or by claqueurs instructed for the service, was an intolerable nuisance. The *chef*, M. Nadaud, was proudly conscious of the great attraction of a successful ballet; and on assuming the authority of the conductorship of the music, he exacted—in vain—strict observance of the style and expression of the music from the already jaded musicians. He himself was a composer; and nothing afforded him greater satisfaction than a request from a leading dancer to write a new *pas* in place of the original music. On other occasions, M. Nadaud would politely consent to the tender entreaty of a bewitching *danseuse* (not particularly well organised in rhythmical feeling, nor possessing a musical ear) to strengthen the accent of her *pas* by the addition of cymbals and big drum. These little innovations were not always made with very good grace when it concerned a *second-rate* terpsichorean; but the little *douceurs* from *les étoiles du ballet* greatly enriched M. Nadaud, and his collection of shirt-pins, studs, and diamond rings was accordingly very considerable.

At the rehearsal of the famous "Pas de Quatre" in 1845, he became unusually excited and anxious to have the music well played. The composition was marked "*Allegro, legato e deciso.*" Nadaud knew little of Italian, and cared less for Italian singers. With an air of grave importance, the *chef* thus addressed the band:—"Messieurs, Attention! Nous commençons avec *Allez-gros, les gâteaux, et des ciseaux.*" A burst of laughter followed, and for a while the *chef* was indignant at the levity of his associates. At last, poor Nadaud was able to comprehend the meaning of his mispronunciation of Italian. Like Vestris, he considered dancing a patrician art, and the *déesses* of the "Pas de Quatre," Taglioni, Cerito, Carlotta Grisi, and Lucile Grahn were the idols of his art worship. The excitement of this union of terpsichorean talent was intense. The theatre was crowded to suffocation on every night the *pas* was given; and Lumley * records this event as the culminating point in the history of the ballet in England. It was certainly the death-blow to *ballets d'action* in this country. Well might *le chef* be desirous of the orchestra playing with attention, *allez-gros, les gâteaux, et des ciseaux,* to second the efforts of *les déesses.*

* Reminiscences of the Opera, p. 117.

After the disastrous close of the reign of Lumley, M. Nadaud succeeded Mellon, leading the dance music at the Royal Italian Opera, Covent Garden, until his decease in 1864. He always discharged his onerous duties with enthusiasm and self-respect, and, in so doing, secured the respect of managers and dancers, and the friendship of his comrades during a period of thirty years' service in London.

PATTI,

BORN 1843.

LA PATTI FAMILY.

IT is somewhat curious to find that the manager of the *Teatro Pagliano* and *Teatro Nazionale*, who first introduced Mdlle. Adelina Patti to the Florentines in 1865, is son of the impresario who first introduced her father * and mother † to the Romans in 1837. Here is the list of the *troupe* for the Roman Carnival of that year:—Soprani, Mesdames Ronzi and *Barili Patti;* Tenor, *Salvatore Patti;* Baritone, Coletti; Basso, Baroilhet (Frenchman).

The issue of this union of the tenor and soprano, now living, were all born in different places, viz.:

* Salvatore Patti. † Barili Patti.

Mdme. Strakosch, wife of the impresario, born at Pesaro; Mdlle. Carlotta, at Florence; Signor Carlo (violonist), at Lisbon; and Mdlle. Adelina, at Madrid. Two deceased daughters were born at Trieste and Odessa.

PAGANINI,

BORN 1784; DIED 1840.

PAGANINI—"THREE TIMES THREE."

AT the dinner given to Lord Brougham, at the Mansion House, after the passing of the Reform Bill, the great musical lion of the season was present. Like most foreigners unacquainted with English customs, he wondered at the hurrahs!—"three times three"—after drinking the health of Lord Brougham. He was told that it was the usual compliment paid to the padrone on drinking his health. On the Sunday following, I sat next to Paganini at dinner, with Lindley, Dragonetti, and a number of noblemen and ladies, at one of the musical gatherings at Lord Saltoun's. On the cloth being removed, the *fêted* lion stood up, and with great unction, said, "Signori miei, 'Alla salute del padron.'" "Evviva," said old

Dragonetti. "Tree times tree—hip! hip! hip! hurrah!" &c. The guests laughed heartily. The ladies were astounded, and to the last day of his life Paganini believed he had only conformed to English custom.

SAX,

NATIVE OF BELGIUM.

INVENTIONS OF ADOLPHE SAX.

" La musique militaire de France deviendra supérieure à celles de Prusse, d'Autriche, de Russie et de toute l'Europe, *notamment par l'adoption et l'introduction des instruments de Sax, que l'on ne possède pas dans les susdites armées.*"—Spontini.

It is the melancholy fate of most men of inventive genius to combat opposition from those whose vested interests are destined to suffer by it. Happily, Sax succeeded, after years of painful anxiety and costly litigation, in obtaining a verdict against the manufacturers of France for pirating his patented discoveries. Confiscation of instruments, with an immense amount of money paid for indemnification, ended the struggle which had occupied the French tribunals fourteen years and brought the patentee to the verge of ruin. Justice triumphed, and for every instrument made by Courtois and other makers on the principle of Sax, the inventor receives a royalty. Erard's invention of the repetition-touch, universally appreciated, and adopted by most pianoforte makers, first met with opposition, not less violent than that which sought to rob Sax of the benefit of his valuable discoveries.

Within the recollection of musicians now in London, the brothers Distin first introduced a band of saxhorns. The mellow tones and novel *timbre* of those instruments excited general admiration. It was the first combination of brass instruments introduced into England, perfectly in tune, and susceptible of modifications of tone. The saxophones form another family of brass instruments—treble, tenor, baritone, and bass. The *timbre* of these instruments is quite novel, and gives an additional colour to the effects of instrumentation. Listening the other day to a very clever arrangement of Gounod's "Faust," played by a French regimental band, I was struck with the beautiful effect of a rich body of sustained harmony by the saxophones, whilst the melody was given to the flutes and clarionets, tastefully varied. The *tout ensemble* was most charming and not overdosed with cymbals and big drums, played irrespective of *nuance*. It is a hopeless task to convey, in writing, an exact idea of tone. That of the tenor saxophones is, in body and sonority, a union of the clarionet and bassoon, but of a peculiar character, from the structure of the mouthpiece and tube.

I am quite aware of all that is said about the

timbre of natural and artificial notes on the French horn. Every variety of musical sound has its distinct power of expression available for effect, which the composer may appropriately employ. The great advantage of the six-valved horn, with separate tubes, patented by Sax, is, that the player, at his option, can produce artificial notes also, by manipulation in the pavilion. Paramount to every other consideration, most assuredly, is the certainty of producing the intervals inconveniently written for the instrument. I need scarcely remind my professional readers of the many failures heard in Handel's use of the horn, in G, playing, "See the Conquering Hero," and in the trio of Beethoven's "Eroica Symphony," and the grand scena of "Fidelio."

On my way home from Vienna, some years ago, I heard at Leipzig, Brussels, and Paris, within one month, the "Eroica Symphony." In Paris only was the horn solo in the trio smoothly and satisfactorily played. Later I heard the "Eroica" at Pasdeloup's Concerts with only one blemish in the entire performance—a failure of the horn in reaching distinctly the top-note of his solo in the trio. The audience, 4500, was much less indulgent than that at Leipzig and Brussels, and a chorus of some 500 voices, *sotto voce*, expressed disapprobation. The following week at Pasdeloup's Concerts, in a composition of Mendelssohn, the horn was slightly wavering, giving the fifth of the key-note in a cantabile. The audience again, in my opinion very tyrannically, "demonstrated;" this unnerved the player, and forced Pasdeloup to engage Mohr, the best horn player in Paris. At the third concert, I heard Mendelssohn's Overture, "Athalie" — how superbly the horns and other brass instruments performed on this occasion, I have not yet forgotten. A grand stream of powerful harmony was produced, with none of those accented blasts of sound which I am doomed to hear from ill-trained trumpeters and trombonists. I ascertained that Mohr plays upon one of the new horns of Sax, and I strongly commend their use in this country.

The new trombones of Sax, with six pistons and independent tubes, after a trial with the sliding instruments, by the unanimous voice of a jury of eminent composers, are now introduced in the band of the Imperial Opera. Ambroise Thomas, in his tragic opera of "Hamlet," is the first to employ the six-valved trombones with separate tubes, "la dernière et une des plus admirables découvertes de M. Sax; découvertes qui semblent appelée á bouleverser la race des instruments en cuivre."—1869.

TOURTE,

BORN 1747; DIED 1835.

TOURTE AND HIS VIOLIN BOWS.

TO the ingenuity of this French Luthier, we are indebted for the discovery of preparing logwood so as to combine elasticity with durability for violin, viola, and violoncello bows. During the war with France, owing to the difficulty of procuring logwood from our colonies, these bows by Tourte fetched enormous prices. They are becoming more scarce, and are increasing in value; yet no violinist, rich enough to possess a cremona, is without his Tourte bow—*la plume de son esprit.* One of these violin bows, mounted in gold, in my possession, cost ten guineas. It is now (1877) as straight, elastic, and perfect as when purchased fifty years ago by the Laird of Elchies, N.B. (Grant), when in India.

VUILLAUME,

BORN 1798; DIED 1875.

VUILLAUME LUTHIER IN PARIS.

THE fac-similes of the Cremona instruments by Vuillaume, and the general excellence of his violins and violoncellos, procured him the *medal* prize of the great Exhibition of 1851, in London. At the Paris Exposition, 1855, he obtained great distinction, and was decorated with *legion d'honneur.*

Every amateur *curious* on the subject of bows and stringed instruments, their size, form, colour, and history, should procure Vuillaume's brochure "Stradivarius," edited by Fétis, containing the biography of the families of Amati, Guarnerius, and Stradivarins. In this publication it is explained that the Cremona Luthiers selected for the "belly" of their instruments the fine-grained wood from the sunny-side of the pine-trees of the Italian Tyrol. This interesting brochure, translated into English, is published by Cocks and Co., London.

MISS WILSON,

DIED 1867.

AN ENGLISH PRIMA DONNA.

ON Thursday evening, January 18th, 1821, in the orchestra of Drury Lane Theatre, I first exercised the profession of music, as a violinist, in preference to quill-driving in an attorney's office. The occasion was very remarkable, the *début* of a young, handsome, and very clever vocalist, pupil of the renowned Tom Welsh. Neither Sontag nor Jenny Lind ever produced a greater sensation than did this English *débutante.* The *Morning Post,* at her second appearance in Arne's opera of "Artaxerxes," thus describes her reception and singing:—"That splendid luminary of the musical world, Miss Wilson, again attracted an audience, which not only filled the house, but literally overflowed every part at an early hour; and the tumultuous expressions of admiration, amounting to enthusiasm, which followed every successive display of her transcendent powers, are proofs of the unparalleled sway she can exercise over the feelings of her hearers. To enumerate the airs in which Miss Wilson was rapturously encored, would be to run over the catalogue of all those which belong to the arduous part she had to sustain." "After encoring the grand air, '*The soldier tired*,' says the *Post*, "the pit rose in a tumult of ecstasy, shouting and waving hats for some time, whilst acclamations rang from every part of the house." The truth is, that the insatiate public soon fatigued the young vocalist, and before long it was discovered that she not only required repose, but further study to complete her vocal education. However, I heard from her own lips, not many years ago, that she earned upwards of £10,000 the year of her *début*, and I know of no other instance of so large a sum being received by a *débutante* vocalist the first twelvemonth of her singing in public. This premature *début* led to her visiting Italy for the benefit of her health, after which she married her instructor and retired into private life. The issue of this marriage was a daughter, a most accomplished musician and linguist, who is now the wife of Signor Piatti. The *çi-devant* Miss Wilson, who died at the close of 1867, a widow, retained to the last her handsome features, and was greatly respected by a large circle of friends. Little did I anticipate, when assisting at her *début* in 1821, that I should be, some forty years afterwards, sponsor to her grandchild.

ELLA PIATTI.

BALZAC in allusion to his father's theory of longevity, states: "Un jour qu'on lisait dans un journal un article sur un centenaire, il interrompit le lecteur pour dire avec enthousiasme :—Celui-là a vécu sagement et n'a pas gaspillé ses forces en toute sorte d'excès, comme le fait l'imprudente jeunesse. . . . Il se trouva que ce sage se grisait souvent, au contraire, et soupait tous les soirs, une des plus grandes énormités que l'on pût commettre contre sa santé (selon mon père).—Eh bien! reprit-il sans s'émouvoir, cet homme a abrégé sa vie, voilà tout!". . . .

In a medical treatise, published some time ago, a statement appeared to the effect that players and musicians, from breathing the impure atmosphere of hot theatres and rooms were generally shortlived. The following list of musicians of my acquaintance attained a pretty good old age :—

Cervetto, violoncellist, 92; Mariotti, trombonist, 92; Dragonetti, contrabassist, 93; Sir George Smart, organist, 91; Neate, 93; Auber, composer, 89.

The following averaged at their death the age of fourscore :—Clementi, pianist; Mahon, clarionetist; Lindley, violoncellist; Anfossi, contrabassist; Mackintosh, bassoonist; Neukomm, composer; Cramer, pianist; Horsley, composer. Of the fifty members of the orchestra of Her Majesty's Theatre, 1822, two only survive (violinists), Oury and myself (1877).

PART III.

MUSICAL REBUS.

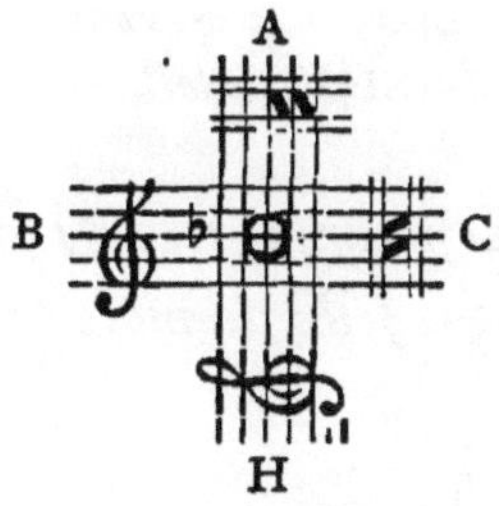

IT should be understood that $B\flat$ in German is simply B, and that $B\natural$ is H. The name of Bach, therefore, is expressed with one note, read according to the different clefs.

MUSICAL SQUIB.

AT the time that Pasta, Galli, and Rubini were considered past their meridian, although enjoying public favour in England, the following squib was posted on the walls of the Scala, in Milan, on the production of "Anna Bolena," in 1831 :—

"LA PASTA *non attacca più*,
UN GALLO *senza speroni*,
UN RUBINI *perduto*."

In this humour the jealous rivalry of the Italians vents itself in harmless *jeux de mots* and epigrams.

MATERNAL ADVICE.

ADDRESSED to a young English lady on her *début* into fashionable life (attributed to the late Lady Dacre).

DAVID AND GRETRY.

AT one of the notorious revolutionary tribunals, the above painter and musician were sitting together *vis-à-vis* to a remarkable looking negress. David, after making a capital likeness of the black lady, handed it over to Gretry to set to music. The latter returned the portrait to David with the following repartee:—

"Une blanche vaut deux noirs."

GRETRY AND NAPOLEON.

AFTER the marriage of the critic, composer, and author, Berlioz, in 1852, to which ceremony I was a witness, with the famed Sax, the most illustrious musicians and *dilettanti* in Paris, including Meyerbeer, assembled in the evening at the residence of the bridegroom. Among other anecdotes, one, in allusion to Gretry, told by Berlioz, as follows, afforded us a hearty laugh:—

"On New Year's day, it was the custom of the Emperor to receive the congratulations of the most distinguished men of science, literature, and art of France. On the first visit of Gretry, Napoleon (who had no partiality for French music) affected not to know him, and thus abruptly accosted him: 'Who are *you?*' 'Gretry, sire.' On the next visit of Gretry, the Emperor again interrogated him: 'Who are *you?*' Feeling rather humiliated, Gretry replied, after a short silence: 'Gretry, sire.' The third year that the composer of "Richard Cœur de Lion" presented himself at the Tuileries, the Emperor again asked 'Who are *you?*' '*Hélas!—toujours Gretry, sire!*'"

THE KING OF HANOVER.

ON the last birthday of his Majesty, when in England, King William and Queen Adelaide conjointly purchased a seraphine for his birthday present. The maker (the late Professor Wheatstone) and myself being commanded to await the arrival of their Majesties at Kew Palace, to attend the presentation of the instrument, we duly repaired thither, and, precisely at the fixed hour, the royal personages drove up. On alighting from her carriage, the Queen ordered the servants to carry the seraphine into the drawing-room. Wheatstone and I followed, and as the King and Queen entered, I played upon it the National Anthem. The Prince affectionately embraced and thanked the Queen, and the latter said something to this effect, "Dear George, this will amuse your dreary hours!" The Duchess of Gloucester then asked the Prince to play upon the instrument, and to my surprise he performed with excellent taste and feeling a charming melody of his own composition. With the exception of Princess Victoria (now Queen), his cousin, every member of the Royal Family was present on this occasion. Professor Wheatstone explained the principle of metallic plates, by a current of air, producing sustained sounds—the original invention attributed to the Chinese. The Professor also exhibited his symphonion of two octaves on the same principle, the air being supplied by breathing through a small aperture. (This pocket instrument is now superseded by the concertina, also the invention of this Professor.) The Prince took great interest in all that was said by Wheatstone, and H.R.H. the Duke of Cumberland informed us that, when a boy, he recollected seeing an instrument similar to the seraphine in the possession of his father, George III. In his attempting to sit down to the instrument, I perceived that the young Prince was nearly blind, and stumbled against the chair. His handsome, tall figure, mild expression of countenance, affable manners, and amiable disposition, coupled with his bereavement of sight, excited a universal sympathy for the afflicted Prince; and I was afterwards told that, on quitting the rural village of Kew, where he was greatly beloved, to reside with his august parent in Hanover, many an eye was moistened with tears of regret. Whilst Crown Prince of Hanover, his Majesty published a most interesting *brochure*,* explaining the effect of music on his feelings, and the imagery which certain suggestive harmonies produced on his imagination. It is worth a persual.—1869.

* "Ideas and Recollections on the Properties of Music."—Colburn, London, 1841.

THE DUKE OF WELLINGTON.

AT a concert in 1830, under my direction, given by the late Right Hon. Sir George Warrender, Bart., the Duke arrived unusually early. After a short conversation with the hero, Sir George desired me to protract the performance as much as possible, as he, at the Duke's request, was going to the House of Commons to vote in favour of Ministers. According to custom, the Duke was seated close to the pianoforte, freely conversing with the ladies near him, and *apparently* paying little attention to the music. The concert proceeded, and for reasons not necessary to explain, it so happened that the performance was curtailed by the omission of two items in the programme, viz., a song by the Italian buffo De Begnis, and a solo on the horn by Puzzi. Returning home from the division of the House of Commons earlier than he expected, Sir George, to his great surprise, found the concert was over, and the Duke taking his departure, who exclaimed, "Capital concert, capital concert, Warrender; but Ella has omitted two pieces!" The Duke's characteristic habit of observation led him to detect failure, which the above artists imagined would have escaped notice.

THE LORDS LYNDHURST AND BROUGHAM.

["Without knowledge there is little sympathy; and he who boasts of having no ear for music may also boast of having one sense less of pure enjoyment than most of his fellow-creatures."]

THE repetition-touch of Erard not having fairly remunerated the inventor at the expiration of his patent, application was made to the Privy Council for a renewal of the said patent, under the then new law, 1835. Being satisfied, after a tedious examination of scientific men, with the importance of the invention and justness of the claim, a renewal of the patent was granted. Lord Lyndhurst very politely requested Madame Dulcken, one of the witnesses present, to oblige him by a display of her known skill on the pianoforte, then in court. Madame had no sooner seated herself at the instrument, wiped the dust off the keys, and played a few notes by way of prelude to a long fantasia, than Lord Brougham interrupted, saying, "Enough, enough, Madame, that will do; that will do." The lady, as may be imagined, retired highly incensed against Lord Brougham, and was wont to say that my Lord Lyndhurst *was* a gentleman.

PROFESSOR OWEN, MRS. JAMESON, AND THACKERAY.

ARIOSTO long ago remarked, that if the villas in the environs of Florence, which seem to shoot up like so many offsets and suckers from the ground, were collected within one wall, they would form a city twice the size of Rome. At the Villa Spence, Villa Bello-sguardo, Villa Salviati, and Villa Ruciano, alike enchanting in position and commanding different views of the city beneath, I met a great variety of amateur talent in the arts—from the prince to the government *employé*—painters, poets, sculptors, and musicians. The genial love and universal appreciation of the beautiful in every art, in the society of Florence and these neighbouring villas, forcibly reminded me of society in an English villa, though less enchanting without, not less instructive within, under the presidency of its learned occupant, Professor Owen, Richmond Park. Among the distinguished guests of this hospitable Professor, on one occasion, was the late accomplished art-critic and affectionate friend of artists, Mrs. Jameson. A discussion arose upon the want of genial intercourse of artists and men of science in England. "Here, in our rambles on the lawn," said Mrs. Jameson, with all the glow of earnest feeling so delightful to behold in an intellectual woman, "you (Professor) have unfolded to us the wonderful provision of nature in these corals strewed among your flower-beds in a familiar and comprehensible lecture. Brought into social contact with your musical friend, both Thackeray and myself have also gained some of the secrets of his delightful art! Painters and musicians seem in London, as it were, to move in a cycle, surrounded frequently only by parasites and amici—*nemici?* The exclusiveness, therefore, of society in London keeps men in ignorance of the genial benefits of art-fellowship enjoyed abroad, and tends to narrow men's minds, and frequently leads to a false estimate of genius." To these remarks replied one who spoke with authority, "The Prince Consort has expressed to me similar observations, and a desire to see the intellects united in congress."

GRISI AND AMATEURS IN FLORENCE.

SEVEN miles south of Florence, on the heights leading to Sienna, I remained some days at the Senator Fenzi's beautiful Villa St. Andrea, where upwards of forty sat down to dinner every Sunday. Here I occasionally heard some good amateur singing. The best was by an English lady, at whose receptions in Florence I heard a Neapolitan duke play "Chopin" very respectably, and Grisi very good-naturedly sang

English, Irish, and Scotch ballads, and an Italian scena. A granddaughter of the above venerable senator (now Madame Oppenheim, 1868) played to me one of Mendelssohn's "Songs without Words," and excused herself from playing another, as she knew but one! At the present time she is proudly in possession of the entire collection, and delights in her further acquaintance with Mendelssohn's music.

On taking leave of music and musicians at Florence, I am bound to admit that, in spite of the general ignorance of *la musica tedesca*, and preference of the Italians for their native operas, in no instance did I ever hear any remarkably good cadence well sung, or a phrase expressively or tastefully performed, escape instant recognition; even in compositions by a German master.

PIETRO THE WAITER.

DILETTANTISM in Florence is not confined to any particular class. Cheap and amusing performances of operas and ballets, accessible for all classes, are nightly crowded. Pietro, head-waiter of our hotel, was an intelligent and a well-mannered servant, ever ready to direct foreigners where to go, what to see, and what to hear. The contents of the museums and picture and sculpture galleries he knew by heart, and was *au courant* of what was in hand in the ateliers of the best painters and sculptors. He also was acquainted, more or less, with the principal vocalists, actors, and dancers. Pietro could sing, from natural instinct, *en amateur*, and was eloquent in discussing art topics. In truth, this dilettante waiter was an authority, an exceptional guide to the sights and amusements of Florence, and a general favourite—with ladies especially.

Pietro, notwithstanding his intelligence and civilities, greatly compromised his good repute by hurriedly removing every vestige of the dinner-service, economising waxlights, and thus depriving the Englishmen of their accustomed post-prandial drinks and discussions at table. When remonstrated with for this habit, Pietro, shrugging up his shoulders, and with that peculiar grimace of the Italian excusing himself of a fault, replied thus: "Ma, signor, mi piace la musica. L'opera comincia alle sette e vado tutte le sere, ed ella sa che bella cosa è la musica." For the fee usually given in English hotels to a waiter at dinner, Pietro had his seat to hear "L'Elisir d'Amore," and a very amusing ballet, with two first-rate ballerini, at the Teatro Rossini. This cheap and popular theatre adjoins the Palazzo Fossombroni, from the drawing-room of which the Count and Countess Fossombroni have access to a stage box, their private property.

During my frequent visits to this palazzo, in the evening I usually joined the family, or some of their guests, to the stage box. Among the *claquers*, most demonstrative in admiration of the performers, in front of the pit, in the centre of a coterie of enthusiastic dilettanti, I invariably saw Pietro. At ten o'clock he would return to his duties at the hotel, and relate particulars of the vocalists and dancers, discoursing with all the technical slang of a professional critic. His sympathy for music was manifested towards me in many acceptable ways, and if this waiter is still Pietro *dilettante*, at the Hotel de la Grand Brittaigne, I commend his services to my fellow-countrymen visiting Florence.

DILETTANTISM IN THE COTTON MILLS.

SCARCELY a week passes without application being made for complete sets of the "Musical Union Records." Several of the early numbers are out of print. In Manchester and the musical districts of the North, several sets have been purchased. This is probably owing to their analytical contents having been made known by Hallè, at his Chamber Concerts in Manchester. In March 1866, I received a letter, containing postage stamps, from a stranger at Stockport, who informed me that, from the age of nine years he had had to work in the cotton mill.

The singular diction of this enthusiastic operative, and his parting with hard-earned pence to buy a

"Record," naturally excited my curiosity and won my sympathy. I returned his stamps, with some half-dozen "Records" of past seasons, containing portraits of celebrated composers and performers. The grateful acknowledgment of the recipient was expressed in a letter couched in language that I should be proud to have written. What most interests me, in the glowing fervour of this humble cotton-spinner's aspirations, is the allusion to the gift of books to form a public library. Judging from the writer's account of his own struggles to acquire knowledge of music, it is no wonder that he appreciates the object sought to be accomplished.

"I rejoice that I have acquired that knowledge which will enable me to direct my children in the right musical path, if it has pleased God to endow them with natural gifts for music. With your "Records" for my guide, I anticipate (God willing) hours of enjoyment, as I sit at my leisure moments in my humble cottage, the walls of which are decorated with portraits of Handel, Mozart, Beethoven, Mendelssohn, Bach, Spohr, Weber, Sterndale Bennett, Shakespeare, and others.

"I sincerely wish you every success in the grand idea you have conceived, namely, in establishing for deserving musical students a musical library and institute. Now I am off to a rehearsal, a distance of seven miles to Manchester.

"I remain, your humble tho' affectionate admirer,

"T. B. B."

"*MY CONSTANCE.*"

THE late George Linley, poet and composer, remarked to me, on our way through Bond Street, "*That's my Constance.*" "Who, which, where?" said I. "*That new shop-front of Chappell's.*" The sum mentioned by Linley, which his ballads brought to the publishers, seemed to me fabulous. That they obtained a more extended popularity than other English songs, I can vouch for. The only *modern* ballad I ever heard in a public musical entertainment abroad, and that, too, at a classical Gewandhaus Subscription-Concert, January 1st, 1846, was Linley's "Constance," sung by Miss Dolby (Mdme. Sainton). It was sung, as this lady always sings, with feeling, taste, and intelligence, and rapturously applauded. The occasion of this Benefit Concert was alike honourable to the *bénéficiaire*, and the illustrious musicians who lent their services to my talented and deservedly respected countrywoman. It should here be mentioned that at Leipzig, Mendelssohn very willingly favoured the engagement of vocalists who had largely contributed to the success of his sacred music in England. The subscribers to the Gewandhaus Concerts, however, being dissatisfied with one or more of Miss Dolby's predecessors, this lady had the honour of being the last English vocalist engaged. Her farewell appearance created a *furore*, and her Scotch ballads were *encored.* The singers who successively appeared in Leipzig were Miss Novello, Mrs. Shaw, Miss Birch, Miss Lincoln, and Miss Dolby.

CAFFARELLI—"BRAVO!"

THE flattering approbation of the favourite singer of Italy, Caffarelli, who visited Rome expressly to hear Gizziello, was more acceptable than all the honours paid to the latter in the eternal city. "Bravo! bravissimo! Gizzielo, è Caffarelli che ti lo dice," said a voice muffled up in a *pellice* in the pit, who immediately quitted the theatre, and set out on his return to Naples the same night. I have some recollection of a schism between the celebrated Garcia (father of Malibran) and Ayrton, the manager of the Italian Opera, when the latter insisted that the band, who were partisans of the vocalist, would desist crying out "bravo!" Upon learning which, Garcia threatened to throw up his engagement, saying, that one "bravo" from the orchestra was worth fifty from the pit, and always gave him the best encouragement. No singer ever gained more *bravi* from the orchestra than Persiani, in some of her exquisitely-conceived and executed cadenzas—the triumph of vocalisation, since her voice was thin and harsh when forced.

TASSO, MOORE, AND GARDINER.

DURING the composition of "Gerusalemma Liberata," Tasso was at a loss to find a suitable word to express the eagerness with which Erminia dismounts on finding Tancredi dying on the roadside (Canto 19, Stanza 104).

Whilst pacing up and down his room, absorbed in thought, most inauspiciously entered a visitor. The latter, receiving no marked attention from the poet, speedily withdrew, and had the misfortune to stumble and roll headlong down the staircase. Tasso rushed to the door, and heard his friend exclaim, "*Mi son precipitato.*" "Bravo! Bravissimo!" shouted Tasso, in great glee, "*ho trovato la parola—non scese, no:* PRECIPITÒ *di sella*"—(Bravo! I have found the word—she did not dismount, no; she *precipitated* herself from the saddle.) This story, told me by Lablache, reminds me of another told me by Gardiner, on dedicating his "Music of Nature" to the Irish bard. In allusion to a particular happy couplet by Moore, Gardiner expressed his admiration of the facility and ease of the poet's melodious versification. "Ease!" said Moore; "why, that couplet you so much admire cost me sleepless nights."

The lines of Moore referred to by Gardiner, if I mistake not, were the following, in "Lalla Rookh":—

"'Tis I that mingle in one sweet measure
The past, the present, and future of pleasure;
When memory links the tone that is gone
With blissful note that's still in the ear;
And Hope from a heavenly note flies on
To a note more heavenly still that is near."

Thus truly sang the great Florentine poet, Dante:—

"——— che seggendo in piuma
In Fama non si vien, ne sotto coltre;
Senza la qual chi sua vita consuma
Cotal vestigio in terra di se lascia
Qual fumo in aere, ed in acqua la schiuma."
—*L'Inferno*, Canto xxiv.

"For not on downy plumes, nor under shade
Of canopy reposing, Fame is won;
Without which, whosoe're consumes his days,
Leaveth such vestige of himself on earth—
As smoke in air, or foam upon the wave."—CARY.

A MEDICAL DILETTANTE.

ON my way to Ischl, 1845, I made the acquaintance of a Viennese, a young man of great classical attainments, who had travelled in the East, and was a remarkable linguist. During our rambles in the lovely neighbourhood of Ischl, and visits to the picturesque lakes of the Salzkammergut country, the clever sketches of persons and scenery of my companion led me to conclude that he was a professional painter of the first class; and his critical remarks on the *chefs-d'œuvre* of the Munich, Dresden, Florentine, and Roman galleries of pictures only served to confirm that impression. Music, naturally, was occasionally a subject of discussion, and I found his remarks on the classical works of the great German masters most judicious; but when he played to me one of Beethoven's difficult sonatas on the pianoforte, I ventured to inquire which of the sister arts was his profession. He replied, "I am a *dilettante* in art, but a medical man by profession." I told him the delusion I had laboured under, recalled to memory the description given of the English by the famous Italian traveller, Beltrami, in 1822, judging the calling and rank of persons in London by their dress, thus: "I see a man of elegant appearance, dressed in black with silk stockings and breeches;—now, then, I think I shall be able to describe a lord—it is a footman. I meet another man with long gaiters, a very plain coat, and a face and manner the most unpretending possible.—That's a very neat-looking servant, I say to myself; I wish ours were as clean. Alas! my dear countess, this is a duke!"

THE CANTATRICE AND THE IMPRESARIO.

IN a different sense from that of the proverb, *vedi Napoli e poi mori*, with the space of twenty years intervening, have I seen Naples and Mori. The latter, a small village near Roverido in the Italian Tyrol, is prettily situated in the midst of luxuriant vineyards and orchards of olive trees, on the high road to the northern extremity of the Lake of Garda. In the autumn of 1865, I was a passenger in the cabriolet of a public diligence, having on my right a smartly-dressed Italian count, and on my left a sentimental-looking donzella, from Mori. Suddenly, a tremendous jerk of the vehicle, as we were being rapidly driven down a steep hill, caused universal alarm. The lady passenger, in her fright, seized hold on me, exclaiming, "Siamo perduti! siamo perduti!" When all fear of toppling over a terrible precipice on our right was at an end, she apologised to me thus: "*Mille scuse, Milord Inglese.*" I assured the bright-eyed damsel that she was much mistaken; I was simply an artist. "Indeed," said she, "I am also an artiste—*cantatrice.*" I replied, "Alas! I was, unfortunately, a director." "Then, sir, I guess you are an impresario" (manager). Mistaking me for Gye or Mapleson, this cantatrice never ceased importuning me to engage her for the Italian Opera of

London, until the end of our journey at Riva. Crossing the lake the next day, I was again accosted by this cantatrice from Mori. She informed me of her intention to go to Milan to secure an engagement for England. Judging by the list of subordinate *rôles* she had sustained in modern operas, I do not think this lady would realise by her voice and talent what she had been told—A FORTUNE. That this is the belief of adventurous musicians abroad I have reason to know; hence the mediocrities that abound in this metropolis, who came advisedly to make fortunes.

A LADY'S MIDSUMMER NIGHT'S DREAM.

SCENE—*Residence of the Director of the Musical Union.* SERVANT *announces a* LADY *in the back drawing-room, wishing to see the Director of the M. U.*

DIR. (*addresses the lady.*) I presume, madame [the lady was middle aged, married, and *far* from handsome], you wish for a subscription-ticket?

LADY. No, sir; I wish to play at the Musical Union. I had a dream last night (*Midsummer*) that I played a sonata at the Musical Union, and I shall never be happy until I realise my dream.

DIR. (*rather alarmed.*) Are you artist or amateur, madame?

LADY. Amateur; but you must hear me play; I

see you have a piano; let me try it, and you will be satisfied with my talent. (*Lady pulls off her gloves, and prepares.*)

DIR. Pardon me, madame; but there is a distinguished foreign pianist waiting for me in the front room, and my time is precious.

LADY (*a little angry*). Sir, you are not gallant!

DIR. I hope, madame, that I am not unpolite; besides which, I beg to impress upon you that the Musical Union is not a place to exhibit amateur talent.

LADY. Some amateurs play quite as well as professors, I can assure you, sir.

DIR. "Buonissimo dilettante non fa buon professore," is a very remarkable fact, which many years' experience has confirmed to the letter; for I have never known a single instance of an amateur becoming a good professor! To amateur music and amateur performances I always listen with an indulgent ear; but you must pardon me, madame, my time is——

LADY (*very impatient to let me hear her*). I won't detain you long; but you *must* hear me play a sonata by Hummel.

(*Madame then opened the piano and played in a style that greatly surprised me for an amateur.*)

DIR. I am sorry, madame, that I must decline your offer to play at the Musical Union. My expenses are very considerable, the subscription very low, and without attracting visitors by the engagement of new and eminent professors from the Continent, I should not be able to pay my artists.

LADY. I perceive you are mercenary, like all the English musicians, and have no love for art.

DIR. Excuse me, madame, but my love for art has cost me a thousand pounds in studying and travelling on the Continent.

LADY. Well, sir (*in a mild and persuasive tone*), I will buy fifty half-guinea tickets if you will let me only play one sonata!

DIR. There are plenty of concert givers who would gladly accept your generous offer, madame; but the Director of the Musical Union will never accept a bribe. My servant will bring you refreshments, you can play upon my piano as long as you please, but I must respectfully wish you a good morning.

LADY. Sir, you are ungallant, mercenary, and not a gentleman!

Lady burst into a flood of tears, begged to be allowed to remain a few minutes alone, and made me promise never to divulge her name; which, by the by, in her impatience to tell me the object of her visit, she never once divulged. I was compelled to leave her to attend a rehearsal, and I afterwards ascertained that she expressed to my servant her regret at having indulged so freely in language which the occasion did not warrant. Thus ended, the Lady's Midsummer Night's Dream. Who, after this, would be a director?

MUSIC AND MATRIMONY.

THE author of the "Music of Nature," Mr. Gardiner, insisted upon the celibacy of all young needy artists. The path to Parnassus is rugged and steep enough, said the old celibataire, without the cares of domesticity to weigh you down and impede your progress. Young artists, fresh from scholastic studies, compelled to devote their whole time to the routine of lesson-giving, toiling eight and ten hours per diem, cannot have sufficient practice to enable them to compete with soloists of established renown. No soldier living only on his pay, said a veteran general, has any business with a wife in camp; and any musician aspiring to high honours as an executant should be content to wed only his muse until he commands position and means of living by his talent. The most original and durable productions of musical composers, said Gardiner, are the offspring of celibacy. This may be said of Handel, Beethoven, Rossini, and Mendelssohn, but not of Mozart.

IL PARADISO E L'INFERNO.

THERE is a proverb in Sicily that Naples is a paradise for men, and l'inferno for horses. This recalls to mind an interview with Lablache, surrounded by his pretty daughters, just budding into life, among artists. Being asked if any of his daughters were destined for the opera stage, the Gros de Naples replied: "Yes, if I could be sure of their becoming *prime donne.* The stage, caro mio, you well know, for a prima donna, è il paradiso—for the seconda donna, l'inferno."

THE PATRICIAN AND PLEBEIAN ARTS.

TERPSICHORE AND EUTERPE.

THE famed ballet and dancing master, Vestris, instructor of half the Courts of Europe, was wont to deplore the decadence of his art. There was a time, said the vain old Frenchman, when noblemen and ladies disported themselves at state balls with grace and dignity, in the "Minuet de la Cour." When told that royalty had commanded a Scotch reel to be danced for their especial delight, at a state ball, the veteran *maître de danse* is said to have shed tears. But rousing himself, he exclaimed, "N'importe—La musique est plébéienne. Une dame ne danse pas avec son cordonnier, quoiqu'elle chante avec son tailleur."

THE ARTS IN FRANCE AND ENGLAND.

IN 1845 a sumptuous entertainment was given to Berlioz by the Princess Alexandre Czartoryska—*née* Radizwill *—the accomplished pupil of Chopin and Mayseder. With that courtesy and good-breeding observed in the patrician houses of my own country, the foreign guests took precedence of the younger members of the family, on being marshalled into dinner. Berlioz, with a provoking amount of national *politesse*, refused to enter the dining-room before me, and whilst we were mutually bowing to each other and uttering all kinds of civilities, the venerable Prince, who preceded us, with the Princess, his daughter-in-law, seeing my embarrassment, *naïvely* observed, "Gentlemen, in matters of art, I believe that England is right in awarding precedence to France." Berlioz smiled at this decision, and I followed in his wake. Elated by congenial society, Berlioz was more than usually brilliant in wit, anecdote, and conversation. Among other compliments that passed towards the foreign guests, "Success to the Musical Union, London" (then in its infancy), was proposed as a toast, to which Berlioz added a singularly prophetic amendment: "Et l'alliance de

* Her father, Prince Radizwill, was a friend of Beethoven, and the composer of music to "Faust."

l'Angleterre avec la France." This interesting event was recalled to my memory in 1851, by the presence of the above Princess and Berlioz at my residence in London, when she delighted the amateurs by her poetical delivery of Chopin's music.

THE SCULPTOR AND MUSIC.

WHEN in conversation with the late Gibson in his studio at Rome, 1842, an itinerant minstrel began to discourse sweet harmony. I asked Gibson if music interrupted his labours; he replied, "On the contrary, I never work more cheerfully than when listening to music." I told him that one studio for music, painting, and sculpture might prove mutually suggestive. "Not exactly," said Gibson, "if our models are emotional." I replied, that to compose it was not necessary to play.

THE PAINTER AND MUSIC.

SMITH, in his "Life of Nollekins," relates that he once found Colonel Hamilton playing so exquisitely on the violin to Gainsborough, that the latter exclaimed, "Go on, and I will give you the picture of 'The boy at the Stile,' which you have so often wished to purchase of me." This picture was a favourite work of Gainsborough, and one which he prized so highly that he repeatedly refused to part with it. I am not acquainted with any living painter who is capable of yielding so much to the emotional effects of music.

THE PREDATORY ANTIQUARIAN.

THE Italians have reason to be jealous of rich foreigners buying up their classical relics of antiquity. At Naples, I know to my cost, that imitation bronzes and terra-cotta objects, manufactured in Paris and elsewhere, are dug up in the ruins of Cumæ and Baja, and sold to the "*pazzi Inglesi,*" as we sometimes are called, for original antiques. On seeing a grave-looking Englishman gazing in silent admiration at the beautiful Campanile in Florence, a boy, with smart utterance of irony, impudently addressed him thus: "Ah! ah! Signor; ma quello non si svita"—"You can't unscrew that."

THE BROTHERS PETRIDES.

IN 1822, the French horns in the band of Her Majesty's Theatre were played by the above two venerable Bohemians. In dress and appearance they resembled each other—both wearing pants fitted tight down to the ankles, a brown wig, an oddly-shaped hat, and large green spectacles. When accused, at rehearsals, of playing a wrong note, each would answer, "*was mein bruder;*" and until the copyist discovered that the parts were wrong, and neither of the brothers was at fault, they would snarl and utter unkind expressions towards each other, with a menacing look. At other times, they were the most united of brothers. By frugality and good conduct, they acquired a modest competency, and retired in 1824 to their native country. I know of no other example of wind-instrumentalists acquiring an independence by orchestral employment, in London. The successors of the Petrides, after a long service in our best orchestras, are now both pensioners of the Royal Society of Musicians. In Paris, after twenty years' service in the Grand Opera band, musicians have a retiring pension.

INGRATITUDE.

THE late Duc de Luynes-Grammont de Caderousse, who died in Rome, in 1867, assisting the wounded soldiers of the Pope, was the generous friend of savans, philosophers, and artists. "Though learned in writing, he was timid in harangue—like our Cowper and Addison. His entire income was spent in pursuit of science and art; a noble use of his fortune, when men were dissipating theirs in vicious and vulgar pleasures. From the artists he befriended, he experienced that keenest stab to the heart—INGRATITUDE." Alas! who is there in power to bestow a favour, that has not experienced ingratitude? Seneca, in his eighty-first epistle, tells us, "In order to shun this danger, you must never confer a benefit while you live." Further on he says, "The usurer still lends his money, though he hath suffered loss by a bankrupt. Life would soon grow dull and stupid in fruitless indolence were we to meet with no rubs in our way." Among his various accomplishments the above French duke was a musician, and performed *con gusto* the fugues of Bach, and other classical works.

PART IV.

MUSIC IN FLORENCE, 1865.

"Of all the fairest cities of the earth,
None is so fair as Florence."—ROGERS.

"As you approach the city from the neighbouring hills the prospect is yet more beautiful. Here you have Florence extended at your feet—her groves and gardens, pinnacles and towers, and the river winding through the famed Valdarno—a golden plain, abounding in corn, and wine, and oil—till the scene is closed by the bold range of the Apennines. Such is the situation of Florence; and within her walls are palaces and museums rich in all the wonders of ancient and modern art; abounding with everything that can delight the fancy or gratify the taste:—

Search within,
Without; all is enchantment! 'Tis the past
Contending with the present; and, in turn
Each has the mastery."

The Classic and Connoisseur in Italy, 1835.—EVANS.

RECOLLECTING the vicissitudes of La Bella Italia in warfare, and the changes of dynasties, so fatal to the healthy progress of the musical art, since the glorious epoch of the Middle Ages, and even since the time of Burney's journey in search of materials for the "History of Music," it is matter of regret to find so little support of late afforded to schools that formerly supplied Europe with such great composers and learned masters. Having satisfied my inquiry on the general state of music in 1842 and 1843, I was anxious to ascertain the future prospects of music in the new capital of Italy, now the seat of government, with an influx of several thousand residents and foreign visitors.

After viewing the churches, picture-galleries, and museums at the Hague, Leyden, Amsterdam, Munich, Innspruck, Verona, and Milan — remaining several days in the mountains of Tyrol, on the right of the Brenner Pass, in a villa some three thousand feet above the sea, and visiting Botzen, Trent, Mori, and Riva on the Lake of Garda — I arrived in Florence on the 10th of October.

ART HISTORY.

["Here am I in Florence, the air warm and the sky bright; everything is beautiful and glorious. 'Wo blieb die Erde,' as Goethe says." *October* 23d, 1830.—MENDELSSOHN.]

WITH much the same feelings as animated the musical historian Burney, in 1770, did I revisit Firenze la bella in 1865, "to hear with my own ears, and to see with my own eyes." "If historians and poets," says Burney, "may be credited, Florence has longer been in possession of music than any other city in Europe." Dante speaks of the organ and lute as instruments well known in his time (the thirteenth century), and in the second canto of his "Purgatorio," introduces his friend Casella, the musician. Villani, the historian, says that his canzonets were sung in Florence by the old and the young of both sexes; and we read of songs, ballads, madrigals, and catches, some of them in four, eight, twelve, and even fifteen parts, being sung by upwards of five hundred masked and richly-dressed persons, on horseback and foot, parading the streets of Florence in company with Lorenzo il Magnifico. In Florence, too, was first made, by Christoforo from Padua, in 1718, that most useful and universally appreciated musical instrument—the pianoforte.

To the long list of illustrious names that adorn the art-history of Florence with Dante and Michael Angelo—ever the presiding deities of Tuscany—may now be added that of one whose musical genius and learning have since shed a lustre on his native city, and to whose memory a suitable monument is now being erected in the capitals of Italy and France—Cherubini, born at Florence 1760, and died at Paris 1842. With the religious and operatic music of this great master, the citizens of modern Florence are, I suspect, at present very little acquainted.

THE ROYAL MUSICAL INSTITUTE.

CONSIDERING how little has been attempted in Florence to promote that branch of the art—classical instrument music—so popular in other cities, it is not surprising to find the present generation little acquainted with the works of Bach, Beethoven, Haydn, Mozart, Weber, Spohr, and Mendelssohn. A movement, however, is now being made in the right direction. The present government supports a Musical Institute, and gives the free use of a commodious building for the gratuitous musical education of the youth of both sexes.

The statutes of the Royal Musical Institute contain very precise instructions for the President, Secretary, Treasurers, Professors, and students.

Article 29 describes the general conditions for the admission of students, viz., morality, good health, natural disposition, and aptitude. No one admitted under nine years of age.

The school is divided into sections:—1. History of music and æsthetics; 2. Harmony, counterpoint, and composition; 3. Accompaniment; 4. Singing; 5. Reading music and solfeggio; 6. The organ; 7. Pianoforte; 8. Minor class for pianoforte; 9. Violin and viola; 10. Violoncello; 11. Contrabasso; 12. Wind instruments (wood); 13. Ditto (metal); 14. A class for choral singing. All education is gratuitous, and each student receives three lessons every week, and the class of each section lasts three hours. The library and musical instruments are free to students.

Before quitting Florence I was shown the valuable collection of Cremona instruments presented by government to the Institute. These consisted of violins, large and ordinary-sized violas, violoncellos, and double-basses, in perfect condition, carefully preserved in a large case, in charge of the President. The latter gentleman and the chief professors expressed a hope, in which I sincerely join, that government would increase the amount of subvention to the Institution.

CHURCH MUSIC.

THE present unsettled question of Church property affords no immediate prospect of re-establishing academies to supply good choristers, organists, and *maestri di cappella*, so much needed in Italy; and with so many splendid churches as there are in Florence, I was grieved to hear so few musical services well performed. The only mass I heard with orchestra was on All Saints' Day, at the Church of the *Annunziata.* The effect was by no means satisfactory; the drums, favoured by the lofty edifice, completely drowned the small band of instrumentalists. In some of the churches are good organs. It is a pity there are not good organists.

ORCHESTRAL MUSIC.

THE sum of £120 is granted by government for the Institute to defray the expenses of gratuitous orchestral and choral concerts. I was present at one on the 5th of November. The programme comprised two masterpieces—Beethoven's Symphony in A, and Cherubini's superb Mass in D minor. The executants, about sixty in the band and sixty in the choir, had had several rehearsals, and the *ensemble* was very good. The conductor, a German, wielded a small *bâton* with decision and intelligence, without such excessive gyrations and violent contortions of limbs and body as are witnessed in some of our London orchestras. The Philharmonic room, in which this concert took place, was well adapted for such a performance, and contained some five hundred persons, among whom were the *élite* of the native *dilettanti*, several English and other foreign visitors, and a goodly assembly of professors and students.

On the 8th of December was given a grand morning choral and orchestral concert to raise funds for a monument to Cherubini. The programme consisted of—

1. Ouverture dell' Opera Faniska (orchestra)........*I. Cherubini.*
2. *Da nobis pacem,* Preghiera (coro ed orchestra) *F. Mendelssohn.*
3. Sinfonia in *Sol minore* (orchestra)...............*W. A. Mozart.*
4. *Kyrie, Gloria e Credo,* della Messa Solenne in *Do* (soli, coro ed orchestra).............*L. V. Beethoven.*

CHAMBER MUSIC.

THE glowing descriptions of Chamber Concerts in the musical journal, *Boccherini*, and the liberal premiums awarded to the successful competitors in composition, had greatly interested me, nor were my expectations disappointed. Prize quartets by Bottesini and Bazzini, artists known for their performances on the double-bass and violin at the Musical Union, are highly meritorious works. These new compositions are printed in full score by *Guidi.**

Two societies for Chamber Concerts are now in full vogue. The first, founded in 1861, led by Becker,† from Strasburg, is strictly limited to instrumental music. The pianists, Mdme. Montignani and Signor Ducci, good and intelligent artists, are not unknown in London circles. The concerted music was satisfactorily played, but the *locale*, in every sense, was ill-adapted for the effect and enjoyment of the music; the room too low and small, and the performers ill-placed. The audience, enthusiastic in their applause, did not include many of the Florentine families. By degrees, however, all classes of amateurs will learn to appreciate the true merits of this style of composition.

* This publisher, to the credit of Florence be it recorded, has done for the interest of art what no English editor hitherto has had the courage to do, by publishing in score the following works:—The first nine Quartets of Beethoven; the Quintet in E♭, op. 16, Piano and Wind Instrument; the Septet, op. 20; the first three Pianoforte Trios; the Serenade Trio, op. 8, and the grand Trio B♭, op. 97. Mozart's Clarionet Quintet, in A, op. 108, and the one in G minor. Hummel's Piano Quintet, op. 87, and Septet, op. 74. Mendelssohn's Ottetto, op. 20. Spohr's double Quartet, in D minor, op. 65. Boccherini's Quintet, A minor, and E♭, op. 47. Prize Quartets of 1862, by Bottesini and Anichini; in 1863, by Croff, and in 1864, by W. Langhans: also other new Quartets by Fiori, Pacini, and Ricordi. There are full scores, too, of the following works at moderate prices, and in octavo form; "Guillaume Tell," "Les Huguenots," &c.

† Engaged 1860 and 1862 at the Musical Union.

The following are the programmes of the first two concerts of the present season, 1865 and 1866:—

SOCIETÀ DEL QUARTETTO DI FIRENZE.

(Founded 1861. Fifth Season, 1865-66.)

Sunday, November 12th, at Half-past Twelve.

1. Trio, op. 1, C minor, Piano, &c.................*Beethoven.*
2. Quartet, op. 74, No. 10, E♭ ....*Beethoven.*
3. Capriccio (3), No. 22, Pianoforte solo, Con acc. di Quintetto...........................*Mendelssohn.*

First Violin......BECKER. Viola......CHIOSTRI.
Second Violin...MASI. V.-celli...SANDELLI and HILPERT.
Pianiste......Mdme. RITA MONTIGNANI.

Second Matinée, November 19th. Fifth Season.

1. Quartet, G minor, Piano, &c..........................*Mozart.*
2. Quartet, op. 12, E♭, con Canzonetta.........*Mendelssohn.*
3. Kreutzer Sonata, op. 47.........................*Beethoven.*

Pianist......Signor CARLO DUCCI.

The more modern Society, established in 1863, is led by a young native artist, Bruni, supported by the best violoncellist of Florence, Signor Sbolci. The pianist, Signorina E. del Bianco, is an excellent player, with plenty of execution and a firm finger. This lady has also been a season in London, playing chiefly in private circles. The Sbolci party is associated with a select vocal society, and the singing of concerted religious music was highly creditable, and far more acceptable than grand dramatic songs, and scenas reduced to a pianoforte accompaniment, at concerts of this character.

LA SOCIETÀ SBOLCI.

(Founded 1863. Third Season, 1865-66.)

Saturday, December 2d, at Half-past Eight.

1. Quartet, No. 1, op. 18, in F........................*Beethoven.*
2. Laudate, Dominum. Coro a due voci di soprani.. } *Gio. Batta. Martini.*
3. Quartet, op. 44, in D..............................*Mendelssohn.*
4. O Salutaris Hostia, per sop. e coro, tre violoncelli obbligati, contrabasso, e organo (harmonium) ....*Bazzini.*
5. Grand Trio, op. 97, B♭, Piano, &c..............*Beethoven.*

Second Concert. Saturday Evening, December 9th.

1. Quartet, G minor, Piano, &c..........................*Mozart.*
2. Credo, a 4 voci ....*Michele Haydn.*
3. Quartet, F minor, op. 95..............................*Beethoven.*
4. Terzetto, sop., ten., and basso (*Faniska*) ......*Cherubini.*
5. Quartet, op. 2, F minor, Piano, &c...........*Mendelssohn.*

First Violin......BRUNI. Viola......LASCHI.
Second Violin...MOUNIER. Violoncello...SBOLCI.
Pianiste......Signorina ELVIRA DEL BIANCO.

The studies and vocalists of this Society are aided by Professor Gaston, Giovacchini, and Geremia Sbolci.

The price of tickets, for each concert of both Societies, five francs.

SBOLCI plays classical music well; his tone is round and powerful; his style is free from affectation, and he phrases his passage with taste. I had no opportunity of hearing him play solos, but a violoncellist that satisfies his auditors in quartets of Beethoven and Mendelssohn has no need to court applause in other kinds of music. The two native violinists, Papini and Bruni, lead quartets with spirit, feeling, and intelligence. They have plenty of execution, and their intonation is irreproachable.

At the concerts led by Becker, the first violin and viola were *vis-à-vis* in front, with the violoncello and second violin at the back. Where I sat, the effect was unsatisfactory, for, between us and the executants was a full-sized grand—Erard! The Sbolci party were placed in a straight line, and I leave my readers to judge of the distance between the first violinist and the violoncellist, more especially in a quintet. At the public Vienna Quartet Concerts, in 1845, the first violin and violoncello sat *vis-à-vis* in front of the viola and second violin! With such arrangements I defy any person, who is not seated *above* the executants, to hear distinctly the four parts of a quartet. At the palace of the late Prince Czartoryski, in Vienna, I first experienced the effect of the quartet played in the centre of a large circle of auditors. Here Mayseder presided, with Borzaga, the violoncellist. Alas! stern death has taken from us every vestige of the happy scenes so often witnessed at the Musical Unions of the above venerable Mecænas of the imperial city.

Considering the slow progress of educating a public in a new style of musical composition, I would suggest to these Florentine societies the advantage of less exclusiveness, and the insertion of a work by the earlier masters, Haydn or Mozart, in each programme, to attract the fashionable *dolce far niente* Tuscans, who at present have no knowledge of high art in music, and look upon these concerts of "*musica tedesca*" as tedious. I have recently heard of the Sbolci party attempting one of Beethoven's posthumous quartets. This is a very great mistake. Let it always be borne in mind that "*l'excès du beau amène le dégoût.*"

ITALIAN OPERA.

THE increased number of Italian singers required to supply the theatres of Europe and America, and the greater remuneration awarded to them out of their native country, long ago elicited a remark from the Venetian heroine in one of Balzac's stories that London and Paris robbed Italy of her best vocalists —"*Paris les juge et Londres les paye.*" The court theatre at Florence, *La Pergola*, receives a subvention of £4000. The two operas given during October and November were "Robert le Diable" and "Lucrezia Borgia." The principal singers are known to the frequenters of the Royal Italian Opera, London—Mdme. Fricci, her husband Neri-Baraldi, and Attry—the latter an excellent French artist. The band, chorus, and *mise en scène*, were very satisfactory. The ballets are well got up, with Mdlle. Brugnoli as principal dancer. The old vicious habit, I perceive, is continued of giving a long ballet *between* the acts of an opera. The King Emmanuel, King and Queen of Portugal, and Royal Family, with a numerous *suite* of military and ministers in attendance, came in full state to witness only the ballet. Opposite the box where I sat were Mario and Grisi, looking supremely happy, with their three charming daughters—de Candia.

The *Pagliano Theatre*,* of immense size, holding upwards of five thousand persons, is usually devoted to comic and popular operas by a second-rate company of vocalists. For ten nights during November and December did Mdlle. Adelina Patti completely fill this enormous theatre. The price of admission was trebled, and the ovations which this fascinating singer and actress received each night of her performance in "Sonnambula" and "Barbiere" were very gratifying. Her engagement was £160 each representation! On the occasion of a Royal visit to hear La Patti, the King of Italy desired her presence in the royal box; and, in return for an album of portraits, presented by the "Amina" in costume, after the first act of "Sonnambula," to the Queen of Portugal, the latter presented her with a massive gold neck-chain and a medallion with pearls and diamonds. The bouquets heaved on the stage were of prodigious dimensions; and, in the Italian fashion, she was

* This theatre ceased to exist, 1868.

called and recalled several times after each act of the opera with uproarious applause.

Although the public are little sparing of censure when displeased with a singer, musical critics are reasonably indulgent. The notices written upon the *début* of La Patti were most flattering. Admitting that she possessed neither the dramatic genius of a Pasta, nor the volume of voice of a Grisi, they were in ecstacies with her vocalisation and admirable acting. Of the other singers, band, and chorus, it is unnecessary to speak; they did their best. I was much more satisfied with the same troupe (*minus* Adelina Patti), under the same management at the smaller *Teatro Nazionale.* Here the famous Neapolitan buffo, Fiorivanti, is heard to advantage in very amusing operas, with a capital ballet. Pit tickets, 10d.; stalls, 2s. 6d.

The fourth lyrical theatre—*Rossini*—gave "Gemma di Vergy" and "l'Elisir d'Amore," by Donizetti, with an inferior set of singers. The ballet, however, was amusing, and the two principal dancers from Milan would not discredit Her Majesty's Theatre, London. Here the pit tickets are 5d., and the stalls 2s. Inferior as was the singing, and boisterous the applause in *encoring* every effective piece of music, or *pas seul*, it was gratifying to see in these cheap lyrical entertainments sober and well-conducted persons, with their families, heartily enjoying the music and dancing, and intent upon watching the incidents of the drama. Surely it were desirable to have such entertainments of secular music in London, rather than have the people allured into music-halls to smoke, drink, and spend much money to witness mongrel exhibitions of the worst tendency, in very questionable society? A lyrical theatre serves many good purposes—poets, singers, instrumentalists, dancers, and scene-painters are legitimately employed. Many artists have sprung from these cheap theatres in Italy, where they first gained experience in dramatic singing and action. The drinking at the London music-halls may be coupled with the gambling at the German Spas, which defrays the cost of entertainments offered to its victims!

Half a century ago it was little anticipated that Italy would ever have recourse to the *repertoire* of the French grand opera to supply her four principal theatres—in Naples, Milan, Bologna, and Florence—with attractive compositions, viz., "La Muette," "Faust," "Robert," "Huguenots," and "L'Africaine." The present dearth of well-written native operas must be attributed to the want of more serious instruction in the higher branches of composition at the chief schools of Milan, Bologna, and Naples. There is no lack of novelty, since not fewer than forty-two new operas have been produced at the last two carnivals in Italy; yet, to speak metaphorically, not one has had sufficient longevity and force to climb over the Alps to the northern cities! The following list comprises the names of those who produced in 1862 a new opera, the first and last only enjoying a world-wide fame—Bottesini, Braga, Bevignani, Bonomi, Cianchi, Chiaromonte, Crescinanno, Capranica, Gentili, Moscuzza, Kinterland, Penso, Rochele, Rota, Savi, Sangiorgi, Varvaro, Viceconte, Zappata, and Verdi.

At the residence of Mdlle. Patti I heard some portion of a charming opera played by the composer, Prince Poniatowski, and on my visits to Signor Pinsutti I found him progressing rapidly with his maiden opera from one of Shakespeare's plays. This Italian maestro has had the advantage of a thorough good musical education in London under more favourable auspices than most of his *confrères*.

At Bologna, "L'Africaine" was given with great splendour and success—quite equal, say the Italians, to the original representation in Paris. Unfortunately, owing to the illness of a principal singer, I did not hear it, as I expected, on my way to Genoa. At the latter city was given "La Fille du Regiment," and at Milan "Il Barbiere;" at both places the singers were second-rate. It should be mentioned that the autumnal season is not subscribed so largely for as the Carnival, and managers reserve for the latter, after Christmas, their most attractive artists. La Patti, for a limited number of nights at Milan, was offered the unprecedented amount of £200 each representation! However inferior are the performances of operas in Italy, to the splendid representations in London, one has the rare satisfaction of hearing the Italian language distinctly and well pronounced. The supply of Italian singers not being equal to the demand in the various capitals of Europe, recourse is had to the surplus talent of other countries, hence the wretched jargon heard, especially in London, of German, French, Swedish, English, and Dutch Italian.

MILITARY MUSIC.

TWICE daily the relief guard at the Pitti Palace, immediately in front of my rooms, afforded me an excellent opportunity of hearing military bands. They mustered about thirty-five when complete, and in fantasias upon opera themes, the soloists showed sensitiveness and good taste worthy of an accomplished *donna assoluta.* The music was well scored, and the masters evidently were skilled and experienced musicians. Several pretty, characteristic, and original polkas, mazurkas, and waltzes were played that would realise a little fortune for any of the London enterprising publishers. On the evenings of the opening of parliament and the state *entrée* of the King and Queen of Portugal, the city, with its duomo, palaces, quais, and bridges, was splendidly illuminated. In the Piazza della Signoria, surrounded by the immortal productions of Michael Angelo, Benvenuto-Cellini, Giovanni da Bologna, and Canova, a military band played from seven until eleven o'clock;

in the Piazza della Trinità and other central situations, upon a stage tastefully draped and illuminated, were seated other military bands. Amidst the assembled thousands of both sexes, *sober* and thoroughly earnest in their attention to the charms of the music, I accompanied some ladies throughout the city, hearing and seeing all that could gratify our senses, without molestation, or much inconvenience. When a favourite *morceau* was played the crowd applauded and even *encored.* After the excitement of the opening of the new parliament, and the picturesque *entrée* of the Portuguese Royal Family through a dense mass of joyful and orderly citizens, nothing could wind up these *fêtes* more delightfully than the inspiring music of these capital military bands throughout the night.

BALL MUSIC.

THE state ball given by the municipal authorities to the King of Italy and the crowned heads from Portugal, was attended by some five thousand persons. Two orchestras were engaged for this occasion; the one in the large state room was numerous, well organised, and played with *verve* and spirit. With the vivid recollection of the orchestras at the Carnival balls in Vienna and Berlin, composed of sixty, eighty, and once of one hundred and ten musicians under the direction of the *late* Strauss, 1846, I have little pleasure in listening to the spiritless accents of inferior bands. *The* Strauss, a master spirit in his way, had great skill in putting together even a few instruments with charming effect, to which I have frequently listened with delight. *Sax* has proved himself a benefactor to open-air music, with his powerful brass horns and Sax-tubas; but when introduced into small orchestras, without a proper balance of corresponding melodic instruments, their effect in a room is decidedly unpleasant. The music of a ball-room requires rhythmical accent well defined; this accent, however, should not *solely* rely upon the loudness of the bass. The Germans understand these matters, and play their waltzes with a rhythmical melodic accent, seldom heard so satisfactorily in other countries.

ITALIAN POLITICS AND ART.

["L'opera del rinuovamento italiano è lunga e difficile: i nemici molti: i pericoli grandi. Pur se guardiamo lo stato d'Italia nel principio del 1859 e lo stato presente, sentiamo risorgere nell' animo nuovo corraggio, e ripigliamo la via col fermo proposito di giungere al fine."—*Marco Minghetti* al suoi Elettori, 1865.]

THE King of Italy is deservedly popular, and has set an example of self-abnegation in yielding the state domains, and sacrificing personal ease and luxury, to benefit his loyal subjects. During my short sojourn of two months, His Majesty made frequent journeys to Turin on matters of state, and, by a very circuitous route, to evade the Papal States, posted to Naples, and visited the cholera hospitals, —coming back to open the parliament in Florence the same week! It is said that, "The Sleeping Beauty of the Arno appreciates fully the honour of her dignified position;" and the loyal citizens of rank and wealth, in whatever degree they differ as to the financial policy of the ministers, are, one and all, agreed on the subject of "Italia Unita." Considering the various and opposing elements already under the obedient control of one central power of government—from Turin to Palermo—it speaks highly in favour of the Italians generally, that they so patiently abide the course of events!

I have faith in the spirit and intelligence of the national government; although temporarily embarrassed in its finances, it is quite alive to the exigencies of the people, and schools are everywhere springing up. On complaining of the want of a catalogue at the Loan Museum of most rare, valuable, and interesting objects of art, and of the incompleteness of various promised improvements in Florence, the custodian shrugged up his shoulders, and with singularly expressive grimace, peculiar to Italians, uttered that universally expletive monosyllable, "Che!" adding what must be received as a satisfactory excuse to persons impatient of the progress of "Italia Unita," "Ma signor, che volete? L'Italia non è che una bambina di cinque anni!" *

In Florence the arts are loved, and talent is appreciated, but neither painters nor composers in Italy are remunerated as in London. The climate, the charms of social life, with the distinctions conferred on creative genius and men of mark and likelihood by the King and noblest of the land, in many instances compensate the want of the greater pecuniary reward of the resident artist in London. Hence, in Florence, Rome, Naples, and Milan, I have known musical instructors content with a modest competence, who, if in London, would obtain for lessons treble the terms given in their native cities. During the autumn and winter at the magnificent villa of the Marchese di Candia (Mario), and elsewhere in Florence, may be seen among the guests, musicians enjoying *en amateur* the harvest of a London season. Throughout all the evils of political strife, Florence has ever preserved her supremacy in taste for the arts; "belle et gaie, elle est demeurée en Italie la capitale de l'esprit."

To the lovers of architecture, sculpture, and painting, I can imagine no greater enjoyment than a tour throughout Italy. Indeed, I can scarcely understand how any English amateur or professional painter with £20 at command, can resist making a month's trip to Florence or Rome! In 1817 Byron visited Flor-

* "L'energie manque en Toscane encore plus qu'ailleurs."—H. TAIN.—*Revue des Deux Mondes, Jan.* 15, 1866.

ence, on his way to Rome. "I remained," he says, "*but a day;* however, I went to the two galleries, from which one returns *drunk with beauty.*" That Paris and London should satisfy musicians by the perfection of their musical performances in every branch of the art, is obvious enough; but with the mellifluous voice and joyous expression of Mendelssohn at Lucerne, 1842, still fresh in my memory, I commend his words to all my brother professors in England—"Visit Italy and see Rome! You will not become a better musician, but will return home a better artist," "and," as an English painter once said to me, "with a new sense."

MUSIC IN VIENNA, 1866.

THE capital of Austria, says Murray, has been proclaimed by many travellers the most dissolute capital in Europe; but there has been much exaggeration in this respect. The streets, however, may be traversed at all hours, by day and night, without encountering disturbance or annoyance of any kind. This opinion I can conscientiously endorse, after three autumnal and winter visits, to this most musical and enjoyable city, and I only wish that in London I could always go to my residence from Pall Mall, through St. James' Park, without disturbance or annoyance, as securely as in Vienna. To publish all my notes on music and musicians in Vienna, 1845-46, 1852, and 1866, would greatly exceed the limits of a moderately-sized volume. I must therefore confine myself to sketches of what I consider most interesting.

More than a quarter of a century has elapsed since the biographer of Mozart, E. Holmes, published his rambles among the musicians of Germany. A more pleasant narrative of what this amiable and accomplished professor saw and heard has seldom been written. This critic, however, evidently made his Continental trip during the summer vacation, when most of the national institutions devoted to the interests of music are closed. Other travellers, less discreet, have hazarded opinions on the taste and intelligence of the Viennese quite erroneous and by no means complimentary. This reminds me very much of what Lady Mary W. Montague writes to a friend about English notions of Fatimas and Greek slaves, derived from ignorant historians, "who never fail giving you an account of the women whom 'tis certain they never saw, and talking very wisely of the genius of the men into whose company they are never admitted; and very often describe mosques which they dared not even peep into." One of our countrymen has recanted opinions which he had hastily formed on finding the three sons of Strauss sole exponents of the divine art, on the classic grounds of Mozart, Haydn, and Beethoven, during the summer months, and drew therefore false deductions of public taste. Even the brothers Strauss, with their compact band of forty musicians, are always worth hearing, and are unique for their effective scoring of dances, Mendelssohn's "Songs without Words," and Chopin's "Notturnos." Nor can there be a more rational pastime for a couple of hours after dinner than sipping good coffee or taking a refreshing ice on a hot summer's day in the Volks-Garden, with the accompaniment of Strauss' band. In the month of November, some four or five swimming-bath establishments are converted into music-halls of grand dimensions for the winter season, where choral concerts and other musical entertainments are given. The Conservatoire has then its weekly practices, the Philharmonic, Quartet, and other concerts begin, and at some dozen churches, masses, with full orchestras, are to be heard. Failing to visit these places when the musical season is fairly set in, no person can judge of the condition of art and the intelligence of the really musical public of Vienna.

In 1845, before the Revolution of 1848 severed from society in Vienna the nobles of Bohemia and Hungary, the imperial city was the most social and, musically speaking, the most enjoyable of any I ever visited.

In 1852 I found it comparatively dull; but, in 1866, notwithstanding its disastrous war with Prussia, Vienna appeared gay, and its magnificent boulevard *Ring-strasse*, on the site of the old ramparts, was filled with happy-looking and elegantly-dressed citizens.

The musical institutions seemed all thriving. At the Royal Opera House, "Faust," "Fidelio," "Zauberflöte," "Tanhauser," and a varied *repertoire*, was given three times a week. The band, some sixty, was first-rate, and the chorus excellent. Of the principal singers, two only are known in London—La Murzka and Rokitansky.

The Philharmonic Concerts, eight in number, had

a full subscription, and the Grand Choral and Orchestral Concerts, at the *Redouten Saal*, under the direction of that most indefatigable and excellent composer and conductor, Kapellmeister Herbeck, gave me more pleasure than I can well express.

PHILHARMONIC SOCIETY IN VIENNA, 1866–1867.

THE concerts of this society now take place in the Court Opera House, which will hold some 1500 persons. Like those of the Conservatoire in Paris, every box and stall is subscribed for, and held, year after year, by the same parties. On my arrival last winter in Vienna, I received from some resident friends their stalls for the first concert. During the performance, I was asked by a lady at my side if any calamity had befallen the owners of the stalls, as they had never been absent, for many years, from a Philharmonic Concert. The band, mustering about sixty musicians, was well conducted by Dessoff, and every composition was executed with the most scrupulous attention to details which often escape the vigilance of our London conductors, with their one hurried rehearsal. I could not but remark the respectful address of the maestro on entering the orchestra with a *bâton* about half the size of those distracting white wands used at London concerts. On mounting the dais, he salutes, in silence and with solemn reverence, his critical audience. At the end of the composition, if satisfactorily executed, enthusiastic applause follows. The conductor then makes a respectful obeisance, and at the third round of applause, the whole band rise from their seats and salute the audience. This custom is far more respectful than the foolish habit in London of the players usurping the privilege of the public in applauding their conductor *before* the music is played. The concerts of this society in Vienna, as in Paris, take place on Sundays. The following selection, without vocal music, as at Pasdeloup's in Paris, afforded me a great treat; the scherzando of Beethoven's symphony being rapturously encored, and Nos. 3 and 4 of Raff's new music deservedly admired.

SUNDAY, *November 11th*, 1866. HALF-PAST TWELVE.

Overture to *Oberon*...*Weber.*
Suite, in C (new)—1. Introduction and Fugue;
2. Minuet; 3. Adagietto; 4. Scherzo;
5. March...*J. Raff.*
Overture *Carnival of Rome*..............................*Berlioz.*
Symphony, in F (No. 8)................................*Beethoven.*

These entertainments terminate at two o'clock, the usual time of dining in Vienna.

THE IMPERIAL CHAPEL.

THE choir of this chapel consists of ten boys, with good voices, admirably trained, five principal tenor, and five principal bass singers: a most compact, perfect choir of first-rate artists.

The band, led by Hellmesberger, including the *élite* of the profession, consists of twelve violins, four violas, three violoncellos, three double-basses, and a complete set of wind instruments, with drums. Never overpowering the voices in accompaniment, yet this little orchestra, with the aid of an organ most skilfully played, in the choruses, is quite powerful enough for the size of the chapel. Of the fourteen masses I heard, on Sundays and Saints' days, at this chapel, by Salieri, Haydn, Mozart, Cherubini, Beethoven, &c., in the winter of 1866–67, the Requiem of Cherubini, and Beethoven's Mass in C, made the deepest impression on my feelings. On referring to my diary, when first I heard Beethoven's Mass in C, at the Concerts of Ancient Music in London, 1836, I find that I recorded the impression of a melodic phrase for the horn and its subsequent harmony in much the same language as I wrote after hearing it in Vienna, 1866. Ex.: "The melodic phrase of the horn, in 'Dona nobis pacem,' Allegro, at the Ancient Concert last night, haunts me—how lovely, simple, and impressive it is, and also the varied harmony into which it leads." That most elegant writer and admirable critic, Holmes, in Novello's edition of this Mass, says truly, "How delighted is the musician, when, after the phrase of symphony by horns and bassoons, in which he naturally looks on the last E as the third of C, to find it taken up by the second violin, and prepared as a discord of suspension in B" (*vide* p. 368, the entire section quoted, with its return to the tonic harmony). If aught would convert me to the Roman Catholic religion, it would be such music as Beethoven's Mass in C. I never listen to such divine inspirations of this great master without recalling to my mind the memorable words of his revelations to the niece of the poet Wieland:—"I have no friend; I must needs live alone by myself; but I well know that God is nearer to me in my art than others; I commune with Him without fear; evermore have I acknowledged and understood Him; and I am not fearful concerning my music; no evil fate can befall it; and He to whom it is intelligible must become free from all the paltriness that others drag about them."

DONA NOBIS PACEM.

Mass in C.—Beethoven.

THE WINTER RIDING-SCHOOL MUSICAL FESTIVAL.

No city contains more convenient and better proportioned rooms for music than Vienna. In the above spacious building I once heard the following selection of music with a band and chorus of some 1200 amateurs and artists:—

PART I.

1. Overture (*Zauberflöte*)..*Mozart.*
2. Vocal Chorus, "Danklied zu Gott, Von Gellert"......*Haydn*
3. Chorus (*Misericordias Domini*)............................*Mozart.*
4. Air, Basso (*Creation*)..*Haydn.*
5. March and Chorus, from the *Ruins of Athens*......*Beethoven.*

PART II.

Oratorio (*Mount of Olives*) ....*Beethoven.*

Vocalists, Madame BARTH, MM. ERLE, and STAUDIGL.
Conductor, NICOLAI.

The accuracy with which the sixty first and sixty second violins led and steadily sustained the fugal theme of the "Zauberflöte" overture, I could not have believed, had I not *twice* witnessed its accomplishment. This overture and a chorus in the "Mount of Olives" were enthusiastically encored by the 2000 comfortably-seated auditors—veritable *connoisseurs.* The emphatic delivery of the words "*Hier ist er. Ergreif und bindet ihn*" (Here he is; seize and bind him), in Beethoven's "Mount of Olives," produced a thrilling sensation, and a thousand stentorian voices shouted, "*Bis! Bis! noch einmal.*" The principal singers, band, chorus, and conductors gave their services gratuitously at this festival, the proceeds of which were in aid of the National Conservatoire of Music. The Imperial Court was present, and the *tout ensemble* of the performance greatly surpassed that of any *monstre* festival I have ever heard. In the same building, November 1866, I attended a choral concert of 1000 voices, with the aid of two superb military bands. This performance, under the direction of Herbeck, was given for the wounded of the late disastrous war with Prussia.

THE GRAND REDOUTEN-SAAL.

THIS beautiful room and its adjoining saloon for small concerts, with white and gold panels, form, with the Ritter-Schule, one angle of the Joseph-Platz. Of its length and height I have no exact information. There is a gallery at each side and at both extremities, having one front row of stalls. In the grand saloon take place the four Annual Orchestral and Choral Concerts of the Gesellschaft der Musikfreunde—Vienna Society—founded in 1814 by Herr Joseph Sonneleithner, friend of Beethoven, and now directed by Herbeck. On the ground-floor are 920 chairs; in the gallery 150 stalls; and standing-room for 1000—altogether, accommodation for 2070. The great orchestra occupies one-third of the room. With this Redouten-Saal are associated the most intense emotions of orchestral and choral classical music I ever experienced. The stalls cost about 5s.; the standing places 2s.

The following choice programme, on Sunday, November 18th, 1866, at half-past twelve, was marvellously well executed:—

1. Overture (*Rosamond*) .... *Schubert.*
2. Concerto, in G, for Pianoforte.......................... *Beethoven.*
3. Old German Songs—en chœur, harmonised by HERBECK.
4. Symphony, in C minor .... *Beethoven.*

For an account of this performance, *vide* p. 212. I am glad to record the opinion of the same writer, on the admirable playing of Mdlle. Kolar. "This lady," says Mr. Kingston, "is already a great artist, and may, perhaps, one day become the first in Europe."

The father of Mdlle. Kolar, a scholar, well known in Prague, is the translator of Shakespeare's works into the Bohemian language. The above handsome Bohemian, Mdlle. Krebs from Dresden, and Mdlle. Topp from Munich, who in 1869 created a sensation in America, were the three promising pianists of the rising German school most favourably noticed by the critics. Had I not already engaged Madame Schumann for the first three *matinées* of 1867, one of the above new pianists would have been heard at the

Musical Union. I regret the more that I lost this opportunity of introducing the above young pianists, as Madame Schumann, to my great surprise, left London without playing at the Musical Union.

THE VIENNA CONSERVATOIRE.

THIS institution educates nearly five hundred students for a mere nominal fee. It contains a fine library, valuable autographs, a small collection of rare and ancient musical instruments, with accommodation for a full orchestra, and a room that accommodates about 600 persons in stalls and boxes. The course of instruction lasts six years, and twice a week the students read classical works under the direction of Hellmesberger. Here, also, are given Hellmesberger's Quartet Concerts. For concerts on a small scale, this room is let out for a very moderate sum. An artist confessed to me that the entire expense of his concert in this room, the singers and soloists giving him their gratuitous help, was under *ten pounds*. In London the printer's bill alone would almost reach this sum.

THE three great summer swimming baths are used in winter for musical and other entertainments. Sometimes the singing meetings terminate with a dance, but invariably with supper and smoking. The band of a crack Austrian regiment, on one occasion, gave a very clever " Spektakel-potpourri," in eight tableaux, played by soldiers in uniform, comprising a most efficient orchestra of sixty stringed and wind performers, under the direction of the composer—Zimmerman. The composition described the scenes of a soldier's march to war, and the supposed incidents attending the battlefield ; and the performance, which would not have disgraced the Philharmonic orchestra of London, pleased the Viennese immensely. This military band of seventy-six executants, belonging to the Duke of Würtemberg's regiment, obtained the first grand prize at the Paris Exposition, 1867. Such a band, heard in London, would produce quite a sensation.

MUSICAL CELEBRITIES IN VIENNA, 1845.

DURING no one of my rambles on the Continent did I meet with more musicians of genius and renown than in the autumn and winter of 1845 and 1846. The following list of contributors to my album within a few days of my departure from Vienna, contains a goodly array of notable professors and amateurs, most of whom were present at all the best musical entertainments I attended. An audience composed of such critical musicians must needs be difficult to please, and its favourable opinion an honour to obtain. Here I should mention that several of the autographs of the most eminent kapellmeisters consist of fugal subjects, *impromptus* jotted down on their morning visits to Diabelli's shop, where I left my album for contributions.

* Czerny, * Thalberg, * Diabelli, Halm, * Nicolai, * Sechter, Hellmesberger, * Proch, Fred. Schubert, * Berlioz, * Mayseder, * Alvars, * Dreyschock, Joachim, * Fischhof, * Assmayr, Vieuxtemps, * Felicien David, * Yanza, * Reuling, * Artaria, * Borzaga, * Haslinger, Mdlle. Müller, * Gyrowetz, * Dr. Schmidt, * Castelli, * Dr. Becher, Bibl, * Füchs, * Lickl, Chotek, Leschetizky, * Prince Çzartoryski, Princess Marcellina Czartoryska, * Baron de Lannoy, * Dr. Sonnleithner, * Ernst, Preyer, Wolf, Blahack, * Drechsler, Pirkhert.

On my last visit, 1873, stern death had shorn the above list of many of its brilliant names.

* Deceased since 1845.

THE MUSICAL SEASON IN GERMANY.

IN most capitals of Germany, as in Vienna and Paris, the operas and concerts extend over a season of six months. In Dresden, the summer season of the opera is said to be the most profitable, owing to the number of travellers passing through, and visitors to the Saxon-Switzerland, residents throughout the summer months. The *congé* of artists and the closing of the Art Institutions, both in Vienna and Paris, are in July, August, and September. Metaphorically speaking, a musical tourist of renown may gather three crops a year by his talent. From October to December, in Vienna; January to March, in Paris; and April to June, in London.

MUSICAL INSTRUCTION IN VIENNA.

UNTIL amateur musical education is pursued in England as on the Continent, with elementary instruction in harmony, and lessons of accompaniment from well-instructed violinists, the latter will always be disproportionably remunerated, compared with other branches of the profession. A foreign writer observes that "in England the pianists grasp everything, live in palaces, and ride in carriages; it is otherwise in Vienna. Lessons from a well-educated accompanist inspire confidence, instil principles of taste and expression, and, to a skilful pupil, advanced in the mechanism of the pianoforte, are of the highest importance." The result of this mode of teaching amateurs the elements of harmony, and to play with violin or violoncello professors, is very satisfactory. The best amateurs in Vienna that I heard could both *play* and *accompany*, with ease and intelligence, at sight. This mode of instruction in Vienna, as in Paris, remunerates sufficiently a superior class of refined artists, independent of orchestral occupation, and who largely contribute to the success of concerts of classical and concerted music in private houses.

LETTER TO PRINCE CONSTANTINE CZARTORYSKI.

"VIENNA, *December* 19, 1866.

"MY DEAR PRINCE,—This, my third visit to Vienna, has confirmed the impression made upon me twenty years ago, and then communicated by me to the English public—viz., that amongst other splendid attributes, this ancient city especially excels in the performance of church, choral, orchestral, and chamber music.*

* (1) Masses at the Imperial Chapel. (2) Choruses by the Vienna Liedertafel. (3) Concerts conducted by Herbeck and Dessoff. (4) Hellmesberger's unique Quartet performances.

"If, in London, we claim merit for massive performances of Handel's oratorios, we must yield the palm to Vienna for tender fidelity to the traditions of Haydn, Mozart, and Beethoven.

"In no city have I heard *chefs-d'œuvre*, in every branch of the art, more satisfactorily executed, nor met with a more intelligent and appreciative public than in Vienna.

"Her national Conservatoire of Music has furnished Europe with four eminent violinists, Ernst, Hellmesberger, Joachim, and Leopold Auer, who have occasionally contributed to the success and glory of the Musical Union, under my direction in London.

"In recognition of this kindly feeling shown towards me by the most distinguished *literati* and professors of music, during my stay in Vienna, and as a trifling token of my regard for, and appreciation of, the above admirable institution, I beg to offer it a volume of my 'Analysis of Chamber Music' and the sum of one hundred florins, to be presented to the pupil who shall obtain the first violin prize during the coming year, at the Conservatoire of Music.*

"The artistic and æsthetic experiences derived from frequent travels on the Continent compel me to admit that so long as my country is without a national school of music, a public institute, and library of music, a national opera, and that governmental support which furnishes an economic basis for

* This was gained by Aldolph Brodsky, a young Russian of very promising talent.

cheap and classical performances, such as I have alluded to in Vienna, under the direction of learned and experienced kapellmeisters, music in England will ever remain, as it now is, a *métier*. In France, it is an art; in Italy, a necessity; and in Germany, a religion.

"The solitary hiatus in Vienna's chaplet of musical excellences will be filled up when the completion of the new opera house * shall enable the imperial residence to emulate London and Paris, in the magnitude and splendour of the temple in which the lyrical muse is enshrined, and the fitness of the attributes dedicated to her service. Worshippers, in this, the seat of her glory, she will never lack; amongst them I trust may be enrolled the name of

"My dear Prince, your faithful servant,

JOHN ELLA,

Founder and Director of the Musical Union,
Hon. Mem. Phil. Acad. Rome, Author of
the 'Analysis of Chamber Music,'" &c.

* This magnificent theatre was inaugurated by the performance of "Zauberflöte," in 1869.

MUSIC IN PESTH, 1866.

THE Hungarian capital, east of the Danube, is flat and uninteresting; but the old capital, Buda, on the west, with its streets along the shore and up steep ascents, crowned with a royal palace, is extremely picturesque. Built on the side of the long range of the Styrian mountains, the effect of Buda at night, viewed from Pesth, is not unlike that of the Old Town of Edinburgh viewed from the New Town. In Buda lived the composer, Volkmann, author of numerous vocal works, sacred and secular, and classical instrumental compositions, long known to me by correspondence and a present of one of his pianoforte trios. At the top of one of the highest buildings, in a secluded spot, lived this celibataire, in a small suite of rooms commanding a lovely prospect of the Danube. He received me kindly, and excused his dwelling in "Alt" to be free from the interruption of idle visitors. In Germany and in Vienna the music of Volkmann finds admirers. At the house of a patron of the arts, I was invited to dine with this composer, his editor (who publishes all Volkmann now writes), the prima donna of the National Opera, and one or two Hungarians known to me formerly in London.

On the wall of the dining-saloon was hung a complete collection of Musical Union portraits, received from a brother in London. In the evening I heard sung various *morceaux* of a highly dramatic character, admirably written, by Volkmann. His trios, heard at Vienna on my return, aiming at novelty in design and character of movements, were interesting.

On certain nights the wild Hungarian gipsy bands of stringed instruments of eight or ten may be heard at the houses of refreshment in Pesth. No description can convey an idea of their extraordinary mode of *vamping* accompaniment, and of inventing variations to a national theme—playing from ear, totally devoid of musical instruction.

A national opera, "Bȧnk-bán," by Erkel, charmed me, and a short German opera, "Leichte Cavallerie," by F. von Suppé, with its pretty melodies, comic music, and Hungarian dances, tempted me to the theatre every night it was given. The peculiar cadence of the Hungarian melodies terminates most of the songs and dances thus:—

The managers of both operas politely sent me free admission. The orchestras were small compared with what are heard in Paris and London, but the Hungarians play with verve and true expression. Indeed, Hungary is well represented by living artists—Liszt, Stephen Heller, Joachim, and Leopold Auer; a refined type of the true musical genius of the country.

In this comparatively small capital of Hungary there are two theatres, one for national, and the other for German operas and plays; also a splendidly decorated and spacious concert-room. Orchestral and quartet concerts are given in the winter, and a Conservatoire of Music affords instruction to some two hundred students. At the grand casino or club, Englishmen are freely admitted, and treated with marked distinction. During the ten days I remained in Pesth and Buda, I never had occasion to dine at my hotel, nor was I at a loss for an evening's entertainment. Now that Hungary enjoys a free constitution, the unbounded resources of its fertile soil will be further developed, and Pesth become a flourishing city.

The picturesque costumes of both sexes in their court-dresses, and the beauty of the Hungarian ladies, are proverbial. The grateful remembrance of English hospitality to the nobles and refugees during the late war, is shown to English travellers in many acceptable ways, and to the editor and proprietor of the *Pest-Correspondenz*—M. Lichtenstein, who was many years in London previous to the Revolution of 1848—I am greatly indebted for much hospitality and many useful introductions.

MUSIC IN PRAGUE.

THE Conservatoire, under the direction of Kapellmeister Kitl, contained some clever students. A young violinist, who gained the prize of 1845, Herr Laub, afterwards made his *début* at the Musical Union in 1851, and is now *chef* in Moscow.*

On my arrival in Prague, during dinner in one of the principal hotels, a compact chamber band entered the room and played, very respectably, movements of Beethoven's Septet. Here I had the satisfaction of being presented to the venerable and learned composer, Tomascheck.

The kapellmeister received me very politely. His room was filled with young men of the best Bohemian families, who were studying harmony, several of whom addressed me in English. Tomascheck originally studied to become an advocate, and pursued music *en amateur*. After the success, however, of his "Leonora," a cantata of Bürger, the Count of Bucquoy, a noble patron of the arts in Prague, persuaded Tomascheck to renounce the bar, and appointed him musical director of his private chapel. From this time to the year of his death, besides numerous MS.

* This admirable violinist died 1876.

works, he published, of vocal and instrumental, sacred and secular compositions, not fewer than seventy works. Among the pupils who studied under Tomascheck, may be cited the following known pianists and composers: — Wurfel, Dreyschock, Schulhoff, Kuhe, Tedesco, and Boklet. He died at Prague, the 3d of April 1850, at the age of seventy-six.

MUSIC IN DRESDEN, LEIPSIC, AND BERLIN.

At Dresden the appointments for the opera and chapel are on the most liberal scale, and the kapellmeisters well remunerated, partly from the King's privy purse. In 1846, Reissiger confirmed what I had heard about the alleged "Weber's last Waltz" being his own composition. He died in 1859, and was succeeded by Rietz from Leipzic.* In no part of Germany are operas, comedies, and tragedies better given than at Dresden. In 1866 I heard "Les deux Journées" admirably performed, and some good quartet playing with Lauterbach and Grützmacher of the party.

At Leipzic there is a good Conservatoire, and now (1868) is opened a new and commodious theatre for operas. The twenty annual concerts, at the Gewandhaus, under the direction of Reinecke, with an excellent orchestra led by David,† have long been renowned for the variety and excellence of the works performed, and the executive talent engaged.

* Rietz, born at Berlin, 1812, has published some forty works—vocal and instrumental.

† Both David and Rietz are now (1877) deceased.

In 1846, at a friendly repast given by David, I met Dr. and Madame Schumann, Moscheles, Gadé (now at Copenhagen), and Mendelssohn.

In Berlin is one of the most beautiful opera houses in Europe. Here, as in Munich and Dresden, operas, orchestral and chamber concerts are well given, and the prices of admission are moderate.*

For an account of popular music in Berlin, *vide* page 150.

* In Munich, 1873, on my way to the Vienna Exhibition, I witnessed an admirable performance of Meyerbeer's "Prophetè." The pit stalls cost about *three shillings*.

MUSIC IN PARIS, 1866-67.

"I beg you will not think that I am one of those German youths with long hair, lounging listlessly, and pronouncing the French superficial and Paris frivolous."—MENDELSSOHN.

THE transition from Italy to France—from the dear and uncomfortable hotels of Florence to the grand hotels of Marseilles—is not more striking than a journey of ten hours from London to "Paris moderne," with its centralised government, cleanliness, sober people, good restaurants and cafés, and personal security at night!

On calling for my letters at Erard's, I found an invitation to the *Muette*, any Thursday or Sunday during my stay in Paris.

LA CHATEAU DE LA MUETTE—PASSY.

THE history of this property is most interesting and little known. The "Paris Guide" states that—

"Louis XIV. issued hence the *Edit de la Muette*, and formerly *La Muette* was merely a hunting-meet, embellished in the eighteenth century. The original structure now lies buried, as it were, under modern additions. The park is still very fine, and the ground alone is worth at this time three or four million francs."

The latter sum has been refused by the present owner, widow of Pierre, nephew and heir of the founder of the house of Erard. In this chateau, on her arrival at Paris, resided the beautiful and unfortunate Marie Antoinette. Crowds daily assembled from Paris to catch a glimpse, through the *grille*, of the stately figure of this betrothed of the Dauphin of France, during her promenades in the long, picturesque alleys of the enclosure. One more eager and curious than the rest was a youth, bright and intelligent in features, and, to all appearance, a mechanic. His name was Erard; at that time he was poor, and struggling against the opposition of the Luthiers in Paris, who were jealous of the success of his clever inventions. Happily, this Strasbourg engineer obtained, shortly after the marriage of Marie Antoinette, a patent from the King for his inventions and improvements of the pianoforte and organ; the latter also signalised by the flattering description given of it in 1797, by Grétry. The Queen, fond of music, engaged Erard to furnish her with his improved pianos and harps, and this protection crowned the efforts of the persecuted inventor with success. The Revolution, alas! which brought Marie Antoinette to the scaffold, threatened also to ruin Erard. Singular to relate, amidst the vicissitudes of events, and changes of fortune, the princely chateau of La Muette and its extensive grounds ultimately became the property of the once struggling mechanic, since which time it has remained in the family of Erard. On Thursdays, during the autumn and spring, may be seen wandering amidst the flowers and statues, where Marie Antoinette was first admired and gazed at by the founder of the firm, visitors from Paris with their families. On Sundays at dinner and weekly receptions, within the last two years, I have seen Rossini, Auber, Berlioz, Costa, Gounod, F. David, Balfe, D'Ortigue, Thalberg, Panofka, Gustave Bertrand, Planté, Massart, Vivier, Kästner, Godfroid, Lubeck, with Jules Janin and the *élite* of Parisian intellect; poets, painters, sculptors, statesmen, nobles, and musicians. The pleasure of associating with such a gathering of artistic minds is totally unknown on this side of the Channel. On such an occasion an artist feels proud of his intercourse with congenial natures, eminent in their several walks of life, and for the most part distinguished by some external order that secures him the homage or respect due to his genius.

It may here be mentioned that the widow of the great Italian composer, Spontini, sister of the late Pierre Erard, resides with the present owner, and gives additional zest to the discussions at table by her brilliant imagination and good sense. I am sure that I echo the sentiments of a very numerous circle of friends in wishing long life to Mdme. Erard, who dispenses her fortune so nobly, and dignifies the position she inherits so very becomingly.

The recent death of Rossini (November 13th, 1868) deprives Passy of one of its greatest musical attractions. In the immediate vicinity of La Muette the illustrious maestro resided in his villa during the summer months, and had weekly receptions of artists and literary celebrities. In this villa he died. Hence Passy will ever be historically associated with the names of Marie Antoinette and Giaccomo Rossini—names sacred to posterity.

THE CONSERVATOIRE.

THE success of the Paris Conservatoire is the result of its direction by men of genius and intelligence from all parts of Europe; and the excellent books of instruction in every branch of musical education attest the wisdom of the directing minds in appointing the right men to the right place. The Institution has been recently improved, and the number of pupils of both sexes, amounting to some hundreds, is now greatly augmented by the admission of military musicians for education as band-masters.

At the distribution of 259 prizes, in August 1868, the President, Marshal Vaillant, minister of the fine arts, in the course of an eloquent address, spoke as follows:—

"Le talent ne s'improvise pas, et le génie lui-même, ce don divin, a besoin d'être développé et soutenu par un profond savoir. Aussi, un écrivain philosophe a-t-il osé dire: *Le génie n'est qu'une longue patience.* La longue patience n'est pas trop une qualité de notre époque, jeunes élèves: méfiez vous des entrainements, et résistez de toutes vos forces à ce besoin d'arriver vite que chacun semble éprouver aujourd'hui. Si vous voulez aller jusqu'au bout, ne cherchez pas trop à abréger la route; on s'égare souvent en prenant les chemins de traverse; marchez donc bravement au but lointain, sans vous en laisser détourner par de vaines chimères ou par des tentations décevantes. Que la science garde sa vapeur! Pour les arts comme pour les lettres, *le temps ne fait rien à l'affaire;* ce n'est pas en hâtant outre mesure, ce n'est pas en employant pour simplifier leur travail des moyens expéditifs et des procédés empiriques que les maîtres ont appris à composer ces *chefs-d'œuvre* qui seront toujours vos premiers modèles—Gluck et Mozart, Beethoven et Rameau, Haydn et Méhul, Cherubini et Meyerbeer, tant d'autres, que je n'oublie pas et dont les noms sont sur vos lèvres, protesteraient en faveur des grandes études et des grandes traditions dont le Conservatoire est le gardien vigilant et jaloux."

Such sentiments inspire one with admiration for the government, and I repeat that, in France, music is an art, thoroughly well cultivated, encouraged, and rewarded.

MUSICAL EDUCATION IN PARIS.

"A statue lies hid in a block of marble, and what sculpture is to a block of marble, education is to the human soul."

FREQUENT travels abroad, attending religious musical services, and visiting public places of entertainment, have confirmed an oft-expressed doubt as to the alleged innate feeling and taste for music attributed by certain writers, as peculiar to any one country in particular. The land of song—Italy—has nothing to recommend it to admiration, in natural talent for singing, among the untutored people; and in more than one instance, in Germany, I have heard a very numerous congregation persistently sing, throughout an entire service, shockingly out of tune, with the accompaniment of a loud organ. On one occasion, I was accompanied by Piatti and two other Italian artists, who were painfully surprised. Yet, by a village choir of *educated* young men and women, we heard some of Mendelssohn's and Schubert's secular vocal quartets well sung, and in tune, in our hotel at Rudersheim, on the Rhine.

Whether a nation is musical, military, commercial, or nautical, depends on the force of circumstances, habit, and education.

In whatever degree France claims to be musical, says a great authority, she owes it to her noble institutions, which, to her credit, have survived in their usefulness the political convulsions of that country during half a century. England, with just pride, boasts of the spirit and enterprise of her people in accomplishing great and useful works without the aid of government, but she has *as yet* no Louvre, no Conservatoire, no National Opera, no institute of learning and fine arts. Even Russia and Switzerland have now a National Academy of Music.

If the French nation is not the most musical of all European nations, she ought to be. Paris has her Conservatoire educating six hundred students, a school of religious music, Orpheon schools for choral singing, and the school of Galin-Paris-Chevé, to teach large masses of the people to decipher music by figures. Marseilles, Toulouse, Lille, Nantes, Strasbourg, Metz, Dijon, Valenciennes, Colmar, Cambrai, and Bordeaux have each a staff of professors, and a complete classification of sections for vocal and instrumental instruction, *gratis*.—1867.

LIBRARY—INSTITUTE—MUSEUM.

In addition to the advantages in Paris of a first-rate education, *gratis*, students and musicians have free access to a magnificent library at the Conservatoire, consisting of several thousands of volumes. Here may be seen private soldiers of the military bands consulting and perusing instruction-books, and full scores of lyrical works, valuable tomes, which are found in no library, public or private, in England—much to our shame. In addition to this splendid library, is another, available on application, at the French Institute. These collections, however, are not so extensive and complete as those in Vienna and Berlin, the latter containing more than thirty thousand volumes of music and musical literature, ancient and modern.

A museum of ancient musical instruments, consisting of some two thousand varieties, is now located in a suitable building at the Conservatoire bequeathed to the Institution by the late M. Clapisson. This curious and valuable collection was once offered to the British Museum.

There is some hope of the late Prince Consort's plan of a public institute and musical library being formed in junction with the Schools of Art at South Kensington.—1869.

ARTISTIC LIFE IN PARIS.

THE cordial welcome which awaits every musician of genius and talent in Paris; the speedy recognition and generous appreciation of his merits by critics of known practical talent and *moral influence of character*, and the social position which is at once secured to him, as in Italy and Germany, are patent to every person accustomed to musical life in that fascinating city. In spite of professional rivalry in Paris, as elsewhere, be he Italian (Rossini), German (Meyerbeer), Belgian (Fétis), or Russian (Rubinstein), the creative, theoretical, and practical musician commands both respect and admiration. Hence Paris, with its immediate vicinity, numbers among her residents artists of celebrity and veteran musicians from all parts of Europe.

However lightly the ribbons and stars of the French Order of the Legion d'Honneur are regarded in England, they form a distinction coveted by both military and civilian; and no man of genius resides long in Paris without being recognised and wearing this national tribute.

"It is not for the mere price of the ribbon or metal that we are to estimate those badges of distinction," said Lord Palmerston, in awarding prizes to his tenantry, "but as the symbols of glory, virtue, and merit." Next to the Prussian Order of Merit, limited to fifty recipients (three only to musicians), the French Institute confers the distinction most valued in Europe by artists and men of science. The Royal Academician painter in England who enjoys the distinction of the initials R.A. would in France be invested with the insignia of Chevalier, and receive the same military salute, on State occasions, as an English C.B. in uniform. This calls to mind the following anecdote, at the Exposition in 1855. The late Roberts, R.A., in company of an eminent painter, was startled on entering the institute at a grand reception, by the salute of the sentinels, and inquired of his companion what it meant; the latter silently pointed to the star in his buttonhole! "*Anch' io son pittore!*" muttered the Anglo R.A. "And for the first time in my life," said Roberts on telling me this, "I felt very proud of being a painter."

In England, distinction is often conferred alike on men of brains and genius, and successful adventurers without either. It were desirable, and I am told it was contemplated by the Prince Consort, to suggest some other symbol of glory, virtue, and merit than the Order of Knighthood, for men distinguished in literature, art, and science.

At the dinner-table of Baugniet, the Belgian painter, last winter, I observed three painters and sculptors of renown wearing the grand cross, and these orders gave them precedence, very justly, before all others of a less rank in decoration.

CONCERTS AT THE CONSERVATOIRE.

"The musicians are all amazement at the honours conferred on me by the Conservatoire. Two days ago my Overture to the "Midsummer Night's Dream" was given for the first time. It caused me great pleasure, for it went admirably, and seemed also to please the audience." Paris, February 21st, 1832.—MENDELSSOHN.

THE symphonies of Haydn, Mozart, and Beethoven (No. 1) were played in Paris so far back as 1805, but no organised society existed in the French capital for the especial performance of first-class orchestral music until 1828. At this period was formed an association of eminent performers under the direction of the late Habeneck.

This "Concert Society," with its unique band of seventy-six performers, on two successive Sundays, now (1868) gives the same programme to different sets of subscribers—1500 at each, in the Conservatoire Theatre. This innovation was adopted last year to meet the wishes of persons unable to procure subscriptions to the original series of seven secular and one sacred concert. The theatre is always crowded, and stalls difficult to procure at ten francs each. The unity of style, equality of *timbre* among the wood, and homogeneity of tone in the brass instruments, give to these performances a charm that cannot escape the admiration of every connoisseur. Thrice have I visited all the best concerts in Germany; and, after twenty-seven years' experience in the best bands of London, I am bound to award the palm to the Conservatoire orchestra.

As members of the Paris Association are engaged in the band, the executants have an individual interest in the success of the concerts, sharing the proceeds at the end of the season. *Esprit de corps* incites them to do justice to the music, and to sustain the glory of the Institution, thereby securing to the *chef* any amount of study and practice. The performance of Beethoven's choral symphony, in 1834, so impressively grand and surpassingly beautiful, was the result of rehearsals extending over several months. It was not until the year 1852 that this complicated work was either understood or effectively executed in London, under the *bâton* of Berlioz, at the New Philharmonic Concerts, after three patient rehearsals by a magnificent band and choir. Of the noble sentiment which animates the Paris Association, and the absence of that jealousy which, in London, so frequently declares itself as to rank, place, and position in an orchestra, one instance has been communicated to me worthy of record. After the death of the principal second violinist, Habeneck, at rehearsal, addressed the *élite* of the first violinists as follows : " *Mes enfans*, you see that a most important place is vacant; who among you will do me the honour of being my second ?" Instantly Alard, the best violinist in France, and pupil of the venerable *chef*, rushed across the orchestra to the vacant desk, amidst the cheers of the whole of the band. He has lately retired. The band is composed entirely of native musicians; and the practical results of a systematic education in the Conservatoire are most striking in the unity of style, taste, and the expression of the performers. To a sensitive artist, the playing of a rhythmical accent with an *up-bow* is both unsightly and unnatural, betraying carelessness, or, what is worse, a defective musical organisation. As said by Lablache of the performances of the famed contrabassist, Dragonetti, " it is a double sensation to watch the bowing, and feel its realisation;" and nothing can exceed the fine effects of the uniformity of bowing in this splendid band. Although the present conductor, Hainl, lacks the spirit and decision of the great Habeneck, the band has lost none of its wonted excellence in the unity of style and details of *nuances*, and other qualities which no other band in Europe possesses. The choir which occasionally assists at these concerts, consisting chiefly of pupils of the Institution, is placed in *front* of the band; and their singing of Mozart's "Ave Verum," with orchestral accompaniment, I always remember as the most delicate, expressive, and perfect rendering of this divine inspiration I ever heard. In short, whatever is here attempted must be well done, to satisfy the crowded audience of amateurs, connoisseurs, students, and professors from all parts of Europe, who attend these unique concerts, among whom I have never failed to see Gounod and the hale octogenarian, Auber. The concerts begin at two and end at four P.M.

PASDELOUP'S ORCHESTRAL CONCERTS.

THESE popular concerts sprang out of an attempt to establish performances of new compositions, and the production of new talent, by an association of young and meritorious artists, under the direction of Pasdeloup. This society, however, failed to excite much sympathy in the public, and in the year 1861 Monsieur Pasdeloup wisely consulted his own interests by supplying a want long felt in Paris by a very numerous class of *dilettanti* unable to have access to the *recherché* concerts at the Conservatoire, and the attractions of works by the great German masters soon proved more remunerative than the trial of compositions by aspirants to fame.

The programme, says Baillot, "C'est le rayon qui vient éclairer la scène;" and at the same time, the index of the public taste. Nothing has more astonished me of late years than the thousands attentively listening to, and enthusiastically applauding, the varied classical orchestral music performed at the Sunday afternoon concerts of Pasdeloup, in the Cirque Napoléon. Annually, from October to April, take place twenty-four concerts. The band, numbering a hundred executants, is vastly improved in its wind instrumental executants, and only second to that of the Conservatoire. Amongst a large and mixed public of 4500 persons, paying from 4s. 2d. to 7½d. for admission, Haydn, Mozart, Beethoven, Mendelssohn, Lachner, Schumann, and Wagner have each their admirers. The enthusiasm, however, displayed after the performance of Wagner's music, convinced me that there is a strong German element at these concerts. The prelude to the "Lohengrin" was rapturously *encored* at one concert; and at another, the overture to "Tanhauser" received three distinct rounds of applause, and a call for Pasdeloup. I must admit that these two difficult pieces were very effectively played, and afforded me more satisfaction than when I last heard them in Berlin and Vienna—the twenty double-basses (of four strings), twelve violoncellos, fourteen violas, and forty violins, and a perfect *corps* of wind instrumentalists well balanced, after several rehearsals, produced these results.

As music is incapable of expressing vice when unwedded to poetry, I hope no one will be shocked if I express a preference to hearing occasionally, after a morning religious service, two hours of sublime instrumental music, to seeing monkeys and hippopotami at the Zoological Gardens.

Another orchestral society is established, consisting of 100 musicians, directed by M. Colonne; the concerts take place at the Chatelet Theatre, also on Sunday afternoons. I have recently heard some splendid performances at these concerts.—1877.

"It was the greatest possible delight to me to hear my Quartet in E♭ performed by Baillot's Quartet party; and they executed it with fire and spirit." Paris, December 20, 1851.—MENDELSSOHN.

THIS branch of the art has always been cultivated by professional association in Paris. In 1827 I heard Beethoven's chamber music played by Vidal and party so soon as the complete edition came from the press of Schlesinger, the publisher. At this period the famed quartet party of Baillot was the rendezvous of all true disciples of the classical art; and more than once has this most intellectual violinist numbered, among his auditors and greatest admirers, Paganini and Mendelssohn. Three organised parties are now supported in Paris by subscription, and conducted on the principle of the Musical Union as to the number and character of the pieces performed. The longest established (with Alard, first violin) enjoys the greatest patronage, and its selections are chiefly from the works of Haydn, Mozart, and Beethoven. The second party, with Maurin, first violin, plays chiefly the posthumous quartets of Beethoven. The time, patience, and trouble which these artists devote to get up their pieces, is evident from the perfection of the *ensemble.* The third society, with Armigaud, first violin, and Jacquard, violoncellist, leans rather to Weber and Mendelssohn's music.

LE QUATUOR.

CARACTERE DES DIVERS INSTRUMENS DE MUSIQUE.

. . . .

"Sous un sceptre nouveau tenant république
Se bornant à toucher pour toute politique,
Paraît *le violon :* ce roi, ce soldat heureux,
Père de ses sujets, ami des malheureux,
Commande, obéissant aux passions qu'il exprime,
Sa voix, soumise ainsi, sa voix devient sublime ;
S'il persuade et désarme ou subjugue en vainqueur,
C'est qu'il a su trouver le chemin du cœur !
Quand le modeste *alto* joint sa voix à la sienne
Pour qu'en un quatuor l'intérêt se soutienne,
Le violoncelle Basse, à ce concert admis,
Devient régulateur de ce groupe d'amis,
Et mêlant ses accens à ceux qu'il favorise,
Sa grave mélodie avec eux fraternise."—BAILLOT.

THE poetical description by Baillot of the four players in a quartet expresses the feelings of an artist acquainted with the *chefs-d'œuvre* of the modern German composers. In some music of Handel, and the early quartets of Haydn, the viola was frequently either in unison with the violoncello, or had but a very insignificant share in the melodic counterpoint of the score, and was commonly played by inferior artists. In modern instrumentation, the case is very different; not only does the viola sustain an equal share in the performance, but the violoncello, which formerly enjoyed the companionship of the double-bass, playing *the same part* an octave below, is now carefully separated. The effects of instrumentation that so captivate modern ears, by this studious employment of each instrument in its peculiar sphere, were quite unknown in the eighteenth century.

THE ITALIAN OPERA. (1700 *SEATS.*)

THE Ventadour theatre, in size and musical appointments about one-third less than the Royal Italian Opera, Covent Garden, is attended by a very critical audience, the *élite* of society, including the Russian, Spanish, and English families, residing in Paris during the winter. The season begins in October and ends in March, and the operas produced, being of Italian origin, with the exception of Flotow's "Marta," this theatre enjoys the rare distinction of preserving its speciality.

IMPERIAL GRAND OPERA. (1811 *SEATS.*)

THIS splendid theatre is supplied in every department with singers, instrumentalists, dancers, and scene-painters chiefly from the schools of the national institutions. The adaptation of German and Italian operas, sung by the foreign artists, has greatly destroyed the *prestige* and nationality of this grand

French lyrical theatre. The orchestra is magnificent; the chorus most efficient; the *mise en scène* superb; and the costumes, down to the meanest individual, classically correct. Unhappily, the scarcity of great vocalists is seriously felt at this theatre, as elsewhere, at the present time; but the combination of a Grisi, Rubini, Tamburini, and Lablache was no less remarkable at the Italian theatre than a Falcon, Cinti, Duprez, and Levasseur, in the halcyon days of the French opera. The ballet, the national pride of the French, is still seen to perfection; and the dance music and *chœurs dansants* in the operas consist of some most exquisite compositions. The subvention to this national opera enables the direction to admit the public (men only) to the pit for about five shillings a ticket. The style in which "Robert," "Les Huguenots," "Le Prophète," "La Muette," "Moïse," "Siege de Corinth," "Guillaume Tell, "L'Africaine," were first represented—the perfection of details in musical execution—I always remember as the most impressively grand representations of these *chefs-d'œuvre* I have ever witnessed. "Hamlet," by A. Thomas, was produced this year (1868), and "Faust," by Gounod, is in preparation. In both these operas Mdlle. Nilsson sustains the principal *rôle*. This lady, Mdlle. Hisson, and Madame Carvalho, are valuable accessions, with Faure, to this theatre. The new grand opera house, a splendid monument of architectural beauty, is now nightly crowded, and is said to produce a monthly surplus of £4000.—1877.

OPERA COMIQUE. (1800 *SEATS.*)

THIS favourite lyrical theatre enjoys a subvention of £4000 from government. Here is witnessed the true type of French dramatic genius in music, singing, and acting; nor do I recollect ever quitting this theatre without having been pleased with the good taste and intelligence of the vocalists and the general execution of the music. "Joseph," "Fra Diavolo," "Le Postillon," "Zampa," *chefs-d'œuvre* of Mehul, Auber, Adam, and Herold, and works of the most varied character, have been given here with perfection. The band is most excellent, the chorus strong and efficient, the *mise en scène* good, and the union of action with singing leaves nothing to desire.

THEATRE LYRIANE. (1600 *SEATS.*)

AT this new and beautiful theatre are produced works by native and foreign composers, with a subvention of £4000 from government. The band and chorus are weak compared with the appointments at the Opera Comique; but it is highly creditable to the director of this third French opera house to produce with good *ensemble* the *chefs-d'œuvre* of Gluck, Mozart, and Weber, in addition to the new works of Gounod.

This theatre is now (1868) leased by Pasdeloup. It is to be hoped that he will be more fortunate than his predecessor. The last opera I heard here was "Romeo and Juliet" by Gounod, admirably sung and acted. My stall cost five shillings. In London, at the Royal Italian Opera, to hear this same opera, my stall cost thirty shillings. What a boon to English amateurs if they could enjoy good national operas at the price paid in Paris, Berlin, Munich, and Vienna! Since the liberty granted to theatres at Paris, in 1866, other theatres give operas, and operettas. Some, not without merits, revivals and novelties.

THEATRE LES BOUFFES. (700 *SEATS.*)

A NEW species of comic opera is given here, the music of which, composed by Offenbach, is much preferable to the general character of the *spectacle.* Offenbach, a German musician, personally known to me in London, 1844, as an excellent violoncellist,* has produced several very successful operettas. Considering the population in Paris, a third less than that of London, this city is well supplied with lyrical entertainments.

* It is said that the rights of authorship and sale of his works the last year realised him upwards of £8000.

MISCELLANEOUS PUBLIC CONCERTS.

DURING the first six months of 1865 were given in Paris 408 concerts. In January, 52; February, 62; March, 90; April, 101; May, 56; June, 47.

Benefit concerts are numerous during a Paris season; but in every case the *bénéficiaire* is the principal performer. Not so in London, where a name is often put up for a certain consideration, and the programme made up of sacred, secular, classical, and frivolous music, in the performance of which the supposed *bénéficiaire* takes but little interest. In Paris, as in London, it is therefore quite evident that the true interests of art are best promoted in the success of societies organised for the performance of a specific branch of music, addressed to the amateurs of cultivated taste, and conducted on sound principles.

POPULAR MUSIC IN PARIS.

A MONSTER gathering of seven thousand pupils of the National Schools for popular vocal instruction was assembled in 1855 in the Palais d'Industrie; and I have heard, in the same locality, performances of military bands by more than one thousand wind instrumentalists. It has been said that there would be no difficulty in combining vocalists and instrumentalists to the number of ten thousand without going beyond the barriers of Paris. For popular, promenade, café, and outdoor concerts, directed by Arban, Strauss, and others, the number of musicians and singers employed nightly exceeds all belief. Add to this the lyrical establishments with their capital bands and chorus, employing, at least, five hundred efficient musicians, and the military bands belonging to the soldiers in garrison, and a stranger may thus form an idea of the musical resources of Paris. In all the cheap places of musical entertainment there is no obstreperous interruption by people resolutely demanding some frivolous, vulgar song, as witnessed in London. Everywhere there is good taste displayed by the solo players and vocalists, and the utmost decorum prevails among the audience.

The attempt, in 1855, to establish in Paris the Christy Minstrels, signally failed. The Parisians could not appreciate the drollery of white men with blackened faces, singing songs with accompaniment of bones and banjo. In Vienna, as in Paris, I have visited every variety of musical entertainment, and I am inclined to award the palm to the French, for the excellence of their cheap *vocal* and instrumental concerts. At the El Dorado this year, I heard a lady sing perfectly in tune and in good style the *Valse* from Gounod's "Romeo et Juliette."

THE ARISTOCRATIC DILETTANTI OF PARIS.

THE resident cosmopolitan society in Paris includes many accomplished amateurs of the fine arts. Among names most familiar to musicians are those of Chopin's best disciple, the Princess Marcellina Czartoryska, the late Prince Poniatowski, Prince Edward Polegnac, &c.

PRIVATE CONCERTS AND MUSICAL RECEPTIONS.

AT the official residences of ministers and mansions of the opulent dilettanti, the best instrumentalists share equal favour with the fashionable vocalists, and at the Chateau de la Muette, Passy, Madame Erard gives, to the *élite* of Paris, evening concerts of vocal and instrumental music, at which are engaged the most eminent artists. These engagements in private and lessons of accompaniment are sufficiently remunerative to keep first-class violonists and violoncellists independent of orchestral employment. The passion for classical chamber music is spreading both in Paris and the provinces. The custom of musicians, painters, sculptors, and *literati* having fixed days and evenings to receive their friends, greatly contributes to the enjoyment of Paris artistic life.

At these receptions a vast quantity of pleasant music is heard, and well played too, especially at the dwellings of musicians. The greater number and variety of these social gatherings, where the sister arts seem to thrive hand in hand, gives to Paris a preference over even Vienna! Indeed, I have come in contact with more thoroughly well-educated painters, sculptors, musicians, and notable men in other professions in one winter in Paris than I have known in London during a residence of forty years, and, although I am proud of being born and bred a British subject, I much prefer a residence in Paris to the plodding routine of a musician's life in London after the season, when, as Berlioz wittily observes, "*si vous cherchez à boire une coupe de pure harmonie; impossible!*"

FRENCH LITERATURE AND CRITICS.

ANOTHER striking proof of the popularity of music in France is the number of literary periodicals exclusively devoted to the interests of the art. In Paris alone there are eighteen published weekly. The oldest established are "Le Menestrel" (1833), "Revue et Gazette Musicale" (1834), and "La France Musicale" (1837.) In several of the daily journals and "La Revue des Deux Mondes" are criticisms upon music from the pen of experienced musicians of renown, scholars thoroughly honest in their opinions.

*MUSICAL STATISTICS IN PARIS.**

ENGLISH people in general, and musicians in particular, do not credit the French for their increased love and encouragement of high art in orchestral music. Orchestral concerts, supported by subscription, are *three* times more numerous in Paris than in London. The average attendance at each of the twenty-four concerts of Pasdeloup, and the sixteen given at the Conservatoire, together, is 6100. At each of the eight philharmonic concerts in London, and Dr. Wylde's five concerts together, there are about 1500. There are several orchestral benefit concerts during the season, and masses performed with full orchestras in churches.

In Paris there is now a party willing to give ear to the works of Lachner, Schumann, Raff, Saint-Saëns, and Wagner. I should be very sorry not to have heard the music of these modern composers. Generally, both in Vienna and Paris, I found *applause* relative to the merits of each composition.

What was said by Reynolds about the popularity of the lower grades of painting, applies to music. A concert of popular ballads in England is more attractive than a programme of the noblest productions of the greatest masters.

* For more details of music in Paris, *vide* "Records," 1859, 1865, and 1867.

MUSIC IN LONDON.

THE FINE ARTS.

"Les beaux arts, en Angleterre, ne consistent pue des choses visibles."—FLORENTINI, 1851.

"The great multitude and hurry of business and employments divert every one from the contemplation of these objects—a contemplation suited to those only who have leisure and tranquillity of mind."—PLINY.

MUSIC, dancing, poetry, architecture, sculpture, and painting originated in the service of religion. The earliest canticle recorded in holy writ was sung after the passage of the Red Sea by Moses and the children of Israel, accompanied by Miriam and dancing women; temples were afterwards erected for worship, adorned with images and embellished with colour. M. Noverre hypothetically suggests that the circumstance of Miriam and the women dancing together implies a previous exercise of the art, and gives dancing a claim to greater antiquity than music. Whatever claim music may have for its antiquity, of all the arts it has been the slowest in its progress. The problems of climate and temperament, of a particular country and people, exercising the greatest influence on art genius, are yet to be solved. L'Abbé du Bos says, "It has been in all times observed that the influence of climate is stronger than that of origin and blood." Mr. Disraeli is of a different opinion, and attributes to Jewish descent the hereditary faculty of musical genius. In the executive art of music, the educated Jews of Germany have greatly excelled; but as for the creative genius, we have the words of Mendelssohn himself when in the sunny south—"Inspiration is peculiar to no country, but 'floats in the air.'" As to the influence of climate, we know that Handel, Gluck, Cherubini, Spontoni, Bellini, Donizetti, Costa, and Rossini produced their greatest works not in the country of their birth.

Whether the climate is now what it was when England was invaded by Julius Cæsar, I leave others to decide, but that different races inhabited this country, at different periods, history affords us most satisfactory evidence. Cicero says, "The ugliest and stupidest slaves come from Britain," and urges his friend Atticus "not to buy slaves from Britain on account of their stupidity and *inaptitude to learn music* and other accomplishments." *

During the Saxon occupation of Britain, we have a very different account of British slaves from that quoted of Cicero. Some Saxon youths being exposed in the Roman market for sale, Pope Gregory I. (the Great), then in a private station, being struck with the beauty of their fair complexions, inquired of the merchants whence they had brought them; being told they were *Angles*, he replied that they ought more properly to be called *Angels*. Inquiring

* "Anthropological Review," July 1868.

further concerning the name of their province, he was informed that it was Deira. "Deira, truly," said he, "they are *De irâ* withdrawn from wrath, and called to the mercy of Christ. But what is the name of their king?" They told him it was Ælla. At length, when he became Pope, he sent Augustine,* with forty monks, to undertake the great work of converting the Saxons. "The conquest of Britain," says Gibbon, "reflects less glory on the name of Cæsar than on that of Gregory the First. Instead of six legions, Augustine, with forty monks, embarked for that distant island, and in less than two years the Pope could announce that they had baptized Ethelbert, King of Kent, with ten thousand of his Anglo-Saxons. On the tomb of St. Gregory is written,

"To English Saxons Christian faith he taught,
And a believing flock to heav'n he brought."

Twenty years after the death of St. Augustine, Edwin, son of Ælla, King of Northumbria, with his people was converted to Christianity by the Bishop Paulinus.

After the death of this prelate, subsequently Archbishop of York and Bishop of Rochester, where he died, 644, he left behind him, in his church at York, James, the deacon, a holy ecclesiastic, who was extraordinarily skilful in singing. This deacon of York, who had a great contempt for tramontane singing,

* Augustine arrived in England 597, and died Archbishop of Canterbury 605.

taught many of the church to sing according to the custom of the Romans.

Here then dates an important epoch in English church music. If we refer to the composers and church services of the Elizabethan period, we shall find secular and sacred compositions of the highest order of merit, and were it not for the baneful influence of the Puritanical spirit of after-times, who knows but England, in every branch of music, might not have taken equal rank with other countries? Barry, the celebrated English painter, deeply impressed with the opinion of Abbé du Bos, Montesquieu, and the Abbé Winckelman, who successively assigned limits to our national genius, says, "They assert that we have no imagination, no taste, no sensibility; that we are cold and indifferent to the powers of music; that our natural capacity for the fine arts amounts to very little, or nothing at all." This opinion of Winckelman, so unjust, so illiberal, Barry endeavoured to refute by the production of his own paintings, which remain a monument, at the Society of Arts, to perpetuate his memory. As to the vicissitudes of opinion among sectarians, in respect to music at places of public worship, we have melancholy evidence in history of the destruction of organs, and aversion "to antiphonal singing of verses tossed from one side to the other," in our cathedrals. In Mace's "Musick's Monument" there is a most graphic description of a large congregation singing Psalms with the accompaniment of "a full-sized, fat, plump organ" in York Cathedral. The writer tells us that during the siege by Cromwell, the Royalists, consisting of some thousand civilians and soldiers, including the best families of the county, sang fervently during the service with such overpowering effect as to transport him above all things earthly. This Mace, a gentleman of Trinity College, Cambridge, declares that he had never heard such a performance before of congregational singing. The revival of anthems and re-establishment of choirs after the Restoration soon brought back our cathedral services to their wonted excellence, and the dominant religious feeling of the English has preserved a general taste in favour of sacred music.

As beforementioned, during my early professional life, six women choristers were brought from Lancashire to lead Handel's choruses, at the King's Concerts of Ancient Music. Thanks to the exertions of Mainzer, Hullah, and other choral masters, there are now thousands of efficient choristers. At the time when Abbé du Bos insinuated that few, if any, truly great painters have been produced in England, neither Turner nor Landseer was living—men of genius, of sensibility, keen perception, and powerful imagination, both natives of this northern climate. The seventeenth century produced a musician in this country, who, had he been born in the present advanced state of the lyrical art, would have rivalled the greatest of German composers—Purcell. The stricter education of the chapel-masters of the seventeenth century, indeed, produced musicians whose church services Englishmen have a right to be proud of. Of our madrigal and glee writers I need not say much. The rapid progress, of late years, of vocal unions, and the immense sale of popular vocal concerted music, and also sacred music for both chamber and churches, at once bespeak the taste of the people. The more fascinating and intensely exciting music of the theatre and concert-room calling into requisition the additional experience of orchestral treatment and license of dramatic expression, is yet in its infancy as a national art in England. Sad results, of late years, have been witnessed in the wreck of fortunes embarked in the attempt to establish a national grand opera in London. The production of grand operas, before we have succeeded in the operetta, of native growth, must ever prove a failure in England. We want both experienced and accomplished creative and executive genius to furnish the means for composition, for singing, and for orchestral resources. These may, to a certain extent, be obtained from persons of a natural aptitude, deriving the benefit of instruction in a national academy. Our neighbours on the Continent, Russians, Norwegians, Swedes, Germans, and French, within the last half-century, though distant from the sunny south, have produced executive or creative genius in all the arts.

It is useless to discuss further the oft-provoked question of musical talent and genius being indigenous. Sir Joshua Reynolds affords us striking evidence, in his lectures, of the beneficial results of English art education in painting, and we need not travel far to see the glorious results of national schools of the fine arts in general, and music in particular. It is hard on the musical youths of England to be obliged to seek complete and superior instruction out of their native country. The course of gratuitous instruction in Paris and Vienna, the two best and most extensive academies in Europe, lasts six years. As I have repeatedly observed, such is the excellence of foreign schools, and so numerous are the students, that the surplus unemployed foreign talent will find its way to London. I have still to repeat the melancholy fact that there is not a single complete orchestra in England composed entirely of English musicians, whilst, in all those countries where a national academy is supported for gratuitous education of musicians—in France, Belgium, Germany, Austria, and Italy—there is no lack of talent to furnish any number of complete orchestras with native musicians.

FOUNDATION OF THE ROYAL ACADEMY OF MUSIC, LONDON.

WHATEVER benefit has been derived from this institution, in the interest of music and musicians of England, all credit is due to the individual exertions and influence of its noble founder, the late Earl of

Westmoreland. From among a large number of candidates, were selected twenty students of both sexes,* of promise to excel in art, and on the 24th of March, 1823, "the Academy opened its doors for their reception." Nothing could be more encouraging than the brilliant commencement of this Academy; but at the close of the fourth year of its foundation the financial report gives a deficit of £400! The committee candidly admit that "they may have perhaps exceeded the bounds of very strict prudence in giving gratuitous instruction, as well as board and lodging, to more pupils (poor, but deserving) than the state of the funds of the institution warranted. A second cause for financial dilapidation may be found in the unaccountable inconstancy of public patronage."

Until the year 1868, this Academy had been struggling for permanent existence with the slender and unreliable support of private contributions. No stronger argument need be used to justify an appeal to government for a liberal grant to support a National Institution of Music, for the church, the concert-room, the theatre, and military service, on a scale worthy of this nation.

Having been sub-professor, inspector of practice, and student in harmony, under Attwood, at this Academy, I have not been unmindful of its progress and decadence. The most active coadjutor of the founder, who, in 1825, was appointed instructor of

* Blagrove of London and Seymour of Manchester (violinists) were of this number, lately deceased.

the harp, and director of orchestra practice, was Monsieur Bochsa. At a meeting of directors, March 22d, 1827, it was resolved "that M. Bochsa's suspension from all connection with the Royal Academy of Music be confirmed and promulgated." It may reasonably be supposed that some cogent reason obliged the directors to adopt this resolution. This is soon explained. The late Mr. Ayrton, a gentleman, scholar, musician, and the critic of the *Examiner* newspaper, strenuously insisted upon the dismissal of M. Bochsa, on the ground of his having been convicted of forgery in Paris, and not being *morally* a fit person to have the direction of a public institution, under the patronage of royalty and the primate of England, for the education of youths of both sexes. The public attention being roused by this exposure, the committee had no alternative but to dismiss M. Bochsa.

This event, and subsequent unfortunate appointments, occasioning revolution in the affairs and management, by degrees alienated the friends of the institution. Both sexes lodging in the same house, and meeting at frequent practices and rehearsals, led to mutual attachments and early marriages, which gave to the Academy the *soubriquet* of "Royal Academy of *Matrimony*." Those students who were so fortunate as to have a long residence and a course of musical instruction have reason to be grateful to the founder of the Academy. Without the existence of this public institution, it is quite possible that we should never have heard of Sterndale

Bennett, the Macfarrens, Howell, Madame Dolby, and other well-educated, intelligent musicians, pupils of the Royal Academy of Music. It should here be mentioned that *Bochsa* was a successful adventurer, a clever man, and the most ready at composition I ever met with ; and in spite of much opposition, he had one of his symphonies once performed at a Philharmonic Concert. Bochsa ultimately died at Melbourne, 1856. His appointment at, and dismissal from, the Royal Academy of Music ought to impress our musical patrons with the necessity of inquiring into the *moral* as well as the professional character of foreigners in this country. I always dated the decadence of the Royal Academy of Music from this exposure by the *Examiner's* critic, and it behoves all those in the direction of public institutions to consider well the *character* of persons selected for the instruction of youths confided to their charge.

THE PEOPLE'S MUSIC.

THE attempt to establish Mechanics' Institutes throughout the country has proved a signal failure, and instead of being arenas for instruction to the illiterate mechanic, most of them have become places of popular entertainment, in which music, in some form or other, holds a large share. Abstruse theories and technical science, however clearly expounded, must ever fail to enlist the sympathies of the great mass of the lower orders who lack the commonest elements of education.

This question of national education, so embarrassing to successive governments, can no longer be overlooked, and until this vital point be settled, I have little hope of government recognising in a very enlarged sense the importance and moral advantages of encouraging throughout the country schools for instruction in the elements of music, as in Germany, and now adopted in France, with subventions to support a national academy in all the principal towns. Whether the people are fond of music or not, one thing is certain, they have no opportunity of hearing good military bands, good secular vocal music, and of cultivating a taste for any kind of orchestral works played by a complete and efficient band, as in the capitals of France, Belgium, Prussia, and Austria.

In the numerous music halls that abound in this rich and mighty metropolis, entertainments are given attended by a very mixed assembly of both sexes, at which songs are sung, occasionally of a very questionable character, and certain dances are applauded which would not be permitted by the censor of morals in the above-named countries. True, on the Continent, as in this kind of entertainment in London, the cost is defrayed out of the profits of the consumption of viands, drink, and cigars. During the last forty years I have attended these places of public resort in cities on the Continent, and I recollect no instance of the slightest breach of decorum or disturbance from drunkenness. I regret that I cannot say so much for the music halls I have visited in London. One exception must be mentioned in favour of Evan's, as conducted by its late proprietor, Mr. Green. Frequently, after a dull theatrical entertainment, I have here passed an agreeable hour, listening to a good choir of boys and men singing a choice variety of glees, part-songs, and choruses. One promising sign of the times is the increase of theatres, and the probability of good lyrical entertainments being produced that will attract some of the music-loving portion of the people who now flock to music halls with little advantage to their moral or physical improvement.

ENGLISH MUSIC AND COMPOSERS.

ANTHEMS, part-songs, polkas, waltzes, and clap-trap ditties crop up in England in great abundance, but I recollect no year so little fruitful of new works of a high character as 1868. No oratorio, no symphony, no opera from the pen of an English composer has been produced, whilst cantatas, in the absence of a national lyrical theatre, seem to engage the creative faculty of our young composers. The latter kind of lyric, the probationary exercise of candidates in Paris for the travelling pension of the Institute, is generally restricted in incidents, and offers less scope for the imagination than the operetta. Without offering any opinion on the relative merits of different English composers, I do not hesitate to say that in the various dramatic essays of Mr. Sullivan there is an individuality of character that gives promise of a brilliant future. If, however, he have no faith in the philosophy of the great German poet quoted below, and fritter away his faculty in composing, for popular favour, songs for the shops, then shall I despair of his producing a great work of general interest.

Let Mr. Sullivan take courage and follow the instincts of his poetical nature, and bear in mind that although "the arts are limited in their means, they are unlimited in their effects." In one or two excerpts lately come under my notice, there was striking evidence in his mastery of effects. He has youth on his side, and I hope he will profit, by the first chance that presents itself, of producing an opera with sufficient variety of incidents to engage his dramatic powers in music of opposite styles.

The affinity of music with other arts implies, of course, only composition: the performers being the mere actors of the drama. In censuring any and every slight deviation from the conventional design, form, and ordinary effects of combinations in musical composition, critics commit a great mistake, and the hackneyed slang of the day, "music of the future," is a very ridiculous expression. Schiller tells us that a musician is to be pitied who seeks temporary popularity. "Der Künstler ist zwar der *Sohn* seiner *Zeit*, aber schlimm für ihn, wenn er zugleich ihr Tägling oder gar ihr *Günstling* ist. Wie verwahrt er sich aber vor den Verderbnissen seiner Zeit?—Er leiste den Zeitgenossen, was sie *bedürfen*, nicht was sie *loben*."

MUSICAL INSTITUTIONS OF LONDON, 1868.

THE following list contains the titles of public institutions specially devoted to particular branches of music, with the dates of their foundation, &c.

Her Majesty's Theatre	1712	Italian Operas and Ballets
Philharmonic	1813	Orchestral and Vocal
Sacred Harmonic	1832	Oratorios (700 executants)
Musical Union	1845	Chamber Instr. Music
Royal Italian Opera	1847	Italian Operas
New Philharmonic—Dr. Wylde's	1852	Orchestral and Vocal
Leslie's Choir (100)	1854	Vocal and Orchestral
Monday Popular Concerts	1859	Chamber Instr. and Vocal
Martin's National Choral Society	1860	Oratorios (700 executants)

LONDON PHILHARMONIC SOCIETY.

OF the thirty original members none are (1877) now living. The members are now thirty-nine, and fifty associates of both sexes, who have the privilege of attending the rehearsals, and the eight public concerts, by payment of one guinea annually. The band consists of twenty-four violins, eight violas, eight violoncellos, eight contrabasses, eighteen wind instruments, and a pair of drums—in all sixty-six

Conductor, Mr. Cusins. About half the executants in the band are foreign artists, German, French, Belgian, and Italian.—1868.

The programme usually consists of five pieces in each act, viz.,—1, symphony; 2, vocal; 3, solo; 4, vocal; and 5, overture. The concerts take place on the alternate Mondays from March to July, beginning at half-past eight, and ending at eleven. These concerts are now given in St. James's Hall with a larger band and some diminution in the amount of subscription.

DR. WYLDE'S PHILHARMONIC CONCERTS.

FIVE subscription concerts take place, usually, in April, May, and June. Symphonies, overtures, and concertos, with the most costly "vocal stars" of the Italian operas, are here heard. The band, chiefly composed of members of the Royal Italian Opera orchestra (about sixty), is conducted by Henry Wylde, Mus. Doc. Oxon., and Herr W. Ganz.

The concerts take place at St. George's Hall on Wednesday evenings.

THE SACRED HARMONIC SOCIETY, EXETER HALL.

ORATORIOS are here performed by a numerous choir and band, consisting of some 700 voices and instrumentalists, under the direction of Sir M. Costa, beginning in November and ending in June.

---

*MARTIN'S CHORAL SOCIETY, EXETER HALL.**

ORATORIOS, cantatas, &c., are here given with some 700 vocalists and instrumentalists, in winter and spring, conducted by the sole proprietor, Mr. Martin.

MR. HENRY LESLIE'S CONCERTS.

CHORAL music, sacred and secular, is given during the spring season at St. James's Hall. Mr. Leslie conducts, and occasionally contributes his own compositions to the programmes.

THE CRYSTAL PALACE, SYDENHAM.

THE annual monster meetings of the Handel Festival Choir, and of the parish schools, numbering at each some four or five thousand vocalists, are interesting. These take place during the spring and summer months. During the winter and spring, the Saturday afternoon concerts are attractive. The band of the company, which performs daily miscellaneous selections, is greatly increased for these entertainments, and the programmes include a variety of orchestral and choral works, not often heard at the London subscription concerts, conducted by Herr Manns.

* This Society is now defunct.

ORIGIN OF THESE SOCIETIES.

THE origin of some of the above existing institutions is worth recording. The Sacred Harmonic Society first held its meetings for choral practice and prayer in a Dissenting chapel. The Philharmonic Society began with orchestral and chamber music. Dr. Wylde's concerts commenced at Exeter Hall, with grand orchestral and choral works under the *bâton* of Hector Berlioz. The Monday Popular Concerts, as the title indicates, began with popular songs sung by Sims Reeves, and popular pianoforte solos played by Miss Goddard (now Mrs. Davison). The Crystal Palace began with a military band of sixty performers. Leslie's choir has varied its programmes, by an admixture of sacred and secular vocal works, with an occasional solo, and other kinds of instrumental music. The Musical Union, with its programme of three classical works, played by the best procurable talent, has never swerved from its original and special purpose.

ST. PAUL'S CATHEDRAL.

THE anniversary meeting, in June, of the charity children in St. Paul's is a spectacle no foreigner should neglect to witness. Berlioz, in a letter dated June 9th, 1851, Crystal Palace, Hyde Park, seven o'clock in the morning, records his impression of the

Festival in the following enthusiastic language:—"J'avais lu il y a plusieurs années ce que M. Fétis a écrit sur cette cérémonie; je m'attendais donc à quelque manifestation remarquable, mais la réalité a dépassée de beaucoup les promesses de mon imagination. C'est la chose la plus extraordinaire que j'ai vue et entendue depuis que j'existe" (*vide* "Musical Union Record," 1851 and 1868).

It is hoped that no attempt will be made to change the characteristic feature of this musical festival of unisonous singing. The service should be specially chosen, irrespective of dates, so that the chants be not long. The sermon should be short, or omitted altogether. In the library of the Vienna Conservatoire, I have read Haydn's statement of the deep impression produced on him by the unisonous voices of boys and girls in the chants, one of which he wrote down in his memorandum book.

LONDON "ENTREPRENEURS."

THERE is very little sympathy for the fate of managers and directors in the public; and owing to the numerous bankruptcies of musical directors and managers in London, I am sorry to say that our credit does not stand high on the Continent. It is a melancholy fact that there is scarcely a performer of renown on the Continent who has not been the victim of some penniless speculator in concerts in London;

and the list of societies—unions and disunions—that have come to grief of late years is quite incredible. "None but a fool or a madman with anything to lose," said a well-known manager, "would ever take a lyrical theatre;" and Lablache was wont to say of a successful manager, that such a man must be a tyrant or a fripon. The enormous expense of band, chorus, principals, &c., is ruinous, without great and permanent attraction. I have long predicted that one of the rival Italian operas must reduce its price of admission to command success. Since London has now no English opera, the two Italian operas have a better chance than hitherto of attracting large musical audiences.

The gains and losses of an Italian opera manager in London are to be counted not by hundreds, but thousands. Ebers lost some £30,000. Laporte, like Lumley, having nothing to lose, had everything to gain. The first, after several unlucky seasons, realised a fortune; and if the latter had retired after the brilliant season of *Jenny Lind*, he would have been wise; but managers, like gamblers, never have the moral courage to leave off. The entrepreneurs of the Lyrical Theatre and the Italian Opera in Paris have lost thousands. Without a subvention from the government, or the municipal authorities in the provinces, no Lyrical Theatre can be carried on without risk in France, Germany, Italy, Russia, or *England*.

CLASSICAL CHAMBER MUSIC.

THIS branch of composition admits of no *remplissage* in its scoring, nor duplicates in its performance. No uneducated musician has ever produced a quartet of legitimate part-writing; and no executant, without mental gifts and refined taste, can faithfully interpret the works of the great masters.

Chamber Music, as its title indicates, is expressly adapted for a room of moderate dimensions; and I agree with a sympathising professor that my private receptions in 1844 were far more social and enjoyable than are the gatherings now in St. James's Hall. Whether the opinion of my professional friend was prompted by a feeling of compassion for my anxious responsibilities, or, perhaps, from a feeling of envy at my success, it is not necessary to inquire; but there is an important difference in the artistic and pecuniary consideration of the subject. Playing very intricate music, without rehearsals, to amuse amateurs *pour la gloire*, and carefully getting up performances with a liberal remuneration for professional service, before a critical audience, are quite distinct objects. Without disparagement to those brilliant *impromptu* displays in 1844, the results of finely-balanced talent, and *careful* rehearsals of quartets and quintets played by the parties engaged now at the Musical Union, have put all comparison out of the question.

Gladly would I now retire from the cares of public life, could I but resume my private receptions, and behold once more that phalanx of genius and talent which assembled weekly in my humble abode in the spring of 1844. To members who were not present at these meetings, it may be of interest to peruse the list of those remarkable men—viz., Mendelssohn, J. B. Cramer, Lablache, Dragonetti, Dohler, Moscheles, Thalberg, Ernst, Sivori, Piatti, Sainton, Joachim, Benedict, Schulz, Osborne, Puzzi, Rousselot, Offenbach, &c., &c.; and when I add that royalty and nobility were regaled with the same species of music that constitutes the orthodox programmes of our present intellectual performances, and in which most of the distinguished professional guests took part, it may reasonably be supposed that the pleasing recollection of those scenes of good fellowship and mutual delight often wafts me to bygone days of intense enjoyment. Seriously reflecting on the condition of art in London in 1844, when no public institution existed to reward eminent professors for playing classical chamber music, it must be admitted that the existence of the Musical Union and its continued prosperity, notwithstanding all its drawbacks as to locality, is a great boon to art and artists in this leviathan metropolis. Three compositions of classical design are everywhere considered sufficient for the power of mental attention, although I am allowed, once in a season, to exceed the cabalistic number of pieces constituting the orthodox programme. When Spohr first honoured the

Musical Union with his presence, after commenting on the analysis of his music, he good-naturedly remarked, in allusion to the programme, "*Das ist gut und kurz.*" A great painter was wont to boast of never losing his time in gazing at a bad picture. Alas! what miserable hours have I been doomed to pass at mongrel concerts, waiting to hear some composition of merit! How often have I envied the painter! Let me hope, therefore, that the concerts of the Musical Union may always elicit from members the compliment of being "good and short," and practically illustrate that principle which impressed me deeply when addressed to students at Rome, "l'economia del gusto."

THE MUSICAL UNION (1877).

"THE origin of this 'Union' dates from the assemblage of a few professors once a week at the residence of Mr. Ella. . . . Thus a mere private recreation of intelligent artists, in the first instance, led to a complete organisation, in which it would be difficult to indicate the persons who derived the greatest advantages, the patrons or the professors; delight and instruction are afforded to the former, fame and profit to the latter. There is a great charm in these morning *réunions.* The players are seated in the centre of a circle, and there is a social feeling displayed, which frees the performance from all formality and stiffness. Profound silence is observed, except that indescribable murmur of applause at some delicate trait in the execution, which never interrupts, but encourages the executants; but at the close critical chat is freely exchanged. The members include royalty, rank, fashion, literary and artistic celebrities."—*Illustrated News*, 1846.

The list of all the artists who have been heard at the *séances* of the Musical Union includes 74 pianists; 102 stringed and 27 wind instrumentalists.—Analysis: English, 48; French, 31; Germans and Austrians, 64; Italians, 15; Belgians, 14; Hungarians, 8; Poles, 3; Russians, 5; Dutch, 8; Danes, 2; Swedes, 1; Spanish and Portuguese, 4; total, 203.

The most recent example of the success of a young *débutant* is that of Leopold Auer, who first appeared at the Musical Union in his seventeenth year, 1863. This young Hungarian has obtained, at St. Petersburg, the most remunerative and distinguished court appointment in Europe—viz., violin professorship of the Conservatoire, leader of the Russian Concert Society, and of the concerts of the Grand Duchess Hélène, with a certain income of three thousand roubles.

"In the musical art, England," says a foreign musical critic, "is the refuge of the past, France the recognition of the present, and Germany the welcome of the future." "This satirical remark," says an English reviewer, "does certainly not apply to the three eminent pianists, Rubinstein, Jaell, and Lubeck, whose portraits embellish the Twenty-third Annual

Record of the Musical Union; since, on reference to the dates of their *débûts* printed in the "Record," we find they were respectively of the ages twenty-eight, twenty-nine, and thirty-three." Notwithstanding the occasional differences of opinion that arise from time to time in arranging public exhibitions of musical talent, I am glad to state that I hold in my possession, from every artist that has been engaged at the Musical Union, letters of cordial assurance of personal friendship at parting.

MUSICAL UNION STATISTICS (1868).

INCLUSIVE of tickets issued to honorary members, artists, visitors, and members—subscribers, since 1845, there have been present at our *Matinées* and *Soirées* upwards of 50,000 persons. The number of members has nearly trebled, and so, also, have the expenses in a corresponding ratio.

"It would indeed be a sad reflection," says a foreign writer, "were no society to exist in the great commercial city of England exclusively devoted to the culture of a class of music that is so well represented at the Musical Union, and which has never ceased to bring together and secure the suffrages of the best educated amateurs in the principal cities of Europe for more than half a century."

"Much patronage makes many enemies and few friends," said a minister in the House of Commons; and a musician who has been critic and director, dispensing more than £25,000 among artists, must necessarily have failed to satisfy all candidates for public favour. In my contributions * to critical literature I have spoken what I religiously believed to be the truth, without wounding the susceptibilities of my brother artists. A musician of twenty-seven years' experience in the best orchestras, personally acquainted with the most eminent artists since 1821, and who has passed five years among musicians on the Continent, is not easily deceived on the merits of executive and creative genius. One of the most distinguished art critics has done me the honour to say that my musical opinions are to be relied upon. I have no exclusive admiration for one particular composer, or antipathy to any novelty in art. Nor need I say, being socially independent, that my choice of executive artists is not influenced by interested motives.

When I first submitted the "Record" of 1845 to the perusal of Mendelssohn, at dinner, chez David in Leipzig—Moscheles, Gade, Schumann present—Mendelssohn was highly complimentary, all the more so, on learning that I sent the programmes to members before the day of the performance. "To peruse the contents during the performance," said Mendelssohn, "would disturb the attention of the auditor, just as one sees a libretto, which they ought to know before going to the theatre."

* "Morning Post," "Athenæum," "Musical World," and other papers.

THE SOCIETÀ LIRICA.

"IN the Società Lirica, with which the public have been made acquainted by the advertisement pages of the "Musical Standard," Mr. Ella has started an institution which may become permanently useful to music. As it at present stands, the sphere of its operations is restricted; and we must look upon it as almost, if not altogether, a private venture; but there seems to be no reason why the band and chorus should not be increased, and the rehearsals made public. That there is abundance of really good operatic music lying upon the shelves of our libraries is very well known, and much of this is very unlikely to see the stage again, on account of the altered conditions of performance. But for all that, it should not be let die if we can find means of keeping it in memory. Almost every opera of modern date has one or more well-constructed finales; and much concerted music of great worth lies buried in these scores. Mr. Ella's object is to draw this gold from the dross which mere fashion thrusts into all stage works; and his scheme includes also the performance of such songs and solo pieces as upon the claim of merit alone appear to be deserving. Of course, so long as the Società Lirica is confined to a small number of performers and private dwellings, its effect upon musical taste must be infinitesimal;

but as large societies have had small beginnings, we may hope that this one will grow until it becomes a considerable public institution. The programme of music in rehearsal does not go back far beyond Mozart, but it contains Mehul's 'Joseph,' Spontini's 'Vestale,' Gluck's 'Orfeo,' and some operas of Spohr and Rossini which are not now performed in this country, together with Wagner's 'Tanhäuser,' which we have not yet arrived at. Our readers may well wish success to the new society."—*The Musical Standard.*

LA SOCIETÀ LIRICA, BELGRAVIA (1877).

THE lyrical branch of the Musical Art, says a French Minister, is a costly exotic that thrives only three months of the year on the Italian stage in England, and most of its *repertoire* is supplied by the National Lyrical Theatre of France! I am, therefore, induced, from pure love of Art, to revive many lyrical gems, with something like orchestral and choral effect, neglected or altogether ignored by amateurs in this so-called musical country.

Season after season London Orchestral Concerts* are becoming few and far between, and the noblest specimens of Sacred and Secular Vocal Music, requiring a complete orchestra, and not unfrequently

* In London 13, in Paris 60, by subscription.

a choir, are sung to a pianoforte accompaniment in our monster halls. Such exhibitions would not be tolerated in any other country.

Vocal societies abound in London for the practice or Oratorios, Cantatas, Madrigals, Glees, Part-Songs, and even Ballads!—in short, for every species of Sacred and Secular Music, except that of the Musical Drama, the most captivating and affecting, as it is the most difficult to sing and to accompany, without sensibility, passion, and intelligence.

The object of this Society is to afford amateurs and professional vocal students the opportunity of practising Italian, German, French, and English Lyrical Works, originally adapted for the Chamber Band and Choir of the late Lord Saltoun's parties, under my direction from 1826 until 1846.

The Operas are scored for violins, violas, violoncellos, double basses, and two flutes, with the addition of the pianoforte, à 4 mains, to give force to dramatic accent of the choral combinations in the Introductions and Finales. The choir is limited to eight female and eight male voices. The vocalists are expected to be acquainted with the Italian and French languages.

The practices take place, Saturdays from 4 to 6, with six monthly programmes; and at each meeting one composition, at least, is read for the first time. The music and instruments are provided, and all expenses are defrayed by the director, whose *repertoire* contains not fewer than 200 scenes from Operas

&c. One guinea from members is paid towards the cost of extra MS. copies of new works.

THE PRINCE CONSORT.

IN 1853 I received an intimation of the Prince's intention to found a Musical Library. The writer of this communication offered the munificent donation of £1000 if the intention were realised, "so as to be a National Institution." In aid of this object, by consent of the late Sir William Tite, C.B., and Thomas Brassey, Esq., Trustees of the Musical Union Institute, 320 volumes of music, six busts of composers, and a full-size portrait of Rossini, painted in 1824, have been presented to the Educational Department of the South Kensington Museum.

THE END.

PRINTED BY BALLANTYNE, HANSON AND CO.
EDINBURGH AND LONDON

www.ingramcontent.com/pod-product-compliance
Lightning Source LLC
Chambersburg PA
CBHW031821270326
41932CB00008B/498
* 9 7 8 3 7 4 4 6 7 9 5 0 3 *